JAPAN'S ECONOMIC INVOLVEMENT IN EASTERN EUROPE AND EURASIA

Japan's Economic Involvement in Eastern Europe and Eurasia

Raymond Hutchings
sometime Editor
Abstracts Russian and East European Series (ABREES)
Croydon

Foreword by Michael Kaser

337.51
H97j

First published in Great Britain 1999 by
MACMILLAN PRESS LTD
Houndmills, Basingstoke, Hampshire RG21 6XS and London
Companies and representatives throughout the world

A catalogue record for this book is available from the British Library.

ISBN 0–333–67986–5

First published in the United States of America 1999 by
ST. MARTIN'S PRESS, INC.,
Scholarly and Reference Division,
175 Fifth Avenue, New York, N.Y. 10010

ISBN 0–312–22004–9

Library of Congress Cataloging-in-Publication Data
Hutchings, Raymond.
Japan's economic involvement in Eastern Europe and Eurasia /
Raymond Hutchings ; foreword by Michael Kaser.
p.   cm.
Includes bibliographical references and index.
ISBN 0–312–22004–9 (cloth)
1. Japan—Foreign economic relations—Russia (Federation)
2. Russia (Federation)—Foreign economic relations—Japan.
3. Japan—Foreign economic relations—Former Soviet republics.
4. Former Soviet republics—Foreign economic relations—Japan.
5. Japan—Foreign economic relations—Europe, Eastern.   6. Europe,
Eastern—Foreign economic relations—Japan.   I. Title.
HF1602. 15.R9H87   1999
337.51047—dc21   98–46224
                                                             CIP

This book is printed on paper suitable for recycling and made from fully managed and
sustained forest sources.

10   9   8   7   6   5   4   3   2   1
08   07   06   05   04   03   02   01   00   99

Printed and bound in Great Britain by
Antony Rowe Ltd, Chippenham, Wiltshire

Contents

Publishers' Note

Sadly Raymond Hutchings died at home in Croydon, Surrey, on 13 November 1998, shortly after completing work on this book.

Foreword

Raymond Hutchings' death from cancer ended fifty years of his research and lecturing on the Soviet-type and post-communist economies. Born in 1924, his study of economics and Russian at the University of Cambridge was interrupted by war service in the Parachute Regiment and was completed by a doctorate at the London School of Economics. He deepened his knowledge of the Soviet economy as a member of the specialist Russian Secretariat of the Foreign Service and in research at the Royal Institute of International Affairs. For seventeen years until his death he edited the Abstracting Service for East European Studies, deploying his linguistic skills in making his own abstracts from Albanian, Bulgarian, Romanian and Russian.

His scholarly publications, in addition to numerous journal articles, fall into two groups: his mainstream texts such as *Soviet Economic Development* (1971; 1982), *The Soviet Budget* (1983), the *Historical Dictionary of Albania* (1996), and an analysis of historical skewness in *The Structural Origins of Soviet Industrial Expansion* (1984), were accompanied by books on tributary themes. An initial venture off the beaten Sovietological track was *Seasonal Influences in Soviet Industry* (1971), an outstanding work of detection from clues in quarterly plan fulfillment communiqués and unguarded remarks by Soviet commentators in the press. The title *Soviet Science, Technology, Design* (1976) responded to world concern with the space and nuclear races, but differed from other books in the same field by wide-ranging attention to design, from the artistic to the technical, within reflections on the cultural environment of a monopoly ideology. *Soviet Secrecy and Non-Secrecy* (1987) appropriately came as the Cold War was about to end and drew attention to the paradoxes of a propaganda machine which vaunted some economic trends but veiled others.

A characteristically idiosyncratic treatment is perceptible in this book, where he takes Japan as his standpoint in briefly surveying 28 post-communist countries through their history, topography, demography, linguistic heritage and customs as relevant to their bilateral economic relationships. Decades of Russian colonial proximity to self-isolated Japan and the significance as much of minor clashes then as of two wars this century throw light on the political confrontation that persists to this day. Among East European countries, Hutchings shows Hungary to be the prime objective of Japanese firms, with Poland following closely, while trade with the Balkan states has been trivial and there has been little investment. His emphasis on Albania may be prescient. The economic vacuum created by internal insurgency in 1997 and the Kosovo clashes of 1998 will begin to be filled when order returns, and Japanese firms cannot fail to be among the new investors. They are already entering the Caucasian states wherever ceasefires allow. Throughout the book Hutchings signalled the strong and weak points of Japan's entry into the post-communist economies and the potential that is still untapped.

In a tit-for-tat diplomatic wrangle in 1971 after 105 Soviet diplomats in the UK were declared *personae non gratae*, nearly all who had ever served in the British Russian Secretariat were banned from Russia. He was in good academic company, the late Professor Alec Nove of Glasgow and Professor Philip Hanson of Birmingham to name but two other economists. At this, he opened up a new avenue for himself – lectures and research at North American and Australian universities. As well as holding visiting Chairs on four occasions, he made twenty-five separate tours of campuses where comparative economics was on the curriculum. More recently his literary and artistic bent (as a sideline he made fashion buttons out of shells) brought him invitations as guest lecturer in Albania and on cruise ships on the Danube: from architectural styles to recognizing birds he would make sure that the tourists' faith in his knowledge was not misplaced.

As the author points out in his Preface, the present work relies substantially on the abstracting work of his later years. The publisher and contributors to that service, now ABREES, were represented at his funeral at Croydon Crematorium on 20 November 1998. I saw there also the affection and respect in which he was held by his family. There were present his widow, Karen, whom he had married in Denmark in 1949, two sisters, four children and their spouses and grandchildren, as well as friends and neighbours. One of his last efforts was to widen the coverage of ABREES to publications in the rarer languages of the twenty-eight countries in its remit, but quality was always as paramount as quantity. The pharse with which the National Association for Soviet and East European Studies initiated such abstracting, nearly three decades previously, remained his watchword: 'a service for scholars by scholars'.

MICHAEL KASER

Preface

This book combines my interests in the Soviet Union and its successor states and in Eastern Europe with a more recent interest in Japan. Though I have visited Japan twice, read widely about Japan and learned some Japanese, enough time to learn more about Japan or to become fluent in the language was simply not available; many thanks nevertheless to Kumiko Jesse for allowing me to attend her evening classes.

When possible I attended seminars given weekly during term at the Nissan Centre for Japanese Studies, Oxford. Unfortunately I could not attend one in this series about Japanese investment in Germany (14 June 1996). The Director of this Centre, Professor A. Stockwin, kindly permitted me to speak in this seminar series, in November 1992, on 'Japan and Romania: A Comparison of Peripheral States' and in November 1996 on 'Recent Japanese Economic Involvement in Eastern Europe'. Both of these tried out some facts and ideas which are reproduced in this book, but in the first the accent was not on economics while the second confined itself to Eastern Europe, nor did it include non-economic comparisons.

I also had the opportunity in May 1995 to lecture in Japan, at Tohoku, Fukushima, Hokkaido and Hitotsubashi universities, and in this connection an most grateful to Professor M. Hakogi, Professor R. Hakogi, Associate Professor S. Tabata, and Professor M. Kuboniwa, respectively, at the universities mentioned, for their help and hospitality. I also gained from them and from their colleagues and students, as well as from the journey itself, useful data and impressions about Japan and Japanese. I also appreciated hearing from Ahira Uegaki at the University of Fukuoka and receiving a copy of his article.

This book was written during a time when the economies of Japan and of South-East Asia were on the whole, and in most respects, success stories. Few writers (though notably Woronoff, 1990) pointed to deficiencies in the Japanese economy. Since then, fundamental defects have emerged and even the 'restructuring' of the Japanese economy is called for. What will be done, and how that will affect Japanese involvement in Eastern Europe and Eurasia, is not at present foreseeable. In certain branches, the Japanese may react by preferring closer involvement in the territories covered by this book at the expense of greater involvement in South-East Asia. An illustration of this is given on pp. 114–35 on Japan and Romania.

I am most grateful to Macmillan for providing encouragement and for extending the deadline more than once. Daniel Re'em (Abstracts Russian and East European Series Ltd (ABREES)) kindly provided printouts of many summary allusions to Japan, put the bibliography into alphabetical order, and installed my new printer. As usual I wish to thank very much my wife Karen. She has had much to contend with this past winter, but had earlier keyed into the computer the ABREES or ABSEES abstracts on which much of this text so heavily relies.

The book is based on multilingual materials, predominantly from Russia and Eastern Europe. Many of these languages make use of accents and to include all of these would require dozens of special signs. This is not practical, nor do I think it necessary or justifiable for readers of an English text. Therefore the majority of such accents or omitted. Those who can read these languages will be aware when, strictly, an accent would be required.

July 1998   RAYMOND HUTCHINGS

1 Introduction

GENERAL BACKGROUND

Japan has normally focused its attention for economic purposes upon itself and then on Asia and chiefly South-East Asia, Australasia, North America, the Middle East and Western Europe, and for political and military purposes on South-East Asia and North America. Africa, South or Central America, Eastern Europe and the former Soviet Union, and now its successor states, have not been in the forefront of attention. *Pace* any change in Japan's economic fortunes, that situation is likely to continue. Japan mainly imports raw materials, including oil and foodstuffs, which to a large extent are obtained from the first group of countries. South-East Asia has been seen as the region with which the Japanese should be the most closely associated, and North America and Western Europe as regions with which they wish to be compared or from which they can learn as regards economics, technology and science. The Soviet Union appeared primarily as a threat while Eastern Europe was neither a military threat nor a very useful economic partner.

The concentration on the First World and certain regions of the Third World mirrored both economic and political preferences. Japan sought the best in economics and technology and, with few exceptions, the former Soviet Union and Eastern Europe did not provide it. These countries were also relatively inaccessible, apart from Russia's Far East. Eastern Europe could be reached by sea but it was scarcely less trouble to voyage to Western Europe. Overland transport via the USSR (Union of Soviet Socialist Republics) was possible but not particularly attractive. Moreover, Eastern Europe was compelled to adopt a type of economic system which the Japanese regarded as inefficient and for which they felt no affinity. Japan was sheltered by the US (United States') nuclear umbrella from Soviet threats and resented the occupation by the USSR of certain islands they saw as rightfully theirs.

Western Europe (most of it) also merged within the economic grouping of the European Community, and now the European Union (EU), which has acquired and is acquiring political powers and functions. Eastern Europe is forming its own groupings, such as CEFTA (Central European Free Trade Association), but individual member-states tend to see this as a half-way house to joining the EU. Cultural aspects, too, pointed towards Western Europe and away from Eastern Europe. Western European languages, especially English, have spread farthest and most ubiquitously. The people of Eastern Europe speak a variety of languages, a number of which are little known except by emigrants outside those countries themselves. Western Europe contains the chief artistic and architectural riches. Of course, Japan's scant interest in Eastern Europe is not a unique phenomenon. It is more or less paralleled by relative lack of interest in this region on the part of Western Europe and United States of America. Even during the Cold War period the Western intelligence community directed its main gaze towards the Soviet Union, far less attention being directed to Eastern Europe.

Thus neither political, economic nor cultural motives pushed the Japanese in the direction of economic involvement with the former USSR or with the states of Eastern Europe. That situation had to change with the disintegration of the Soviet Union and the Soviet bloc. It is changing in the direction of encouraging Japanese economic involvement, which now takes a variety of forms. The change is not taking place rapidly, partly because such a fundamental change was so unexpected. Previous studies by Western specialists generally assumed the continuation of the USSR for the indefinite future, and hence made little effort to forecast how Eastern Europe might change if that were untrue. For example, the booklet *Japan in the Year 2000: A Future View* (Occasional Paper no. 18, Asia Program, Wilson Center, Smithsonian Institution Building, Washington DC 1983) hardly mentioned the Balkans or Eastern Europe. Its predictions are largely made irrelevant by the disintegration of the USSR. Likewise the article 'Prospective Changes in Japan's Trade Pattern' by M. Noland (1990) made no mention of either the USSR or Eastern Europe; one could easily conclude from this source that there were no such territories. However, an excellent account of Japan's economic relations with the USSR up to its date of publication is found in J. Glaubitz, *Between Tokyo and Moscow* (1995).

Japan's total direct investment in foreign economies grew steeply and at an almost uniform rate between 1960 and 1988, from about 0.1 billion dollars to about 40 billion dollars (Komiya and Wakasugi, 1991, Fig. 1, quoting Japan's Ministry of Finance). Table 1 in the same source does not distinguish the Second World, nor does the article even name the USSR or any countries of Eastern Europe. Investment in 'Europe' rose from 1.1 per cent in 1951–60 to 18.7 per cent in 1986–8 (ibid., p. 52). The great bulk of this was almost certainly in *Western* Europe, including Britain as one of the chief recipients.

Due to the novelty of Japan's economic engagement with countries of the former Second World and unfamiliarity with the ground rules of a frequently varying situation, which also differs appreciably between the post-Soviet states, up to now the trend of increasing Japanese economic involvement in successor states to the former USSR and Eastern Europe has made limited progress and affects only some of those states. However, the territory formerly included within the Soviet bloc was so extensive and the countries comprised until the reunification of Germany within that territory – twenty-eight – so numerous that the subject has to be large in scope. (Twenty-eight appears to have been correct; Chechnya, 'Tatarstan' or the 'Republic of Sakha' are not considered here to be separate states).

This book covers all types of Japanese economic involvement and all the 28 states, although the degree of involvement and consequently also the degree of detail included here are very uneven. The situation is evolving and must supply material for more intense and voluminous studies. This book sets as its objective to relate what has happened and to offer explanations based on the so far limited factual material.

This is believed to be the first book to be devoted to Japan's economic involvement in Eastern Europe and Eurasia. As such, it may be needed. The author asked a much respected colleague, a specialist on the Soviet economy but also knowledgeable about Turkey, China and Thailand, which country in Eastern Europe he thought had been the chief target for Japanese economic interest. Evidently puzzled, he replied 'Would it be Poland?' It has been, overwhelmingly, Hungary. His reply tended to confirm that Russian specialists had little information on the subject and that their opinions were likely to be erroneous. Specialists on Western Europe are not likely to be better informed. As for Japanese economic relations with the former USSR or with its successor states, very little has been published on that topic.*

DEFINITIONS AND ARRANGEMENT

'Eastern Europe' includes here the European countries apart from the USSR which during the communist era belonged to the Soviet bloc at one

---

*A large proportion of references to newspapers and periodicals is taken from *ABREES* (*Abstracts Russian and East European series*, formerly *ABSEES*) of various dates. The serial record number in *ABREES* or *ABSEES* of that reference is indicated in the text immediately following the original source with the prefix RN=. One may then look up the issue of *ABREES* or *ABSEES* which contains that record number. For example, RN=21314 refers to an item in *ABREES* issue no. 104 (no. 4 of 1993). In a few cases the reference takes the form RN=H 4/89 (89) and then one should look up that date in the *ABREES* or *ABSEES* volume no. shown in brackets (in this case 89). Also, some RN, were left unknown at the time of the author's death in November 1998.

time or another. Thus, Albania is included, although it broke with the USSR in 1961, whereas Greece, Turkey, Finland and Cyprus are excluded. Only occasional allusions are made to these. 'Eurasia' covers both the former USSR and all its successor states. 'Economic involvement' includes trade, aid, credits and loans, joint projects, advice, investment, transport and communications and other economic relations. These cannot all be expressed in a single indicator; consequently it is not the aim, nor will it be possible, to range countries in a precise sequence of 'degree of involvement'. This can be only roughly estimated. The primary focus is on the post-Soviet era, but there is also mention of any necessary or interesting background commencing even before this, and – exceptionally – in the case of Russia, long before. Far Eastern states apart from Japan, or economic involvement in the region by countries other than Japan, are not covered, apart from occasional allusions usually for the sake of comparison.

DIFFERENCES BETWEEN EASTERN EUROPE AND EURASIA

It may be convenient at this point to summarize the differences between Eastern Europe and Eurasia. In the present context these may be summed up as follows:

1. There are historical links between Japan and Eurasia (the Russian Empire), but virtually none between Japan and Eastern Europe.
2. Eastern Europe has never been invaded by nor experienced any warlike operations on the part of the Japanese, whereas Eurasia has.
3. Japan did not see any threat to herself arising from Eastern Europe, but did see a threat from the Soviet Union (and possibly now a lesser threat from Russia).
4. There are obvious complementarities between the economies of Japan and Eurasia (especially Russia) but less obviously between the Japanese and East European economies.
5. Literature connecting the Eurasian (in this case, Russian) and Japanese economies is more abundant than literature connecting the Japanese and East European economies.

FOCUSES OF THE BOOK

The primary focus here is economic, but some material of a non-economic nature had also been gathered and it seemed legitimate to include elements of this, because the non-economic material sometimes sheds light on economic aspects, because it was thought this might be interesting in its own right, and to leaven the subject-matter. These sections are signposted and readers who are solely interested in economic material in the strict sense should skip over them.

The bulk of the material is presented in country sections, headed 'Japan and [the name of the country]'. Japan's economic involvement has been very unevenly distributed among the various countries within the region, and this means that while some country sections are fairly long, a number are short or even very short. There seemed no point in padding out such a section if there was essentially nothing to say.

Each of these country sections has two subsections: 'Comparisons' and 'Relations'. (Only certain country sections have subsection on 'Historical Background', below). The 'Comparisons' part puts down some basic measurements, especially of areas and populations, and salient aspects where that country differs from or resembles Japan. A problem here was to avoid starting what was too simple or obvious; the accent is on providing information. It is supposed that these comparisons will introduce some material which is novel to many readers, including those who have expert knowledge of one or the other partner but not of both. In most sections there is no subsection on 'Historical Background', but this is included for a few countries where that background has been significant or has extended over a long period. Until rather lately there has been little connection between Japan and most of the listed countries.

Countries are listed under their current names, except that, to avoid confusion with former Yugoslavia, the presently named 'Yugoslavia' or FRY is called Serbia/Montenegro. Macedonia is assigned its current name of FYROM (Former Yugoslav Republic of Macedonia). Where a country has newly emerged from being part of a larger state, that is from the former Soviet Union (FSU), the former Yugoslavia or the former Czechoslovakia, a section for each of those no-longer-existing states is included as well. While in Eastern Europe since 1989 the preservation or subdivision of formerly existing states has been the chief order of the day, and in Eurasia simply the subdivision of a formerly existing one – the USSR–German reunification involved abolition of the independent German Democratic Republic (GDR). This being a unique case and for the sake of avoiding a possibly confusing subdivision into disjointed country sections, the section 'Japan and Germany' includes separate subsections devoted respectively to pre-division Germany, the (former) Federal German Republic, the (former) GDR, and Germany post-reunification.

INTER-COUNTRY COMPARISONS

As already noted, the book also makes certain comparisons of a non-economic nature between Japan and other countries or societies. In correspondence with one leading Japanologist it has been found necessary to justify such an approach, the view being encountered that no valid comparison is possible. Since Japan, too, is inhabited by human beings, some similarities of behaviour had to be expected, but other resemblances were thought too random or insignificant to permit useful comparison. Or, as a less extreme view, it was recommended that comparison should be made with certain countries only, chiefly with the United States.

Of course, Japan is highly individual. To a Western visitor it appears Asian and alien; but the former is obviously true of other Asian countries and the latter of many Asian and non-Asian ones. Unlike many of these, Japan also exhibits certain Western-like features. Indeed, Japan sets some trends which the West may well follow, or is following. Its history, traditions, language, culture, and so on, are distinctive, yet not entirely lacking in similarity. Thus it is asserted here that more varied and adventurous comparisons are justified, and may bring to light relationships or characteristics which would otherwise have stayed undiscovered, may show them in a clearer or more meaningful light, or may suggest what other nations need to do to make them more (or less) like Japan. To attempt comparisons between Japan and certain other nations, therefore, does not seem futile, and may even be useful. This assumption underlies the inclusions of such comparisons in the present book.

Which sorts of comparisons should then be attempted, or with which countries? Comparisons should be most fruitful when there are both points of similarity and points of contrast. If there are only the former, we would in effect have found another Japan. If there are only the latter, it would be impossible to determine which differences dictated the overall dissimilarity. Also, one should not confine oneself to comparing countries which have often been compared before, for whatever of interest might be discovered has probably been discerned already. A more original comparison may then make a bigger addition to the stock of knowledge or understanding than one which is less original, even if the latter might be intrinsically the more valid.

The United States, Britain and Germany are the usual objects of comparison (though comparisons with Germany are uncommon); comparisons with Romania and Albania are highly unusual. Even certain eminent Japanologist do not see the point of comparisons with these latter countries, particularly Albania; but perhaps – dare it be said? – they do not know enough about Romania or Albania. Certain other countries are also compared here with Japan, in one or more respects. The request to the reader is: until you have seen what results from the comparisons, please withhold judgement. Some notes follow now about possible comparisons, not all of which are pursued further.

As pointed out by Clive Holland (1911, pp. 185–6), the Jews and the Japanese are perhaps the only, certainly the chief, nations which have evolved their own religions.

Japan and Germany is surely a meaningful comparison. Both Japan and Germany are large, modern, industrial, dynamic states, belonging within the category immediately beneath a superpower, and located in the northern hemisphere. Both have populations within the range 75 to 125 million. Both are very important trading nations. Both are either neighbours or near-neighbours of Russia (formerly the USSR): Germany to its west, Japan to its east. There are also substantial differences between them. Germany is a continental power, though with coastlines on the North Sea and Baltic Sea, whereas Japan consists of islands (four large and numerous small), all in the north-west Pacific Ocean. Their histories, too, are very different, Germany not being unified until 1870, whereas Japan has been a single state for much longer. At one time pagan, Germany is now Christian (Lutheran or Roman Catholic); Japan both Buddhist and Shintoist. Both took part in the two world wars, but in the First World War on opposite sides, in the Second World War on the same side (though not with any joint command). More precise comparisons centre on their histories during the run-up to the Second World War and during that war. Both began the war as aggressor states (even if justified in their own eyes); Germany by attacking Poland (allied with Britain and France), Japan by attacking the United States, Britain, France and the Netherlands. Both gained quick and almost decisive successes, but failed to carry them through and ended by being utterly defeated. Both later experienced foreign occupation, lost territory temporarily or (it would seem) permanently, became democracies on the demand of their conquerors, and currently are allied with the United States and its supporters. Both are capitalist (plus considerable government intervention) and wealthy. Both have strategic situations. Since the Second World War neither has focused on rearmament, although both have now rearmed with Western encouragement (or even insistence). Neither has regained political influence commensurate with their economic strength, but recently that difference is becoming less marked: Germany within the framework of the European Union (emerging as one of its leading proponents), Japan by acting independently or as a member of international economic bodies (or as a prospective member of the Security Council).

The similarity between the two countries was closest during the run-up to the Second World War, yet here too there were differences. Japan, unlike Nazi Germany, did not develop a new political philosophy. There was no exact parallel in Japan to Nazi anti-Semitism. Japanese society in this period should be called militarist rather than fascist (Fairbank, Reischauer and Craig, 1973, p. 725). Japan's advance to war was less systematic even if not less premeditated. Nazi Germany dictated its own timetable, whereas Japan's was affected by the war situation in Europe and expectations of colonial enlargement therefrom, and of breaking the oil blockade initiated by the United States. Germany's attack against Poland surprised the Polish government, yet within the general strategic context could not be called unexpected, while by attacking Pearl Harbor Japan achieved strategic surprise. Japan's declaration of war was timed to just precede devastating attacks against her main enemies, and especially against her strongest enemy, the United States. By contrast, Nazi Germany assaulted first, and without warning, the weakest member (Poland) of the opposing alliance, then paused for half a year before unleashing another shattering blow, and then a further year before attacking (outside that alliance) the Soviet Union.

The two countries' defeats in the Second World War also took place in different circumstances. Germany was overwhelmed by land attacks from east and west and south and simultaneous very destructive air-raids. The Japanese mainland was not invaded: island-hopping US forces fought themselves nearer and nearer, heavy maritime losses were inflicted, and then devastating air-raids including atomic bombs against Hiroshima and Nagasaki. In the final days Soviet forces burst into Manchuria.

Postwar circumstances were also different. The German government was toppled. In Japan, General MacArthur's rule interrupted continuity and made fundamental changes, yet the Japanese government, headed by its Emperor, remained essentially intact (apart from the trial and execution of some war criminals).

In literature, comparisons of Japan with other countries other than the United States of America (USA), Britain and Germany have been slow to emerge. In their chapter 'Imperial Japan: Democracy and Militarism', Fairbank *et al.* (1973, pp. 682–725) explain *inter alia* Japan's motives and attitudes towards the USSR, state the Japanese perception of events and probabilities in Europe, and compare Japan with Nazi Germany (pp. 702, 722–5). A major step was taken by Gianni Fodella (ed.), who, in *Japan's Economy in a Comparative Perspective* (1983), compared Japan and Italy. The book has eleven contributors. The subject-matter of Fodella's book is limited to the two countries' economic systems, plus some attention to politics. Within Europe the country that most closely resembles Japan as regards economic system is probably Italy, though in other respects there are big differences between the two countries. (Italian and Japanese vowels are pronounced rather similarly and in each language a vowel ends most words, but in other respects the languages are, of course, quite unalike.) Fodella points out that

all comparisons conducted so far have been made with the U.S., with rare and recent exceptions, or with advanced countries of the West like Britain because the majority of the Western scholars are Americans. These studies are certainly useful but they could yield more useful results if the country compared to Japan had a certain number of basic characteristics common to it, as would be the case of Italy or, to some extent, of West Germany (Fodella, 1983, p. 5).

This author agrees, but thinks non-economic comparisons can also be useful.

Until now only one person, the Japanese scholar Kazuhiko Yamamoto, whose interest in Albania is recent but extremely keen, appears to have attempted any comparison of Japan with any East European country. (See also below, in the country section 'Japan and Albania'.) And his comparison, though profound, is limited in scope. Undoubtedly, with Albania or other East European countries, only certain comparisons are useful. Japan is so different that with most of the East European countries one can make little useful comparison. Yet the scope is wider than may be thought at first sight, especially if sufficiently broad bases are adopted. The basis for comparison might be not only economics but traditions, history, religion, folklore, and so on. These other comparisons, which were thought appropriate, are included here within the relevant chapters.

2 Japan and the Russian Empire, the Soviet Union and the Russian Federation

2.1 JAPAN AND THE SOVIET UNION

2.1.1 Historical Background

The process of making contact between the Russian Empire – Tsarist Russia – and Japan extended over almost two centuries and was fraught with many difficulties and vicissitudes which derived from distance, unequal strength of motive (the Russians needed a nearer source of supply than European Russia for their pacific settlements, whereas Japan, with no such need, pursued an exclusion policy), disasters, ignorance of the other country's language and customs, and the stiffbacked regimes of both parties; on the other hand there were useful accidental contacts, both national and individual initiatives, and acts of benevolence. (See, in this connection, Lensen, 1959.)

Although Japan's isolation was finally ended by the American William perry in 1854, the Russians might have forestalled the Americans by some fifty years. certainly, Perry's eventual success was preceded by other efforts by non-Japanese which helped to bring about that result. Throughout this long period the impetus – including economic motives – came from the Russian side and often from entrepreneurs of adventurers; the Japanese were chiefly concerned to preserve their identity, national honour and territorial integrity. Individual Japanese too played an important part. The Japanese then or later showed no interest in settling on the pacific shore, and even now Hokkaido is the only Japanese island that is not densely populated. Exchanges of goods were small and not regulated by any agreement. There are no statistics of trade nor was there any significant investment. This earlier history is nevertheless fundamental since it lays the basis for present-day political relations between Japan and Russia. This history has no parallel in Japanese relations with Eastern Europe or with non-Russian republics of the former USSR. While it has only limited relevance to subsequent economic relations, the kurile Islands – which the Russians used as stepping stones on their way to Japan – remain of small economic significance. On the other hand, the island of Sakhalin – which the Russian also coveted, though showing restraint – has substantial economic weight due to its oil, as has the timber-rich far eastern mainland, though the full, potentialities of these areas are still not exploited.

During the present century, Japan and the Soviet Union, or its predecessor Tsarist Russia, have been once allies (in the First World War) but twice enemies: 1904, when Russia was easily defeated, and in the final days of the Second World War when the USSR already stood on the winning side. The frontier forces of Japan and the Soviet Union clashed heavily on occasion during the 1930s, such as in 1939, though this did not result in full-scale war, and Stalin felt able to transfer from the eastern to the western front troops who first, in December 1941, compelled the German invaders to retreat. The Soviet invasion of Manchuria in 1945 was considered (at least ostensibly) in the USSR to have been the decisive reason why the Japanese sued for peace. At present Russia occupies land which Japan regards as properly her own (the islands of Etorofu and Shibomai); southern Sakhalin, too, has changed hands more than once during this century.

2.1.2   Comparisons

Japan and the former Soviet Union differed sharply from one another in almost all superficial respects. On 1 January 1986 the USSR had an area of 22 402 200 sq km (square kilometres), Japan one of 372 000 sq km, so the USSR was 60.2 times larger. The population of the USSR (on 1.1.86) was 278.784 million, of Japan (1985) 120.760 million; the USSR's population by this reckoning being 2.3 times larger. Japan's density of population was 26.2 times the greater. There were many more profound or subtle differences. (Further comparisons are included in the section 'Japan and the Russian Federation'.)

Both countries suffered very severely in the Second World War: Russia mainly from invasion, with all its accompanying ills; Japan from hostilities along an extended oceanic perimeter, the blockade and air-raids. Only Japan was the target of atomic bombs. Throughout the Cold War the former Soviet Union became America's opponent, Japan America's ally. The international weight and influence of the USSR was based much more on military than on economic power, Japan's much more on economic than on military power.

While the huge capital expenditures required for any great expansion of Russian–Japanese trade and economic co-operation were a powerful opposing factor, only non-economic factors could sufficiently counteract the economic magnet between Japan and Russia, and these existed in the shape of political antagonism. This has delayed the strengthening of economic relations, but not to the extent of fully counteracting various positive circumstances.

2.1.3   Relations

Soviet trade with Japan was, however, small relative to Japan's population or economic strength. Neglecting earlier dates, in 1985, according to Soviet statistics, trade turnover between the two countries amounted to 3215 million (mn) roubles, equalling 2.27 per cent of total Soviet foreign trade turnover. This was somewhat less than Soviet trade with Italy (3793 mn) or France (3778 mn), though more than Soviet trade with the United States (2702 mn). In that year Soviet trade with the Federal German Republic amounted to 7086 mn roubles, with Cuba to 7989 mn with the GDR to 15 205 mn. Japanese foreign trade amounted to a much bigger share of Chinese than of Soviet foreign trade (Glaubitz, 1995, p. 114).

Soviet trade with Japan was to an unusual degree unbalanced, Japan's exports to the Soviet Union greatly exceeding Soviet exports to Japan. In 1985 Soviet imports from Japan amounted to 2287 mn roubles, exports to Japan to 928 mn. In contrast, Soviet exports to Italy and France exceeded imports from those countries, while with the GDR exports and imports were almost in balance. Soviet exports to Japan comprised 1.3 per cent of total exports, while imports from Japan comprised 3.3 per cent of total imports. Thus Japan's share in Soviet imports was not altogether negligible. The composition of Soviet trade with individual countries is not given for all years in Soviet statistics, but machinery and equipment must have comprised the main part of imports from Japan, while probably a fairly large share of Soviet exports to that country consisted of timber.

There were no joint enterprises or joint projects, except towards the very end of the Soviet epoch, which are mentioned later in this chapter. Various large-scale projects were mooted, but did not come to fruition, for different reasons which included the huge investments demanded from the Japanese side and objections from China and the United States. Furthermore, the Japanese wanted their territorial aspirations to be satisfied first.

There was one interesting semi-unofficial intervention in 1959. On the basis of interviews with over 20 Japanese businessmen, V. Syrokomskiy refuted the suggestion that Japan's trading future lay with China rather than with the USSR (*Literaturnaya gazeta*, 30 May 1979, p. 14 – RN = 03118).* This article appeared in a literary journal, not an economic one, enabling one to suppose that it did not necessarily presage any change in Soviet policy. More authoritative allusions from the Soviet side to any desirability to enlarge Japan's involvement blew successively cold and hot. The Soviet Communist leader L.I. Brezhnev (in 1977) claimed that the Soviet Union could develop the Far east making use solely of its own resources – foreign assistance would merely enable it to be done more quickly – whereas Gorbachev in July 1986 'produced the impression that the Soviet Union was desperately dependent on foreign assistance for the development of its Far Eastern regions'. He condemned the region's dependence on oil supplies from distant sources in the USSR and 'bemoaned' its small contribution to exports (Glaubitz, 1995, p. 109). About this time (1986–7) we also encounter reports of dissatisfaction with the working of certain of the USSR's far eastern ports, though without any mention of Japan (Shirmanov, 1986 – RN=13104; Bratchikova, 1987 – RN=13108).

However, before the break-up of the USSR, Japan was one of its main creditors, and had granted loans of $30 billion (Zhagel', 1997, p. III – RN not yet known). Credits from Britain, France and Japan aided Khrushchev's maize (corn) campaign in 1959. (Keep, 1995, p. 110). A debt of US$1.5 billion was contracted by former Soviet ministries and enterprises which, following the break-up of the USSR, no longer existed (Agafonov, 1993, p. 3 – RN=21233). (Throughout the text 'bn' is consistently used to mean 'billion', i.e. one thousand million.)

Siberia's overland bridge between the Far East and Europe gained prominence. Across Russia, or formerly the USSR, is the shortest and quickest route between Japan and Eastern Europe. Consequently an agreement between Japan and the USSR in 1968, which inaugurated container traffic across the USSR, had great importance.

In 1970 several major Japanese corporations – notably C. Itoh & Co., Marubeni-Ida, Mitsui & Co. and Sumitomo Shoji Kaisha – signed an agreement with the Soviet government to allow them to operate

---

*Certain correspondents have specialized on reporting Japan's economic involvement. Thus, A. Trom reported many times about Hungary, A. Khoroshilov about Russia. Although few of the names listed in the Bibliography have been noticed in other contexts, G.P. Szego (Hungary) figured in 1990 as one of the editors of the *Journal of Banking and Finance*; at the time he was at the University of Rome. N. Mikheyeva (Russia) reappears as a co-author with J. Thornton, and spoke at the Slavic Research Center at the University of Hokkaido.

container transport using the Trans-Siberian Railway. For this purpose they co-operated in the construction of port and container facilities in Vostochny port (in Wrangel Bay) to handle 120 000 containers annually. Cargoes of Japanese machinery, industrial equipment, consumer durables and other goods are regularly shipped westwards in 20-ton containers (Wilczynski, 1976, p. 89).

Curiously, Wilczynski does not itemize this transport, or indeed any transport in his index, and seems to attach only limited importance to it. Neither is Japan itemized). 'At about the same time Schenker Trans-Siberian Container Service (FRG) began similar operations from Western Europe to Japan. . . . The number of containers transported between Japan and Western Europe increased from 4000 in 1971 to 51 000 in 1974' (ibid., note 1). However, the Japanese totals of the numbers transported are smaller than the Soviet ones (Glaubitz, 1995, p. 99). (By the Trans-Siberian between Japan and Western Europe, transport costs were 20–25 per cent lower than by sea transport by the shortest route, and the transit period 20 days compared with 26.) (Wilczynski, 1976, p. 89, note.)

2.2   JAPAN AND THE RUSSIAN FEDERATION

2.2.1   Comparisons

On the dissolution of the USSR the Russian Federation (Russia) succeeded to the territory of the former Russian Soviet Federal Socialist Republic (RSFSR). In geographical respects, Russia and Japan are extremely dissimilar. Russia is huge and mainly northerly (more northerly than the USSR was, on average), while Japan is far smaller and, though embracing a range of latitudes, on the whole more southerly. Thus Japan's climate is on the whole much warmer. Japan comprises islands, Russia a vast mainland. Japan consists mainly of mountains, Russia mainly of plains. Russia has many long, wide and navigable rivers, Japan not one. Demographically and socially the two lands are very different. Russia includes many minorities, Japan only two (the Ainu and the Koreans) of significant size. In religion, Russia is overwhelmingly Orthodox Christian (or nothing), Japan Shinto and Buddhist and, in only a tiny degree, Christian. The Russian and Japanese languages are totally unalike. (In this latter connection see 'Japan and Bulgaria'.)

The two economies are among the world's biggest and most varied, yet have little else in common, except that both territories contain timber (Japan vastly less than Russia, and partly of different types). Russia has abundant coal, oil and natural gas which Japan (except for some coal) lacks. The importance in both of hydro-electric power is an element in common. Both have large and diversified heavy industries, though Japan far surpasses Russia in shipbuilding. In recent years Russia has been contracting its defence industry and adapting it for other purposes, whereas Japan's defence output has increased. Yet Russia's arms industry remains much the larger. Both transport systems rely largely on railways, but Russia concentrates on long-distance freight, Japan on rapid or very rapid passenger movement. Japan depends far more on foreign trade but has more diverse and higher quality manufactures to offer. As for cereal diet, Russia relies on rye, wheat and maize (corn), Japan on rice. Russia's agriculture is based on extensive cultivation mainly without irrigation, Japan's on intensive cultivation with irrigation (rice paddies). The Japanese eat far more fish per head; the Russians more fish than one might expect, but not according to Japanese recipes. Similarly, both drink tea, but only one has the tea ceremony! Both countries are food importers, Russia about 40 per cent though of different sorts (Shchurov, 1995, p. 1 – RN = 23286).

While the yen is a hard currency, the rouble is not quoted on foreign exchanges and still may not be exported or imported.

The Japanese work longer hours. According to a Russian source, in 1994 the average Russian spent 1441 hours a year at work, while the Japanese average was 2017 (Mikulskiy, 1996, p. 25 – RN not yet known). A more exacting work ethic raises Japanese labour productivity still further, but in Russia women have wider work opportunities.

2.2.2   Relations

In sum, the two economies have need of or can benefit from or learn from one another, the Russian economy especially. Adjacent and large in scale, they have, especially during the Soviet era, largely concentrated on different things. The need is to find a *modus vivendi*.

Mutual Trade

As reported in September 1992, Russia was one of the few countries to have a positive trading balance with Japan. (Russia must be differentiated here from the USSR, which some years earlier had had a negative balance

– see 'Japan and the Soviet Union'). During 1991 (while the USSR still existed), imports from Japan amounted to $2.114 bn, while exports from Russia to Japan were $3.317 bn. Japan became Russia's third most important trading partner (after Germany and Italy) in volume of trade turnover ($5.431 bn in 1991). But in the first half of 1993 the trade turnover with Japan was 39.6 per cent less than in the same period of 1991. This was a greater fall than in Russia's total trade turnover, which fell by 30 per cent in this period (Anichkin, 1992, p. 4 – RN=20333). According to figures for the first half of 1993, Russia's trade with Japan had stopped shrinking for the first time since 1988. Whereas Japanese firms had been reluctant to deal with their Russian counterparts, mainly due to economic crises in Russia and failure to get payment for goods already delivered, at the start of 1993 the Russian government resumed paying off interest on loans taken earlier, and substantially improved trading conditions.

Trade between the two countries had been declining for a number of years, in 1993 dropping to US$3 bn, which was just 0.5 per cent of Japanese total foreign trade. Japanese businessmen were now interested first of all in the US$1.5 bn debt contracted by the FSU ministries and enterprises, which no longer existed. Japanese corporations, having failed to get back the money on their own, were now making claims of accumulated accounts at the government level. The new tactics proved successful, and a couple of months earlier (at the start of 1993) some corporations managed to get back interests charged on their credits. The businessmen also expressed concern over Russia's very complicated administrative tax and banking systems, which made all kinds of hard currency operations very difficult. It was rumoured in Tokyo that the Russian authorities had completed a plan for the economic development of the far east of the country; Japanese businessmen would like to learn directly from the Russian officials about the part they would play in it. Other projects, such as timber industry in Siberia, gas and oil production in Sakhalin, and building of roads, were being considered. (Several of these are examined elsewhere in this chapter.) Though deliveries to Russia were just 0.4 per cent of total Japanese exports, experts predicted a considerable increase due to the huge demand for Japanese goods in the Russian market. However, as lately reported, Russia's trade with China surpasses her trade with Japan (Portanskiy, 1997, p. 1 – RN not yet known).

In 1991 over 90 per cent of Japanese exports to the USSR and Eastern Europe were engineering (machine construction), high-technology and light industrial products. Japanese imports were non-ferrous metals (32 per cent), fuel (12 per cent) and other raw materials (15 per cent) (Anichkin, 1992, p. 4 – RN=20333). One may reasonably suppose that

the share in imports from Japan of 'machine construction, high technology and light industrial products' was not smaller for the USSR than for
Eastern Europe. As reported in August 1993, Japan's exports consisted
in the main of steel pipes, equipment for the oil and gas industry, ferrous
metals, electric generators, metal constructions, plastics, trucks, and so
on (Source Anon., August 1993).

Imports from Japan into Russia amounted to US$707.2 mn during the
first half of 1993, which was 54 per cent more than in the first half of 1992
(Anon., 1993b, p. 2 – RN=21536). Russia therefore fell into debt to Japan.
The Russo-Japanese Economic Committee estimated Russia's debt to
the Japanese as US$7.6 bn. The debt of individual enterprises to the Jap-
anese amounted to US$1.6 bn (Sveshnikov, 1993, p. 1 – RN=21534).
The Russians were reluctant to pay – late payments to Japanese firms
amounted to $1 bn in 1991 (Anichkin, 1992, p. 4 – RN=20333) – conse-
quently Japanese entrepreneurs became reluctant to enter into direct
contact with their Russian colleagues. Many Japanese firms preferred
to act through trading companies, which knew the local market. For example, the trading representatives of Toyota and Nissan in Russia were
the Japanese trading companies Toyota Tsuse, Nisso Boeki and Misui
(*ibid.*). These seem to have supplanted other major Japanese trading
companies, which either had become bankrupt (as reported by Zhagel',
1997, p. III – RN not yet known), or perhaps more probably had with-
drawn from the Russian scene due to unpleasant experiences. Another
consequence was that the Russians became very interested in possibilities of obtaining credit.

Credit Relations

Russia (still the USSR at that time) received $6.1 bn of medium and
long-term credit from Japan in 1991, including $299 mn of direct private
investment (Anichkin, 1992, p. 4 – RN=20333). As reported five years
later, international negotiations with Eximbank, the Export-Import
Bank of Japan, ended with an agreement to allocate a credit of $500 mn
to Russia. This figure forms part of the loan of $1.2 bn promised at the
beginning of the 1990s, $700 mn of which has already been allocated.
Eximbank insists that at least 15 per cent of the cost of a project should
be borne by the borrower-state. This protects the interests of both sides.
The Russian government produced a list of projects which included a
baby food enterprise in Khabarovsk and a hospital in Irkutsk. The Japanese side hoped that there would be no repetition of the problems in
finalizing agreements which occurred with the first group of projects,

due to peculiarities of Russian taxes and import duties. While keen to be involved in joint projects, they wanted to ensure that these were sound investments.

Before the break-up of the USSR, Japan was one of its main creditors, and had granted loans of $30 bn. Russia was responsible for the $12 bn (at the contemporary exchange rate) which remain from the debt dating from before the break-up of the USSR. Out of this sum, $7 bn are owed directly to Eximbank. Most trade with the USSR was through Japanese trading companies, many of which went bankrupt. Negotiations between the Russian government and the Tokyo Creditors' Club in 1996 were due to be concluded in 1997. The writer added that, as a result, Japanese companies' interest in investment in Russia was increasing. The projects attracting interest included: Sakhalin oil, transformers near St Petersburg, and the car industry (Zhagel', 1997, p. III – RN not yet known). Sakhalin oil is referred to below (subsection 'Sakhalin and Neighbourhood'), also cars, any more detailed statement about interest in transformers has not come to notice.

Far Eastern Business Relations

Past agreements between Russia and Japan included clauses whereby Japan supplied machinery and equipment in exchange for timber goods from the Russian far east. In August 1994 an agreement KS-5 (KS were the initial letters of the surnames of the first negotiators) was being negotiated to renew this trade, and a group was appointed to resolve questions arising from the preparation of documents. Present at a meeting were, on the Russian side representatives of *inter alia* Sakhalinlesprom, Dal'lesprom, Dal'les, Primorskles, and Roseksportles (in these abbreviations 'les' means timber, 'Dal'' means far); on the Japanese side from firms which had traditionally traded with Russian timber enterprises: Marubeni, Mitsubishi, Nisse, Itochu (a later name for C. Itoh) and Kamenatsu corporations and KS Industri. Subgroups would be formed to deal with the supply of equipment and spare parts from Japan; with Russian timber exports; and with financial matters. The project would take about five years, with a possible extension. Agreement had not yet been reached on prices, and other problems had to be solved. For instance, the Russians wanted to be free to use equipment from other countries which would be less expensive than Japanese equipment. The agreement was due to be signed by the end of 1995 and work was planned to start in 1996 (Levina, 1995, pp. 1–2 – RN=23896). In October 1995 it was announced that Russian and Japanese timber undertakings were to resume negotiations after a three-year break. The meeting would take place on 17–19 October when the possibility of extending the supply of Russian timber to Japan would be discussed. It was hoped that wider use would be made of wood in Japanese housebuilding. At a preliminary meeting it was decided to lower the prices of pine, fir and deciduous timber (Khoroshilov, 1995, p. 2 – RN = 23897).

The Japanese market is very important for timber enterprises in Khabarovsk *krai* (*'krai'*, literally 'borderland', is a territorial division applied to certain less developed and extensive regions of Russia and the former USSR: Yukon 'territory' or the 'Northern Territory' of Australia are approximate parallels). It is illustrative of Japan's importance that a fall in the price of wood on the Japanese market plus introduction of the 'hard-currency corridor' rule led to a sharp fall in the foreign exchange income of these undertakings in Khabarovsk *krai*'s Solnechnyy *raion* (district) (Khoroshilov, 1996b, p. 1 – RN = 24702).

A conference took place in Khabarovsk *krai* in May 1996 on how to attract investment from Japan, which in the past had been a traditional partner in extraction of timber in the Russian far east, in difficult regions. Unlike the Republic of Korea, Norway, the USA and others, the Japanese had made no move to extend their activities. In April it became known that the reason was some trouble in the enterprise Kiyama-Avia, going on over a two-year period, the Japanese partners having been accused of cheating. The Association of Japan–Russian Trade asked the head of the administration of Khabarovsk *krai*, within the Federal Court, to investigate. So far no answer had been received. Consequently the Japanese had not invested in the *krai* and future relations were looking difficult (Khoroshilov, 1996a, p. 1 – RN = 24671).

The disintegration of the USSR seriously harmed Khabarovsk *krai*'s timber industry. Dal'lesprom reported a fall in the export of timber which affected production in timber-working and furniture enterprises. They received 3000 cubic metres (cu. m.) less than in the previous year. Exports of timber in the *krai* had halved. High transport and fuel costs had lost them markets, especially in Central Asia. The non-westerly consumers of 'near abroad' (former republics of the USSR) could not afford timber from the *krai*. Transport of fuel and food was also disrupted to the far north. Tunsk Furniture Factory raised its prices for prepared panels and Zarya combine therefore produced its own panels. Prices for ash wood had also been raised and furniture makers bought raw materials elsewhere (Khoroshilov, 1997a, p. 2 – RN = 25672).

The situation in the Japanese market now closely affects the timber industry in the *krai*. As reported in April 1997, demand for timber for housebuilding in Japan had dropped. The Russian–Japanese enterprise Ladoga had failed in its first programme for treatment of woodpulp, and now valuable equipment was standing idle. Sales of their goods suffered because the overseas partners kept a strict control on prices, timber assortment and production. The home partners' task was to find cheap sawmill material for them. High prices and the low spending power of the Khabarovsk population was the reason why storage depots were full of unsold goods. In Zarya combine they held furniture worth 3.5 mn roubles (Rs). The *krai* had great assets but now a surplus of enterprises. The far eastern market wanted to buy the better, more 'comfortable' (which presumably here means higher quality, or more consistent) products from western Russia and abroad. Japan, South Korea and South-East Asia needed Russian roundwood, but this had to be prepared on the spot. Khabarovsk *krai* was changing into a raw material supplier for its economically developing neighbours. (During the Soviet time, furniture – normally a bulky commodity in relation to its value – was transported from the far east to treeless regions of Soviet Central Asia.) Their furniture industry could only regain its Central Asian market if the government lowered transport tariffs (Khoroshilov, 1997a, p. 2 – RN=25672).

A Finnish firm, Tkhomesto, has become involved. Exporters of coniferous timber from Irkutsk *oblast*, the Buryat Republic and Krasnoyarsk and Khabarovsk *krais* met representatives from Tkhomesto to discuss exports. The firm had spent considerable sums on creating local enterprises capable of preparing 1.2 mn cu. m. of timber annually. A large part of it was in roundwood and was exported to Japan, where most Russian firms directed their business. Tkhomesto had become well known as a middleman for supplying coniferous timber to the Japanese market. At their timber terminal at Nakhodka they had electrical equipment to evaluate and measure exports and to stamp each log with its own number, the details of which were entered on a computer. This made the suppliers' work easier if disputes arose. The firm put forward a proposal to treat wood against pests with a preparation 'Sinesto B'. Treated wood earned an extra $5–10 for each cubic metre. Some members said that it was far more profitable to export sawmill material than roundwood in present circumstances (Kalinkin, 1997, p. 3 – RN=25685).

Japanese Exports to Russia's Far East

What are the Japanese sending in return? Cars, as one would expect. Vladivostok is full of Japanese cars, according to Michael Palin (BBC, 31 August 1997), although this city has been open to foreigners only since

1992. Probably electronic goods have been supplied, too, but confirmation and details are lacking.

Communications with the Pacific Coast

The Russians now show a better understanding of the advantages to be gained from better links between the timber regions and the Pacific coast. As reported in March 1996, the first 10 kilometres (km) of a motorway had been started in Khabarovsk *krai*, linking villages in the *taiga* (dense coniferous forest) and ultimately Komsomol'sk with the ports of Lazarev and De-Kastr. By summer the roadbuilders expected to have reached Nizhnyy Tambov so that the road could be used by nearby timber industries. This was important because roadbuilding in timber areas in the deep interior of Khabarovsk *krai* had almost ceased and timber enterprise roadbuilders had been disbanded. Work on the new road was government-funded, but would proceed slowly because of the difficult terrain. The road was vital for the lower Amur where timber exports could come by water only during the summer navigation. Also, improved timber haulage roads were needed to get wood out of the interior to the seaports. Funds might be allocated for this because talks were going on to make the far east route through Lazarev from Sakhalin and Japan one single highway (Khoroshilov, 1996d, p. 2 – RN=24789; see also below). Later, it was reported that work on the road Lidoga–Vanino, joining the *raions* of Khabarovsk *krai* with ports on the Tatar Straits, was being carried on from both sides. The shareholding company Dal'lesstroi began with reconstruction work on a 40 km section of timber road used by the Tyumen' Timber Industry. After 163 km, the workers reached untouched forest where wood had never been felled. The Vice-President of Dal'lesstroi said that in two years the whole 360 km route would be given over to felling, and future investors would not lose out. The area could become a centre for international trade. (It is not clear what this meant; it sounds over-optimistic.) In April work commenced at the Vanino side with a 19 km forest road. In June work brought them to the River Ikche, and brigades of the 9th Bridge Unit joined in the work to erect a 5 km bridge of many spans (Khoroshilov, April 1997b, p. 1 – RN not yet known). Other communications projects affecting the Pacific coast have been mooted, such as to bring railway freight cars to Magadan by sea (Bikmukhametov, 1987, p. 1). This was during the Soviet *perestroika* period, and no Japanese participation was mentioned. Magadan was at that time still a closed city.

Sakhalin and Neighbourhood

There were unsuccessful attempts to develop these oilfields with Japanese involvement in the 1970s. Several oilfields on the Sakhalin shelf were discovered without foreign assistance in the 1980s, but Russia could not develop them independently because special platforms, not produced in Russia, were required to overcome the problems of ice and climate (see also later paragraph). In the late 1980s the American company MacDermott, the Japanese company Mitsui and the American company Marathon, formed a consortium known as 'MMM', but no business resulted because of inflated demands from Sakhalin's governor. The Sakhalin Island administration favoured a rival bid by Exxon and the Japanese company Sodeco (standing for Sakhalin Oil Development Corporation). Only after pressure from the federal government in early 1992 was MMM awarded the tender (Glaubitz, 1995, p. 116; Watson, 1996, p. 443). In 1984 the consortium, now joined by Shell and Mitsubishi, finally signed the agreement on the Sakhalin II project. Sakhalin I was signed in July 1995 to develop a neighbouring group of oilfields off the island (*ibid.*, p. 433). Although the Sakhalin I agreement was signed after that for Sakhalin II, the former project has a much longer history, negotiations having been begun as early as 1977 (*ibid.*). Putting into effect Sakhalin II was delayed for two years to allow the Russians to prepare appropriate legislation, in particular on the division of production. The first licence for the development of deposits to be based on an agreement on the division of production was granted not long before June 1996 to the company Sakhalin Energy (created from the shares of all investors as the operator of the project). This licence cannot be revoked.

In June 1996 it was reported that Sakhalin II would be going ahead. This project had attracted $10–12 bn from Western investors for the development of the Pil' tun-Astokhskoye and Lunskoye oil and gas deposits. Depending on the yield, the Russian side stood to gain $16–23 bn, having made no investment except allowing foreign involvement, while the foreign side stood to gain $9–16 bn. It was proposed to transport the gas to the shore, 20 km away, through a pipeline. This would then continue south to Korsakov, where a compressed gas factory would be built. Up to 70 per cent of contract work would be done by Russian contractors, including the military-industrial complex. It was pointed out that speed was necessary to gain a hold in the market for gas, and that legally binding documents, as well as legislation, were needed for everyday business (Leskov, 1996, RN=24670).

It is probably for this project that an oilrig platform for Sakhalin has been reported under construction at Amur Shipbuilding Works. (Earlier it was noted that Russia could not then build such a platform, but evidently she now can.) The construction was popular with the workers, who probably found it more remunerative than work for the Russian Defence Ministry, which was owing Rs 42 bn in wages (!), as a strike at the works took a strange form, being limited to certain workshops only. The workers wanted to put pressure on the Defence Ministry while at the same time hurrying on with producing an oilrig platform for Sakhalin. The management did not know what to do with the unfinished submarines that occupied 60 per cent of the production area (mothball, complete or recycle them?), which was preventing work on civilian projects (Kunilovskiy, 1997, p. 3 – RN not yet known). It may be surmised that the Japanese had been instrumental in ensuring wages for the oilrig builders, and it is interesting that this put pressure on armaments production.

Within Sakhalin itself, negotiations were reported as early as March 1992 with the Eastern Japan Railway which was helping to put in a new communications system, and which offered to deliver 26 diesel trains. In March 1992 fifty local railway specialists were preparing for a spell in Hokkaido, and the Japanese were sending ten experts (Arkeyev and Martynov, 1992 – RN=19763). Later, the Sakhalin railway was scheduled to renovate Japanese-built narrow-gauge diesel trains with Russian (military) tank engines. (Anon., 1993c, p. 1 – RN=21276; cf. Martynov, 1992, p. 2 – RN=20057). Twenty diesel trains were promised as a gift by the Mitsui company. Representatives of Mitsui and of the East Japan Railway (which was handing over the trains) visited the island and decided that the track rehabilitation already achieved would allow these diesel trains to operate without problems (Moskvin, 1993, p. 1 – RN=21529). Sakhalin has in fact become the recipient of Japanese trains (probably 20). Their arrival caused a sensation, due not only to their provenance but to their brilliant colours, being painted yellow, white and blue (Russian trains are normally drab). During the winter of 1994–5 they could not be used because of the heavy snow and low temperatures, but with the spring they reappeared, connecting South Sakhalinsk and Korsakov, serving leisure resorts. Residents of the western shore also benefited with services to Nikolaichuk, and the trains appeared in the north of the island (Moskvin, 1995, p. 2 – RN=23592).

Probably emboldened by this generosity, the regional body tried to apply leverage to the federal government with the aim that it should help the local economy. The purport of a telegram addressed to President Yeltsin by the Chairman of the Assembly of Sakhalin and the Kurile

Islands was that if the Russian authorities did not take urgent steps to help their people, Sakhalin's regional assembly would be forced to turn to Japan and other countries with an urgent appeal for help (Anon., 1994c, p. 1 – RN=22396). It was (allegedly) rumoured in Tokyo that the Russian authorities had completed a plan for economic development of the far east, and that Japanese businessmen would like to learn directly from Russian officials the part they would play in it (Agafonov, 1993, p. 3 – RN=21233).

Another project is to link Russia and Japan by rail bridges, via Sakhalin. The Russian mainland is 7 km from Sakhalin at the nearest point, while Sakhalin is 42 km from the northern Japanese island of Hokkaido. The cost of construction has been put at the enormous sum of 7 trillion Japanese yen or 65 billion dollars (Anon., 1993g, p. 3 – RN=21838). This seems a visionary project, the benefits from which could not in the foreseeable future repay the cost, and nothing more specific has been heard of it. According to a later statement, 'in the more distant future' the mainland might be linked with Sakhalin; this would require a long tunnel, and Japan was not mentioned (Brezhnev, 1994, p. 2 – RN=22762). This too seems unlikely, or at least not taking place in the near future. But a new air service has been established between Sakhalin and Hakodate (Hokkaido, Japan). The flights are regular and make use of AN24 aircraft, which take one hour and 45 minutes. Sakhalinskiye Aviatrassy (Sakhalin Airlines) had ordered more modern aircraft which should reduce the flight time to one hour (Anon., 1994a, p. 1 – RN=22135). Hakodate (south Hokkaido) was chosen as the destination probably because, besides being Hokkaido's chief port, it is the final stop on the train route to the main Japanese island of Honshu, via the world's longest undersea tunnel; its airport also runs direct air routes to Honshu.

Sakhalin has evidently received some help from the Japanese, but this is more than offset by its other disadvantages, such as its remoteness from European Russia. A Russian parliamentary hearing on the 'Social and Economic Position of the Far North of Russia' reported the almost complete collapse of the region's economy. Sakhalin had not done as badly as some other areas mentioned, yet its average fall in production had been 15 per cent, compared with 5 per cent for the Russian Federation as a whole. Draft laws to help the North were incomplete (Pis'mennaya, 1997, p. II – RN not yet known). Sakhalin will doubtless seek a better deal from Moscow as well as more aid from Tokyo. The economy of Sakhalin remains susceptible to shocks: for instance, a 'petrol crisis' in the summer of 1997 which is thought to have been deliberately engineered to force up the price (Tarasov, 1997 – RN not yet known). Such problems basically stem from the collapse of the central supply system of the communist era, with stable market relations yet to be achieved. Japan's proximity might alleviate future crises of this sort.

Japanese business interest has its chief focus in Russia's far east regions, which are now linked to Japan in multiple ways. Thus in December 1996 Sumitomo was engaged in realizing in the Maritime *krai* a 'whole packet' of economic schemes. As reported in December 1996 it had already invested US$20 million in the Terney-Les firm, which operated in the depths of the forest (ITAR-Tass, 1996, p. 2 – RN=25381). It sounds unlikely, but the Japanese have shown interest in growing mushrooms in the *taiga*. No details are given in the source, which reported that Khabarovsk *krai* was widening contacts with foreign firms. New Zealanders showed them ways to protect the roots of young seedlings in nurseries and greenhouses, and this – as well as the fact that the Canadian government had financed a model timber undertaking in Khabarovsk *krai* – was the context of the Japanese interest (Khoroshilov, 1996c, p. 2 – RN=25100).

Wider-Ranging Activities

However, other Japanese business interest has ranged farther afield. Even within the Soviet time (the *perestroika* period) a Soviet–Japanese timber-working plant was built in Irkutsk *oblast*, with Japanese specialist help, in one-third of the usual time, and productivity there was expected to be almost double the branch average. (This is referred to in more detail below.) The Khanty-Mansi peoples of the West Siberian plain, living to the east of the Ob'river, were to get video equipment installed by Marubeni Corporation. One can only speculate why this Finno-Ugrian group, who until recently were mainly 'hunters and fishers, with some interest in reindeer-herding' (Brown *et al.* (eds), 1994, pp. 34, 45) should be singled out, but in their frozen wastes they surely appreciate being able to watch something.

Japan mounted its largest ever trade and industry exhibition in Moscow in April 1992. Three-quarters of the participants are said to have found new trading partners in Moscow. This was probably an exhibition of a general type, and if so most likely concocted specially for the Russian market, as in Japan itself all trade exhibitions are now specialized. Russian specialists have received training in Japan, for which the Japanese state paid 200 mn yen ($1.6 mn) in 1991 and 540 mn yen ($4.3 mn) in 1992. It also provided economic and humanitarian assistance and $200 mn to support the development of trade projects, guaranteed by the Japanese government (Anichkin, 1992, p. 4 – RN=20333).

Japanese water-heating systems are being built by Tulachermet (Tula ferrous metals, Tula being a town south of Moscow which used to specialize in armaments) by agreement with three Japanese companies: Nisso Iwai Corporation, Paloma Industries Ltd. and Ube Industries Ltd. Nisso Iwai had already supplied equipment worth US$30 mn. The first 4721 heating systems were produced in 1992 from Japanese spare parts. Despite their relatively high cost (18 000 Rs each), the products had sold because of their high quality. The planned capacity had not yet been reached because the Russian side had not yet finished building works. If everything went as planned, Tulachermet was to generate 3000 mn Rs of profit annually, and would recoup the investment in four years. By the end of 1994 output was allegedly to be increased to 50 000 water-heating systems annually, and by 1995 new types would be developed that did not require pipes. Aleksandr Zotov, head of the project's Russian side, regretted that completion of the production line was hindered by the slowness of local builders; this circumstance did not allow fixing the retail price (Matkin, 1993, p. 10 – RN=21531).

As reported in August 1997, Toyota was hoping to start producing their vehicles in Russia within the next 2–3 years. They were planning to start assembling Haieis minibuses at Tushino Machine-Building Factory 'soon'. The company intended to set up a trading branch in Moscow. Japanese journalists reported that there were plans to assemble 5000 Toyotas per year in Moscow, from Japanese parts. The first could appear by the end of 1998. In order to carry out these plans, Toyota intended to set up a joint enterprise in Moscow, for which it would supply 70 per cent of the company capital (Charodeyev, 1997 – RN not yet known).

Japanese Exports to Russia

Among the items for which promising prospects have been seen were Japanese fax machines. Geotek aimed at opening up the Russian market to high quality Western equipment, especially the Japanese companies Mita and Murata. Geotek had no regional distributors, but among its customers were banks and enterprises of Moscow, Omsk, Yekatarinburg, Chelyabinsk, Rostov-on-Don, also Moldova and Yakutiya (Semenov, 1993, p. 2 – RN=21232). In June 1993 about 150 Japanese businessmen came to Moscow to take part in a forum held by the Joint Committee on Economic Co-operation; presumably they had exports in mind. Japanese car-tyre manufacturers are preparing to expand in Russia. The world market for tyres is saturated and there is room for serious competition only on the Russian market. Moscow dealers report increased interest in imported tyres, which are better quality than Russian ones for a similar price. Half the tyres sold in Moscow are imported. The Japanese company Bridgestone, which has mainly supplied tyres for the mining industry, has the most serious plans for the Russian market. This company trades in tyres for lorries, buses and cars not only in Russia but in Ukraine and Belarus. A network of 13 main dealers has been created, which work with 80 trading organizations. Since February 1996 the Japanese have entered the Russian market for car tyres. They sell 15 000–20 000 car tyres per month and 800–900 for buses and lorries. All the tyres supplied to Russia are made in Japan. Neither Goodyear nor Michelin are serious competitors on the Russian market: the main competitors are Russian, Eastern European and Scandinavian companies. Russian manufacturers are likely to lose out, as unlike car manufacturers they do not have sufficient influence in government circles to stem the flow of imports. They lack the modern technology to compete with Western manufacturers as equals, although there are some successes (Yevplanov, 1996, p. II – RN=25101).

The Japanese are also emerging as suppliers of rails. As reported in August 1996, Russian rails had quite good physical and mechanical properties, compared with US rails, but the better equipment of US railways with track maintenance machinery gave US rails a longer life. Converted to dollars, Russian-made rails were at that time 10–15 per cent dearer than foreign. In 1995, 10 km of Japanese rail were bought for the BAM (Baykal-Amur-Mainline) Railway, and now the Far Eastern Railway was thinking of ordering 100 000 tonnes of Japanese rails. For the high-speed lines which Russia was contemplating, a radically improved type of rail was needed (Pan, 1996, p. 2 – RN=25149). Apparently more rails may be ordered from Japan.

Russian coal miners, who formerly bought from Promtractor, a tractor factory in Cheboksary (209 km east of Nizhnyy Novgorod), have switched to foreign tractors – 'Caterpillar' (US) and 'Komatsu' (Japan). The number of tractors sold by Promtractor dropped from 780 in 1993 to 230 in 1995. (Yakovleva, 1996, pp. 1–2 – RN=24720). Thus Promtractor suffered severely from the US and Japanese entry.

The ship design bureau Vympel (undoubtedly Russian – the word in Russian means 'pennant') is completing technical documentation of a ship designed to process liquid radioactive waste. By agreement between Russia and Japan, Japan will provide money for the design and construction of this vessel in Russia. The ship will process up to 7000 cu. m. of contaminated water at Zvezda Works in Vladivostok (presumably this would be one loading). Construction of the ship's sections is proceeding at Khabarovsk (ITAR, 1997, p. 3 – RN = 25684).

At the other side of Russia, as reported in November 1997, Novorossiisk Shipping Line (Novoship) has taken the unprecedented step of ordering, from Sumitomo in Japan, a high-capacity tanker of 100 000 tonnes or larger. Four units of this type are envisaged, and possibly two more; the first unit will cost $41 mn which is regarded as quite a bargain, and the construction time nine months is regarded as minimal. Novorossiisk Shipping Line had previously ordered smaller tankers from Croatian shipbuilders, and has also ordered from Croatia chemical carriers. As Novoship has been unusually profitable among Russian shipping lines and in recent years has been expanding, whereas most Russian shipping lines have been contracting, it is not very probable that other Russian shipping lines will follow suit (Kalashnikova, 1997 – RN not yet known). However, this remains to be seen. It is possible, too, that this deal may affect the morale or fortunes of the shipping interests of other Black Sea nations, such as Romania, and/ or the probability of construction of the pipeline so far tentatively envisaged from Turkmenistan towards Japan (see section 3.13 'Japan and Turkmenistan'). This whole topic requires expert examination.

Telecommunications

The Japanese are interested in improving telecommunications, or at least in building them. Sumitomo also has a leading role in building a Moscow–Khabarovsk telecommunications link. As reported in October 1993, the contract was worth $235.3 mn. The tender was won by a consortium consisting of Sumitomo, NEK (Japan) and Siemens AG (Germany). Other foreign firms took an active part. Sumitomo became the general contractor for building the Moscow to Khabarovsk radio relay network. The line would include 10 500 high-quality communications channels. A compulsory condition for the tender was the availability of concrete proposals for finance. The Japanese partners of the winning consortium played an active role in obtaining preferential loans from Eximbank (Sveshnikov, 1993, p. 1 – RN = 21534).

As then reported, the telecommunications line was to be operational by mid-1995. At least in the first stages, construction apparently went ahead according to schedule. A subsequent account placed this scheme within the context of building a modern international communications network in Russia. The first of three stages in this construction was a digital international communications system between Russia and Denmark

and a 7680-channel fibre-optic line from Russia to Finland set up in
1993. The second stage was the opening in February 1995 of the eastern
complex in Khabarovsk. This is based on an underwater fibre-optic digital
communications line between Russia, Japan and the Korean Republic.
The third stage is connection with a terrestrial fibre-optic line from Moscow to Rostov-on-Don to Novorossiisk, and a 3540 km underwater fibre-
optic line from Novorossiisk to Odessa, Istanbul and Palermo. Total
investment in the southern project is $50 mn or 70 bn Rs. The section
from Novorossiisk to Rostov-on-Don (555.5 km) was completed in
December 1995 and would provide 30 000 telephone lines between the
cities. The three areas of international communications would be linked
by a radio relay line from Moscow to Khabarovsk (8000 km). This would
be constructed in stages. In March 1996 international communications
centres were opened in Samara, Yekaterinburg and Novosibirsk. The
capacities are: Samara 10 320 channels and lines including 2160 international ones, Yekaterinburg 3480 and 1500, Novosibirsk 7200 and 1620,
respectively. The construction of fibre-optic communications lines from
Kingisepp to Tallinn was completed in 1996, and work was continuing
on fibre-optic lines from Khabarovsk to Harbin and from Moscow to
St Petersburg (Baskayev, 1996, p. 1 – RN = 24793).

New Investment Trends

Toyo Engineering Corporation (TEC) of Japan has begun executing a
US$120 mn contract with Tekhmashimport on installing a modern oil-
processing line with an annual capacity of 1 800 000 tonnes. The contract,
which is to be paid by the main client – Novokuybyshev oil-processing
plant – was ratified in 1992, but only now, according to the Moscow head
of TEC, Fumitaka Abe, have all problems been solved. About 800 Japanese companies are involved in the project, supplying highly efficient
and environmentally friendly equipment produced on American licences.
The new line, planned to be fully operational by 1996, would be the only
one in Russia producing high-octane fuel on Western equipment,
which would open up possibilities for export. The Japanese side were
also to train their Russian colleagues. The rest of the oil-processing
lines were using equipment made in former socialist countries or FSU
republics. The contract with TEC was seen by many as a sign of changing attitude towards Russia by Japanese investors, which might prompt
investment from other Japanese companies (Kravchenko, 1994, p. 10 –
RN = 22748).

Conversion of the Defence Industry

Japan, with her postwar experience of abandoning military production to concentrate on civilian output, must have gained expertise in defence industry conversion. One might suppose that this would be useful to Russia in the post-Soviet era, yet only one such venture has been reported, which is a study by the private research institute Namura of a machine-building factory in the Russian town of Murom, this study having been sponsored by the Japanese government. Before 1993 the factory had been employing 11 500 personnel and 6000 units of modern equipment, 95 per cent of all orders being from the Ministry of Defence. In 1993 it was privatized – 51 per cent of shares remained at the factory, 20 per cent went to the State Property Committee, and the rest were sold at a voucher auction. The factory lost 90 per cent of its military orders and subsequently was reported to be specializing in refrigerators, machinery, tools for agriculture, and toys. The Japanese experts who arrived in April 1994 recommended setting up a number of independent small headquarters for each production line, creation of a marketing department, and gradually turning to mono-production, in this case to refrigerators. They proposed to cut the number of people in the main headquarters from 20 per cent of all personnel to 5 per cent, and getting rid of unprofitable properties of the factory – it owned a library, a number of camps for children, tourist camps and a medical centre. Mr Tamada, Director of the research institute, informed the factory personnel that even well-known Western companies such as Japan Victor Company and General Motors were compelled to undergo structural changes, reducing their workforce and output. Apparently it will not be easy to follow the Japanese experts' recommendations in Murom because, although in a market economy a factory cannot go on producing simply because it has enough resources and personnel, the former military factories in Russia have unfortunately been doing so, according to Dzokayeva (1994, p. 9 – RN=22758). The Japanese advice appears good, but nothing further has been heard about this, nor has any other instance of advice about defence conversion come to the author's notice.

Joint Ventures

These have not got under way in large numbers. As reported in August 1989, joint ventures with Japan numbered 19, as compared with more than 100 with the Federal German Republic (Glaubitz, 1995, p. 116). The first joint Russian–Japanese enterprise was founded in 1987, during the Soviet era. This was Igrima-Tayriku, for which the 'Protocol of Intentions' was signed 'a few months earlier' than 13 June 1987 (the date of the report). This new development was made possible by *perestroika*, which modified various Soviet institutions. (This newspaper report adopted the future tense, but in the current text it is assumed that these predictions were fulfilled; see also below.) The product would be sawn timber and the predicted annual output 90 000 cu. m. The All-Union Timber Industry Association Irkutsklesprom would provide 51 per cent of the capital. The factory would be built on the territory of Igrimin Timber Industry undertaking in Novaya Igrima urban village in Irkutsk *oblast*, with the participation of Tayriku Trading. The Soviet side were to do the building while the Japanese would provide the complex technical equipment, spare parts, installation and operational machinery. Financing would be by credits provided by the participants. No further details were given, except that the period of expiry would be five years. April 1988 was designated as the date for commencement of production. D. Ivata, President of Tayriku Trading, was interviewed. It had been three years earlier that they had made the first proposal to the Soviet side. Other Japanese firms would monitor their progress and if they were successful in securing concessions that question would be raised with the 'competent authorities'. They were planning to build houses for the workers, as well as shops, kindergartens and so on. M. Busygin, Minister of the Timber, Cellulose-Paper and Wood-Processing Industry of the USSR, commented that pay would be different from what was normal (presumably his meaning was that it would be above-normal) but within Soviet legislation. As regards personnel, the Minister had nominated as general director I. Podashev, born in 1941, and having had experience of directing a large timber industry association. Mr Ivata had nominated as director K. Yamaguti, born in 1931, who had 25 years' experience of importing Soviet timber and selling it in Japan. He 'knows your country, the Russian language'. The directorate would include five Japanese specialists (Shmyganovskiy, 1987, p. 4).

Two later reports about this enterprise are to hand. As stated in December 1987, supplies of first-class pine and fir timber to the enterprise were not assured, because of past over-felling in the immediate vicinity. Timber had to be despatched from further afield (Kalinkin, 1987, p. 1 – RN = 14428). This was clearly not the fault of the enterprise itself; if anything, it confirms that it was producing efficiently. As reported in March 1988 the factory had been built in only eight months rather than the two years which would have been normal – a difference which particularly impressed the Russian reporter. At the busiest time there were 350 people at work, including 30 Japanese. Three shifts were worked.

Projection and building, in stages, went on simultaneously. The assembly teams came from Moscow, and, thanks to their quick construction of the building's carcasses, installation of the equipment could be done in a warm atmosphere. The factory's complement was 163, including five Japanese specialists. (These might well have been the five mentioned by Ivata at the earlier date.) Output per head was nearly double the branch average. The contract was for 30 years, which might nevertheless be prolonged or terminated prematurely. The correspondent visited the port of Vostochny, in Vrangel (or Wrangel) bight, built with Japanese co-operation and officially opened at the beginning of 1974 (Glaubitz, 1995, p. 99) and saw how timber was being exported at much lower value than that produced by Igrima-Tayriku. All waste products had to be used, which the Japanese already knew how to do. The bringing into operation of the Igrima-Tayriku plant was an important event. Timber was the main item in Soviet exports to Japan, and Irkutsk *oblast* was in the lead in supplying the *taiga*'s riches (Yermolayev, 1988, p. 1).

Negotiations between the two countries to produce timber – apparently this is separate from Igrima-Tayriku – are said to have dragged on for years. The initial agreement was for the Japanese company K.S. Sange to supply the technology while the (Russian) Roseksportles, Eksportles and Dal'les would supply the timber. Agreement was reached concerning personnel and delivery times of machinery, and concerning the amount and kinds of timber goods to be supplied to Japan and their price. Agreement over funding, however, was not reached. Russia was to receive $100 mn worth of equipment through a credit of Eximbank, Japan, guaranteed by the Japanese Ministry of Industry and Trade. The credit was to be cleared off in five years through Russia's supply of roundwood amounting to 3 mn cu. m. Setting the terms of the basic agreement was said to have been made more difficult by the entry into the Japanese market of other Russian timber organizations. A proposed variant of the agreement would have more regional than governmental significance (what this meant is unclear). Both sides were wanting to settle, but major difficulties were caused by the number of borrowers involved, price-setting, and how the credit liquidation scheme was to work. Details of the project were needing to be worked out more fully in view of the complexity of the financial and credit arrangements (Levina, 1987, p. 2 – RN not yet known).

There were almost 60 joint Russian–Japanese joint enterprises by April 1992 (Anichkin, 1992, p. 43 – RN=20333). This is three times as many as three years previously. Details of most are not available. More recent data are not available either, but unless there has been extremely rapid growth, which is unlikely, their number falls far short of the number of Russian–Chinese joint enterprises, which is stated to be about 1000 (Portanskiy, 1997, p. 1 – RN = 25980).

Fishing

A fishing agreement has been signed. Russian catches in the Pacific Ocean were to be about 4.5 mn tonnes in 1996, 1 mn tonnes higher than in 1994. Russian quotas are not auctioned abroad. Any exchange of quotas is agreed at government level, taking into account the different countries' preferences. The agreement with Japan allows Japanese fishermen to take 100 000 tonnes of fish from Russian waters and vice versa. The Japanese can pay for an extra 80 000 tonnes of quota, excluding certain catches. The distribution of internal quota is determined by industrial criteria (50 per cent), social criteria (20–25 per cent), incentives (10–15 per cent) and competitive sales (10–15 per cent) (Svistunov, 1996, p. II – RN = 25369).

In actual fact the official fishing arrangements have been in substantial degree ignored. The price of crabs in Japan fell dramatically, due to cheap supplies from Russia. Russian experts estimated that 2 bn worth of sea products bypassed customs officials. In a successful, but illegal, joint enterprise the Japanese processed sea products caught by the Russians, and it was thought that crabs could completely disappear within 2–3 years if this enterprise continued to work at the rate then reported. It was subsequently reported that the Japanese police had started to take action against Russians and Japanese involved in illegal fishing, which made a farce of the current intergovernmental discussions of 200-mile zones and quotas.

Russian Ventures in Japan

Russian ventures within Japan are few and in their infancy. In January 1992 a catering business, the firm Volna (meaning 'wave') which belonged to the Kosyritsi family and which already had food shops and cafés in Russia, and subsidiaries in the USA and West Germany, was reported to be opening a restaurant in Tokyo (Prelovskaya, 1992 – RN = 19463). There is no further word of this, and in both 1991 and 1995 there was no visible Russian presence in Japan (present author's experience).

Trans-Siberian Transport

According to the head of the Russian Federation Transport Ministry's transport co-ordination department, the Trans-Siberian container service has lost its attraction to foreign shippers, thanks to the mess it made of things during the *perestroika* period. Nowadays a Japanese exporter prefers to send shipments by sea via the Suez Canal to Rotterdam, thence by smaller vessel to Finland, where freight would be trans-shipped and sent by highway to Moscow or St Petersburg. No longer were 150 000 import–export containers sent annually over the Trans-Siberian; until there was a firm rates policy, proper legal foundations and a responsible and reputable management, this eastern traffic would be unlikely to return (Shchukin, 1996, p. 2 – RN=25446). This is consistent with a more recent report: at a session of the Co-ordinating Council for Trans-Siberian Traffic, held at the Railway Ministry and attended by representatives from participating countries and carriers, anxiety was expressed at the loss of traffic to competing routes. From Japan to Fin-land a container sent by the Trans-Siberian took 35–40 days, about the same time as by sea, whereas via China and Kazakhstan only 25 days were needed; this latter route was already carrying 1000 containers monthly. Shortened transit times, largely through elimination of unne-cessary port and customs delays, and a lower unified tariff, were badly needed (Chibisov, 1997, p. 1 – RN not yet known). Russia also wishes to take part in the Singapore–Europe Mainline Project, which would head first for Beijing, but at the time of the report its onward route was as yet undecided: it might go via Mongolia and the Trans-Siberian, alternatively via Kazakhstan and the Trans-Siberian, or avoid Russia through Iran and Turkey (Anon., 1997b, p. 1 – RN not yet known). See also Chapter 3, section 3.13 'Japan and Turkmenistan' regarding prospective pipeline transport across Asia.

Air Routes and Services

One legacy of the Cold War is that the flight paths of most (but not all) aircraft plying between America and the East tend to take a circuitous route avoiding former Soviet airspace. As much as 3000 km could be saved if such flights passed over the Arctic and Russian airspace. Plans are being mooted to take advantage of this (Yaroslavets, 1997 – RN not yet known). Japan could be one of the beneficiaries. Meanwhile, Aero-flot flies from London to Tokyo via Moscow very cheaply (in 1991 the return fare was £560) but the journey is rather arduous so informed travellers prefer to pay more – to go by KLM, for example – for the sake of more attentive in-flight service (this is based on the author's experi-ence). But Aeroflot is starting to provide freight services between peripheral foreign countries. Co-operation with a Norwegian export company started in 1995. In February 1997 it reached the point where Aeroflot could sign an agreement to transport fresh salmon twice a week directly from Norway to Japan (Rosich, 1997, p. VI). At the opposite end of Russia from Japan, a Russo-Japanese joint enterprise 'Aeroservice' was founded in 1989 to organize Aeroflot's ground service at Moscow's Sheremet'evo airport. Aeroservice has made Sheremet'evo by far the best of Russia's airports for freight transfers and despatch. Among its varied activities is a Japanese restaurant (Shitov, 1995, pp. 16–17). This contrasts with Sheremet'evo's indifferent service to air travellers and uncomfortable layout (of course non-Russian airports, too, are often not ideal).

PARTICIPATION OF THIRD COUNTRIES IN RUSSO-JAPANESE ECONOMIC ARRANGEMENTS

Tkhomesto has already been mentioned. Certain American firms have aided Russo-Japanese exchanges by vouching for the quality of the Russian products. 'One American timber company sells Siberian pine to Japanese trading companies by inspecting timber stands and monitoring timber quality . . . Japanese and Korean trading firms that normally buy pine from New Zealand are prepared to buy Russian logs from the American company because of its reputation for consistent quality' (Thornton and Mikheyeva, 1996, p. 111).

In summary, this chapter has revealed a fairly wide variety of types of Japanese economic involvement in the post-Soviet Russian Federation.

BIBLIOGRAPHICAL NOTE

Russian studies of Japan have been extremely numerous, and (up to its date of publication) are covered by E. Stuart Kirby (*Russian Studies of Japan*, Macmillan, London, 1981). This book does not cover Eastern Europe. So far no successor to it has been noticed.

3 Japan and the non-Russian Successor States of the Former Soviet Union

3.1 INTRODUCTION

In this chapter the successor states to the former USSR, apart from Russia, are listed alphabetically. If formed into regional groups approximately in order of their nearness to Japan, the Central Asian States would come first: Kazakstan, Kyrgyzstan, Tajikistan, Turkmenistan, Uzbekistan. Second would come the Caucasian states: Armenia, Azerbaydzhan, Georgia. Third would come the southern states: Moldova, Ukraine. Fourth would come the western states: Belarus, Estonia, Latvia, Lithuania. A conjecture that distance would tend to dilute Japanese economic involvement was found to have some justification.

3.2 JAPAN AND ARMENIA

3.2.1 Comparisons and Relations

Armenia, a small (Christian) Caucasian state long in conflict with Azerbaydzhan over Nagorny-Karabakh, has 8 per cent of Japan's area and 2.8 per cent of her population, so Japan's density of population is three times greater. In recent years Armenia's economy has plumbed the depths of an exiguous existence. Shoddy goods came in from Poland, Turkey and the UAE (United Arab Emirates) (Arutyunyan, 1994, p. 2 – RN=22830); the source mentions none from Japan. Armenia did acquire the trust of international financial institutions by repaying its debts precisely (pi. 1995c, p. 19 – RN=22828) but despite this there is no sign of Japanese economic involvement.

3.3 JAPAN AND AZERBAYDZHAN

3.3.1 Comparisons and Relations

Azerbaydzhan's area is 86 600 sq km and its population (1 January 1991 estimate) 7 137 000: thus its area is 23 per cent of Japan's and its population

6 per cent, making Japan's density of population almost four times greater. Azerbaydzhan's coastline is on the Caspian Sea. The climate is warm and largely dry. Industry and mining (especially oil extraction) are the chief sectors of the economy, though there is also agriculture including viticulture. In 1992 production slumped and prices rose (Mamedov, 1993 – RN=20724); military expenditure has been high (Useynov, 1993 – RN=21342), as is natural, given the clash with Armenia. There has been no report of Japanese interest.

3.4   JAPAN AND BELARUS

3.4.1   Comparisons

Belarus, with an area of 207 600 sq km and a population of 10 008 000 in 1985, had a density of population seven times less than Japan's. Other differences compared with Japan were hardly less pronounced.

Following the disintegration of the USSR the Belarus economy went into steep decline. In December 1993 its local currency was heading for hyperinflation (Shimov, 1993, p. 32 – RN=21631). By mid-1995 the economy was slipping into economic crisis: many enterprises stood idle, the shops were full of goods that nobody needed, prices were rising, 24 per cent of enterprises made a loss. In this plight, Belarus moved closer to Russia: a customs union was established between the two countries (Debski, 1995, p. 6 – RN=23437). The latest budget trends are more favourable (Demchuk, 1997 – RN not yet known).

3.4.2   Relations

There appeared to be little basis for direct trade between Belarus and Japan, and so far there is little sign of Japanese economic involvement; this is indirectly confirmed by a report in August 1997 that in the past Belarus had no trade with China because of distance and because trade was concentrated in the Siberian region, whereas now negotiations (about decorative parts for furniture) were taking place between Belarus Timber and Paper Industry and a Chinese overseas trade firm (Vysotskiy, 1997, p. 2). Japan is one stage farther away from Belarus than China. Some Japanese goods have doubtless reached Belarus due to its customs union with Russia. The Japanese 'Bridgestone' company trades in Belarus in tyres for lorries, buses and cars (Yevplanov, 1996, p. II – RN=25101).

3.5   JAPAN AND ESTONIA

3.5.1   Comparisons

Estonia (area 45 215 sq km with many marshes, lakes and islands, and 36 per cent forested) has 12 per cent of the area of Japan, but normally appears very small on a map because of its closeness to Russia. Its population, some 1.6 million, is about 1.2 per cent of Japan's, making Japan's density of population ten times greater. In the Soviet period Estonia's economy was relatively prosperous, being based on oil shale, peat and phosphorite ore (exported largely to Russia), timber-related industries, electronics and engineering, and consumer goods. Soviet consumers valued Estonian products for their higher quality and attractive design, but Japan has its own domestic traditions of high-grade products. History, culture, religion and language have no resemblance to their Japanese analogues. The Estonian language is related to Finnish (thus not at all to Russian or to Japanese), and of 97 functioning joint ventures as of 1 April 1991, many involved partnership with Finnish companies (Anon. (ed.), 1992d, pp. 531, 533). The Estonian economy has exhibited a less favourable trend than that of Latvia, but better than that of Lithuania. As reported in July 1997 the average wage in Estonia was almost $250 per month, compared to $217 in Latvia and $188 in Lithuania. The average pension is higher than in the other Baltic States, at $75 per month. The cost of living is high and there is a huge gulf between rich and poor, according to one Russian account, which might perhaps be biased (Lashkevich, 1997, p. 4 – RN not yet known).

3.5.2   Relations

All three Baltic countries are very unlike Japan, and there are few reports of Japanese interest in them. The trade deficits of all of them increased substantially in 1994. All three countries have been trying, since they declared independence from the then USSR at the beginning of the 1990s, to transform their economies, which were then oriented towards trade with the rest of the then USSR (Anon., 1995d, p. 20 – RN=23228). They were doubtless wishing to import Japanese goods, but at the time it was not clear how they would be paid for. The typically exportable consumer products of Estonia (see above) might be appreciated by the Japanese, but are unlikely to be known about and would scarcely be needed. In any event, there has been no sign of Japanese investment or other economic involvement.

3.6   JAPAN AND GEORGIA

3.6.1   Comparisons

Georgia, with an area of 69 700 sq km and a population (1 January 1991) of 5 464 000, had in that year a population density of 78.4 persons per sq km. Thus Georgia had an area 18.7 per cent of Japan's and a population of 4.4 per cent, making Georgia's population density less than a quarter of Japan's. Georgia stretches east to west, the western Rion plains and Black Sea littoral having a humid subtropical climate, the eastern part a more continental one (Anon. (ed.), 1992d, p. 540). Georgia produces tea and subtropical fruits and has deposits of manganese; also oil and hydropower.

3.6.2   Relations

Despite these assets, or more exactly because of its dependence upon them, following the disintegration of the USSR Georgia experienced all the hardships of a small territory abruptly separated from its markets. Despite its favourable geography and attractive scenery, during the first half of the 1990s the new country's economic situation became appalling: there was inflation, soaring interest rates, barely functioning railways (though their bureaucracy stayed intact), unimaginably low living standards (Russu, 1993 – RN=21667 and 21668; Gogidze, 1994 – RN=22292; Chonkidze, 1995 – RN=23179). The socio-economic crisis caused by the break-up of the Soviet Union resulted in a larger fall in GDP in Georgia than in any other ex-Soviet republic (81 per cent) (Chaplygin, 1997). A hopeful sign appeared for 1995 in the shape of a balanced budget (Namtalashvili, 1995 – RN=22876). Up to the time of writing no report has been seen of any Japanese economic involvement.

3.7   JAPAN AND KAZAKSTAN

3.7.1   Comparisons and Relations

These two countries are extremely unlike geographically, historically, or as regards religion or population (Kazakstan has 7.3 times Japan's area and only about 7.6 per cent of Japan's population, so the population density in Japan is nearly 100 times greater). Few or no Japanese dwell in Kazakstan, which is nevertheless the only successor state of the former Soviet Union apart from Uzbekistan to include significant numbers of ethnic Koreans – about 100 000, some hundreds of whom were present at the World Cup football match between the two nations (*Sunday Telegraph*, 12 October 1997, p. 4S).

Despite or even because of this dissimilarity there is not very ample evidence of direct economic involvement of the one country in the other. However, in December 1996 it was reported that Kazakstan was selling the Yermak power station to the Japanese. Kazakstan was also selling other former Soviet properties, including the Karaganda Metallurgy Combine to the British (Vinogradov, 1996, p. 1 – RN=25311). Japanese goods, electronic or otherwise, would surely find a market in oil-rich Kazakstan which – as the next paragraph suggests – will in future find a means to pay for them.

Since Japan signed an agreement with Kazakstan in 1994, it has spent $50 mn on oil prospecting, modern equipment and training of local experts. As reported in April 1997, activities were to be expanded to include Tereskenskaya Ploshchad' as well as the Priaral'e (territory in the vicinity of the Aral Sea). Three private Japanese companies had formed the joint company Japan-GIT Oil (Kazakstan). This company had extended the original agreement and signed contracts for oil extraction and division of output. The Japanese would invest $1358 mn over 30 years. The volume of working capital required was $3870 mn. Kazakstan should obtain $4273 mn receipts to the budget (Kuz'menko, 1997, p. 2 – RN not yet known). But these totals, while huge, are improbably precise and therefore problematical.

There is one other clear sign of Japanese commercial interest. A group of Japanese companies intends to invest US$250 mn for the production of chromium in Kazakstan. According to a contract concluded for five years, the Japanese companies have obtained control of this industrial sector. The contract, representing in effect the rehabilitation of chromium production in Kazakstan, has been signed by Mitsui Mining and Smelting Co. Ltd and Japan Chrome Corporation; these two companies would also take over the 2 bn Teng (Kazak currency) debt of the sector, equalling US$32 mn. Responsible sources declared that the government was prepared to consider the Japanese proposals for privatization of these two companies, if they proved within five years that they were able to invest (Anon., 1995b, p. 21 – RN=23518).

While no report has been seen of Japanese involvement in Kazak aluminium, its production and export are to be expanded and 'other Far Eastern countries' besides China are noted as a possible export destination (Samarina and Kuz'menko, 1997). Japan might be one of those countries.

Kazakstan would be interested in the creation of a Trans-Asian mainline railway linking the Caucasus, Middle East, Turkey, Central Asia and the Pacific, which would make the Trans-Siberian no longer the chief east–west artery. The signing of a memorandum for the construction of a railway from Yeralievo in western Kazakstan, through Turkmenbashi to Turkmembender in Iran, is a further stage in this process (Tuchkov, 1996, p. 2, RN=25022). Japan is a possible final destination of such a mainline. In June 1997, at a conference (in Tashkent, probably) attended by delegates from many countries, almost certainly including Japan, on the transit potentialities of Kazakstan, the Kazak Transport Minister said that with its 13 000 km of mainline railway, the country had great potential as a transit route between Chinese ports and Europe. The new Trans-Asian route using the Druzhba-Alshan'kou line over the Chinese–Kazakstan frontier would reduce the distance between Germany and Japan by 2500 km compared to the Trans-Siberian route. Renovation of rolling stock, electrification, track rehabilitation and attraction of foreign investment would enable the railways to take advantage of this opportunity (Lavrinenko, 1997, p. 2 – RN not yet known). This too would help to bring Japan and Kazakstan closer together.

3.8 JAPAN AND KYRGYZSTAN

3.8.1 Comparisons

Kyrgyzstan (during the Soviet time called Kirghizia), with an area of 199 000 sq km and a population of 4.5 million (26 per cent ethnic Russian), hence a density of population 7 per cent of Japan's, is extremely unlike Japan in virtually all respects.

In early 1993 Kyrgyzstan was in economic crisis. In July 1993 most factories in the capital, now called Bishkek, were at a standstill or working only three days a week. Ways out were being desperately sought. To the extent that private enterprise took a hand, illegal poppy plantations boomed and a great volume of drugs was smuggled in from Afghanistan. Multilateral co-operation has been sought with adjoining Uzbekistan and

Kazakstan, and Kyrgyzstan, which became independent in 1991, may envisage its future chiefly within this regional grouping.

3.8.2   Relations

Only bare mention has been found of economic relations between Japan and Kyrgyzstan. A total credit of US$240–60 mn was promised by Japan, Turkey, the USA, and the European and Asian development banks (Trofimov, 1993, p. 2 – RN=21159). It was subsequently clarified that Japan had lent $60mn at 2–3 per cent annually. The loans did not seem to have improved the still catastrophic economic situation (Kozlonskiy, 1993, p. 4 – RN=21466).

3.9   JAPAN AND LATVIA

3.9.1   Comparisons and Relations

All three Baltic countries are very unlike Japan. The trade deficits of all of them increased substantially in 1994. All three countries have been trying, since they declared independence at the beginning of the 1990s, to transform their economies which were then oriented towards trade with the rest of the then USSR (Anon., 1995d, p. 20 – RN=23228). They were doubtless wishing to import Japanese goods, if they could pay for them.

Some alleviation of Latvia's foreign exchange situation must have occurred, as in 1996 over 27 per cent of that country's car sales were Japanese. In the three Baltic states as a whole, in the first nine months of 1996, car sales included 641 Toyotas, 364 Nissans and 333 Hondas, which may be compared with sales of 526 Fords, 368 Opels, and 71 cars manufactured by the Russian Tol'yatti plant. Russian sales of cars were in third place (Lashkevich, 1996, p. 1 – RN=25323). A requirement in Latvia that money earned abroad has to be spent abroad, as reported, for instance, concerning Daugavpils Locomotive Works (Dannenberg, 1997) must encourage imports, although Japan is not specifically mentioned here. Latvia might lead the way in any reorientation embracing Japan among other new partners, as its economy has exhibited much more favourable trends than those of Lithuania, but neither Japanese investment nor other Japanese economic involvement has been reported in any of the Baltic countries.

Riga, capital of Latvia, is to become a fuel port (pi, 1995b, p. 20 – RN=23230), and the Baltic States are pursuing integrated transport plans (pi, 1995a, p. 21 – RN=23236). These transport developments might interest the Japanese if they were to extend marketing in or near the region.

3.10 JAPAN AND LITHUANIA

3.10.1 Comparisons and Relations

Lithuania has an area of 65 200 sq km (17.5 per cent of Japan's) and a population of about 3.57 mn, making its density of population about one-sixth of Japan's.

The Lithuanian economy has exhibited the least favourable economic trends of any of the Baltic States, though an upturn was visible in February 1997 with more lively stock exchange activity (Skripov, 1997, p. 5 – RN not yet known). The foreign country which has invested most in Lithuania is Britain, though in other economic indicators the leading foreign country is Germany (Lashkevich, 1995 – RN=23234), perhaps due to the fact that Memel, now Klaipeda, used to be part of Germany (having been annexed by Hitler in 1939). No sign has been seen of Japanese investment or other economic involvement.

3.11 JAPAN AND MOLDOVA

3.11.1 Comparisons and Relations

Moldova (sometimes called Moldavia, but that name should preferably be reserved for one of the republics of the former USSR or for one of the regions of present-day Romania) is extremely unlike Japan in virtually all respects. Its area is 33 700 sq km (9.1 per cent of Japan's), its population (in January 1991) 4 367 000 (3.5 per cent of Japan's). Moldova's language is Moldavian, which is Romanian, written during the Soviet era and until lately in a Cyrillic script but now in a Latin one. If there are non-economic resemblances between Japan and Moldova, these are subsumed in section 4.11 'Japan and Romania' (Chapter 4).

The economy is concentrated on agriculture, especially viticulture and related industries, plus some textiles and chemicals. Before independence, the Soviet Republic of Moldavia (slightly larger than present-day Moldova) derived 3.4 per cent of its Net Material Product from exports to other countries (Anon. (ed.), 1992d, pp. 476, 478). There has been no report of Japanese economic involvement in Moldova.

3.12   JAPAN AND TAJIKISTAN

3.12.1   Comparisons and Relations

Tajikistan has an area of 143 100 sq km and a population (1 January 1986) of 4 648 000, the population density being therefore 32.5 per sq km (one-tenth of Japan's). The country is very poor and backward, with high unemployment, and it was decided that privatization should be reversed (Petrov, 1993, p. 3 – RN = 21607). The Tajik economy is based on cotton and certain other raw materials (aluminium), also fruit and vegetables, but even if these just possibly might form a basis for mutual trade there is no indication of Japanese interest.

3.13   JAPAN AND TURKMENISTAN

3.13.1   Comparisons

Turkmenistan, which consists mainly of desert and semi-desert, is very sparsely settled (population 3.3 million in 1986, area 488 000 sq km, thus a density of population only 2 per cent of Japan's). It is economically backward and underdeveloped, mainly Muslim and with an Islamic culture; it has virtually nothing in common in Japan, yet does have something (natural gas) which Japan may want.

3.13.2   Relations

Turkmenistan's transport system is claimed to have been reborn since independence, at which time its transport facilities were in a 'state of ruin' (Vels, 1993, p. 2 – RN = 21610). Furthermore, as reported in February 1995, among projects where foreign investors would have priority was a pipeline to transport natural gas to Japan. This would be 6700 km long and have a capacity of 28 bn cu. m. (Infocentrum/German Agency BFA, 1995, p. 7 – RN = 23374). No further details are available of what, if implemented, would have to be a mammoth scheme, though the following year a Russian journal did mention that a pipeline to Japan was under consideration, among other pipeline destinations (Sukhonos, 1996, p. 2 – RN = 24862).

3.14   JAPAN AND UKRAINE

3.14.1   Comparisons

Ukraine, with a population of 50 million, about two-fifths that of Japan, is by far the most populous of the non-Russian successor states. Japan and Ukraine are nevertheless very unalike, in geographical features as well as in language, religion, history and economic system. The Ukrainian economy has been in crisis, including grave monetary plight, with no genuine economic reform under way before 1995.

3.14.2   Relations

There seems actually to be little basis for direct trade between Japan and Ukraine. Japanese economic involvement in Ukraine, if present at all apart from the loan mentioned below, must be very recent and does not appear to include any specific projects. The Japanese Bridgestone company trades not only in Russia but in Ukraine and Belarus in tyres for lorries, buses and cars (Yevplanov, 1996, p. II – RN not yet known).

At a meeting in Paris on 24 October 1996, organized by the World Bank, a group of 15 donors and eight international organizations decided to grant Ukraine assistance of US$3 bn for 1997. Out of this sum, US$1.2 bn was promised earlier. The International Monetary Fund (IMF) and World Bank undertook an obligation to grant Ukraine at least US$1.4 bn, including a medium-term facility by the IMF. At least US$400 mn had to be found in Europe, the USA and Japan in order to consolidate support for the radical economic reforms undertaken by the Ukrainian President; these would include, especially, an important fiscal reform in 1997 (the allusion being no doubt to the launch of a new currency, the *hrivna*). It was not clear how much Japan would contribute (Anon., 1996a, p. 3 – RN=25497).

3.15   JAPAN AND UZBEKISTAN

3.15.1   Comparisons

Japan and Uzbekistan differ not greatly in area, Uzbekistan being 20 per cent larger (Japan 372 000 sq km, Uzbekistan 447 400 sq km) but very much in population (Japan 124 mn, Uzbekistan 19.81 mn in 1989). Japan's density of population is therefore on average seven times

Uzbekistan's, but this has little meaning as some areas of Uzbekistan are densely settled but others uninhabited. While large areas are semi-desert, the territory also includes the broad, fertile and densely populated Fergana valley. There is one curious demographic similarity, that both have substantial minorities of Koreans – Uzbekistan over 200 000 (1995). Koreans reached Japan during a remote epoch, whereas Uzbekistan's Korean diaspora dates from the 1930s (Ochil, 1995, p. 1 – RN = 23412). (See also section 3.7 'Japan and Kazakstan'.)

3.15.2   Relations

Among successor states of the FSU, Uzbekistan might be described as the largest of the smaller ones (cf. Hutchings, 1971, p. 119). In the Soviet era Uzbekistan made a big contribution to total Soviet exports, being possibly second only to the Russian Soviet Federal Socialist Republic or RSFSR. Cotton, and secondarily karakul (that is dressed lambskin, or astrakhan) pelts were the effective agents (ibid., p. 117). Uzbekistan has very ample supplies of natural gas (ibid., p. 126), which might be of interest to Japan if suitable transport (such as by pipeline) could be provided. (A project to build a pipeline from Turkmenistan to Japan is of interest here – see section 3.13 'Japan and Turkmenistan'. However, as reported in 1992, Uzbekistan was having to import much of its energy, including liquefied gas (Anon., 1992c, p. 1 – RN = 20417), so at that time could not have traded with Japan – also an importer of energy – in those commodities. Uzbekistan is an exporter, Japan an importer, of cotton which conceivably might form a basis for trade exchanges. Japan of course produces manufactured goods in wide variety. Uzbekistan's industrial output has included textile machinery, excavators, graders, centrifugal pumps, armoured cable and machine tools, also hosiery and wine (Hutchings, 1971, pp. 118, 122); all these would have been Soviet style, and whether any of them today could interest Japan would require lengthy examination; there are no reports on the subject but one has to be sceptical.

The biggest international business is, however, tourism. Japanese are enthusiastic tourists, and Uzbekistan is a possible and (as far as this author knows) so far scarcely exploited destination for them. The 'Silk Road' international conference of the Worldwide Tourist Organization (WTO) continued its work in Tashkent on 4 October 1994 under the regional chairman for Europe of the WTO. Representatives of China, Kyrgyzstan, Iran, Greece and Kazakstan reported on the work being carried out in their countries to develop tourism. High-level Uzbek representatives reported on the development of tourism in Uzbekistan, on restoration of the ancient architectural monuments in Tashkent, Samarkand, Bukhara and Khiva, or the need for more hotels of international standard, the training of specialists and the creation of amenities for foreign tourists. The UNESCO administrative director for intercultural projects expressed his opinions on the 'Silk Road' concept and announced a new journal which would include information about the co-operation of countries within the boundaries of the project. The representatives of Japan and Turkey expressed their views on improving the project and made proposals of their own. The following days' session in the Sherdor Medersa ('Medresa' should mean an Islamic seminary: the spelling in Turkish is *medrese*) of Samarkand's Registan complex saw the adoption of the 'Samarkand declaration on tourism along the Silk Road' (Uz, 1994b, p. 1 – RN=22819). So Japan shows interest in tourism to these destinations and its citizens should soon be (or may already be) on their way.

Representatives from Japan, South Korea and Germany were among those attending a conference about new road and rail links between Uzbekistan and China, via Kyrgyzstan. At the Chigirchik Pass (2500 m), they saw the physical challenge to the new arteries that are intended to shorten the distance between Chinese ports and the West. The new routes would form part of the revived 'Silk Route'. As parts of the new road (Andizhan–Osh–Kashgar) already exist, completion of the road could be early, but the Kyrgyz government required supplementary financing for part of the work (Kucherenko, 1997b, p. 2 – RN not yet known).

Some years before, on 13 December 1993, the Uzbek President (Karimov) received a Japanese delegation comprising representatives of the Ministry of External Trade and of Japanese enterprises, headed by Uzhi Kiekawa. President Karimov endorsed the idea of setting up an Uzbek–Japanese Economic Commission, hoping it would create wide opportunities for development of bilateral economic co-operation (Uz, 1993, p. 1 – RN=21917). During the three-day state visit by President Karimov to Japan in May 1994, discussions with companies, banks and funds led to the signature of agreements with Mitsui, Mitsubishi and Marubeni, these being among Japan's biggest trading corporations (Agzam, 1994, p. 2 – RN=22516). The Japanese were to fund a passenger coach repair works in the suburbs of Tashkent, which would enable Uzbekistan to repair its own railway coaches; this works might well also take orders from Tajikistan and Turkmenistan (Kucherenko, 1994b, p. 2 – RN=23119). This is again reported in March 1997: Central Asia's biggest rolling-stock repair works would take shape from the end of the year, financed by a Fund for External Economic Co-operation of Japan $60 mn credit. It would stand on the site of the existing passenger car depot and when reaching full output in the year 2000 would be capable of 400 passenger-vehicle capital repairs annually. Furthermore, a Japanese private investment group had approved a project for building an electric locomotive repair works on the basis of the existing Uzheldorremash (meaning in Russian: Uzbek railway repair) combine; this would involve a credit of around $120 mn (Kucherenko, 1997c, p. 2 – RN not yet known). Mitsubishi figured again in February 1995. This firm had begun working with Mercedes-Benz, Nissan (misspelled in original, but presumably meant), Daewoo and a number of Swiss banks (the Russian ZIL and KamAz automobile plants, and the Latvian Dzintars cosmetics company also being mentioned) (Tell, 1995, p. 4 – RN=23405). The project, mentioned at the time of President Karimov's visit, was made more concrete.

As noted above, Japan's Fund for External Economic Co-operation allocated more than $60 mn for modernization of the Tashkent wagon repair works (more precisely, the previous allusion was to $60 mn, so an overhang must have been permitted); tender documents were being prepared. Japanese and local specialists worked out a prospectus for modernization of the Uzbekistan Works to make the latter suitable for repairing electric locomotives. The same fund was also negotiating the possibility of backing a plan of the Uzbek government for wholesale electrification of the rail network (Kucherenko, 1997a, p. 2 – RN=25516), which sounds ambitious.

By January 1996, although Russia remained Uzbekistan's chief trading partner, the position was changing. In 1996 Uzbekistan's trade turnover with 'near abroad' (former republics of the USSR) would increase by 3.3 per cent and with 'far abroad' (the rest of the world, thus including Japan) by 12.3 per cent. In the last two years, major foreign companies had been attracted by Uzbekistan's natural resources. In the spring of 1995 the Export-Import Bank of the USA and Eximbank, the Export-Import Bank of Japan, jointly announced $160 mn of credit for an oil and gas project. Japanese businessmen were interested in construction projects, and Japan had granted a credit of $150 mn for telecommunications development (Bezverkhov, 1996, p. 3).

Although Japan's involvement in the Uzbek economy is growing, Uzbek economic co-operation with the Republic of Korea appears to be on a much greater scale. (Much information is given in Uz, 1994a, p. 1 – RN=22513.) The Uzbek President, visiting Korea in February 1995, recalled the Korean diaspora in Uzbekistan. Co-operation between Uzbekistan and Korea had been developing unexpectedly fast, and of the $100 mn invested by Korea in the Commonwealth of Independent States (CIS), $80 mn had been in Uzbekistan. This investment was for the development of motor car and electrotechnical factories, and other enterprises. Korean businessmen were not in a hurry to invest capital in Russia, because peace and harmony ruled in Uzbekistan. The necessary circumstances had been established for foreign investors, and their activity enjoyed legal protection. People were not firing at each other and spilling blood, as in some republics, but working. (The Uzbeks like to draw attention to their superiority in these directions.) Much had been achieved since the opening of diplomatic relations. In particular, there was air communication between Uzbekistan and the Republic of Korea. Private cars produced by the Daewoo Corporation, minibuses, televisions and electric apparatus were well known to the Uzbeks of today. At accelerating speed, the Uzdaiwooavto factory in the town of Assak in Andizhan region was moving towards production of up to 200 000 cars a year. If total trade between the two countries was $83 mn (this apparently means in 1993), in the first eleven months of 1994 it was $200 mn.

Co-operation with German firms (Siemens, Mercedes-Benz, etc.) has also been prominent. As reported in June 1994, the first 100 Mercedes-Benz lorries had been assembled by the joint Uzbek–German enterprise for vehicle production in the town of Druzhba in Khorezm region (*Druzhba* means 'friendship' in Russian). It had taken three months to master the firm's technology. As the correspondent complacently noted, German specialists working in Khorezm and training the local workers for their new employment acknowledged that the production process had not been successfully mastered in such a short time by a joint enterprise of Mercedes-Benz or one of its subsidiaries anywhere else in the world. Specialists from Mercedes-Benz, examining the assembly line and conditions in May and studying the degree of qualification of the cadres, decided to issue the 'certificate of quality' to vehicles assembled in Khorezm. It was planned to assemble no fewer than 400 vehicles by the end of the year. When the enterprise was operating at full capacity 4000 vehicles would come off the assembly line annually (Khasan, 1994, p. 1 – RN=22514). Speaking at a reception in honour of the German President on his state visit to Uzbekistan in April 1995, the Uzbek President maintained that fresh horizons had been opened up with independence. Siemens, Daimler-Benz, Alcatel, Thyssen, Lufthansa and many other German concerns had established themselves, and financial co-operation too was growing. The trade turnover between Uzbekistan and Germany had grown fivefold in three years and would exceed 1 billion DM (Deutsche Marks) in 1995 (Karimov, 1995, p. 1 – RN=23410). Given this activity by South Korea and Germany in Uzbekistan, Japan was evidently not then in the forefront. It is not clear whether the gap has since been made up, but it seems unlikely.

In one sphere, however, Japanese advice might produce a spectacular result. As reported in December 1994, Uzbekistan was growing 500 000–600 000 tonnes of rice annually, when demand amounted to 700 000–750 000 tonnes. The area under rice was at that time 174 000 hectares, but a yield of 40–45 metric centners (1 centner = 100 kg) per hectare – which would have enabled Uzbekistan to supply itself fully – was rare and usually the yield was 30–35 or even 20–25 metric centners. Experts were saying that to raise productivity the rice-growing *kolkhozes* had to be reorganized into small farms by taking the land on long-term lease. Though that was legal, nobody seemed willing to take the plunge, as whoever did so needed highly productive grain, modern technologies, and so on. Uzbek scientists had spent many years on selecting highly productive strains of rice and developing new agricultural technologies, and had been making great strides, but their results were accepted very slowly by rice-growers, and often never emerged from experimental plots. For that reason the Uzbek Academy of Agricultural Sciences invited a delegation from the Agricultural, Timber and Fishing Ministry of Japan, headed by the coordinator of the International Research Centre of Agriculture, Mr Mitsunori, who said that the main aim of the visit was to start close co-operation with Uzbek scientists and specialists to study the climate and productivity of Uzbekistan, and finally to work out a project on introducing modern technologies in this field (Galimov, 1994, p. 5 – RN=23104). The Japanese would surely have much to offer. If Uzbekistan could meet its own consumption needs in rice that would be a great boon to its economy, and if it were the Japanese whose advice achieved that result their status would soar.

BIBLIOGRAPHICAL NOTE

This chapter is largely based on Russian language sources; partly also on Czech, English and French language sources. Some basic data here and elsewhere are from Anon. (ed.), 1992d.

4 Japan and Eastern Europe

4.1 INTRODUCTION

The first problem – if not opportunity – to confront was the paucity of literature on the subject of Japan's economic involvement within this area. Japanese statistics about trade with the 'Communist bloc' naturally included the USSR, China, and so on. For what these statistics were worth, such trade in 1985 comprised 9.2 per cent of Japanese exports and 6.5 per cent of Japanese imports (Murakami and Kosai (eds), 1986, Graph 40, on an unnumbered page; source: Japan Tariff Association, *Summary Report, Trade of Japan*). Books about Japan and Europe are fairly numerous, but what they have had in mind is always or almost always *Western* Europe. Historically, Japan had had little connection with Eastern Europe; geographically the two areas are not near to one another, culturally there is little resemblance. (The last aspect will, however, be examined for certain countries elsewhere in this chapter.) From an economic angle the Japanese saw Western Europe, not Eastern Europe, as advanced and attractive. I had virtually reached a conclusion that nothing systematic had been written on the subject in English, when I found Iliana Zloch-Christy (ed.), *Privatization and Foreign Investments in Eastern Europe*, (Praeger, 1995), which contains very relevant articles by Ken Morita and Gabor Bakos. Those focus directly on Japanese involvement; other articles in the same book make briefer allusions. Also very informative about earlier Japanese–Soviet and Japanese–East European economic relations is J. Wilczynski *The Multinationals and East–West Relations* (Macmillan, 1976, reprinted 1979). These sources, more particularly the last, are used here especially to sketch the historical background.

At any rate, almost right up to modern times there were few or no links between Japan and Eastern Europe. As regards current dealings this may be on the whole advantageous. Western European links with China have been bedevilled by history (one need only mention the Opium Wars). As already explored, relations in previous centuries between Japan and Russia had been partly antagonistic, and within the present century this continued in the shape of armed confrontations and wars, whose aftermath still hampers Japanese–Russian economic relations. It is only during the past five to seven years that Japan has really become conscious of Eastern Europe and of the individuality of its member

51

countries, and knowledge by Japanese of this region of the world remains far less than their knowledge of the United States or of Western Europe. (This gap enabled me to deliver several lectures in Japanese universities in 1995 about those countries.)

Any political links between Japan and Eastern Europe have generally involved Russia (or the Soviet Union) as a third or even as the dominant player. Certain aspects were mentioned in the section 2.1 'Japan and the Soviet Union'. 'The enemy of my enemy is my friend' applies normally in international relations, although less conspicuously in Balkan history. Russia (or the Soviet Union) has at times been the enemy both of Japan and of one or more East European states. The most notable instance is Japan and Poland, just before the Russo-Japanese War of 1904. Japan (an independent nation), and Polish nationalists striving to make Poland again a nation, saw Russia as their common enemy, though it was not in practice possible to reach any common alignment. (See section 4.10 'Japan and Poland'.) The view held by many Poles of Japan in 1989 was also, for similar reasons, very favourable. Hungary's adherence to the Anti-Comintern Pact, to which Japan also belonged, and the participation of Hungary or Romania in Germany's invasion of USSR in June 1941, probably made no great impression in Japan at the time or afterwards: Japanese attention was focused on her own warlike plans, and then operations. Hungary's or Romania's participation also did not coincide in time with the very brief Soviet offensive against Japan in 1945. There exists one book on Japanese relations with Hungary in 1935 (see Bibliographical Note at end of chapter), but apparently no other (at any rate that is accessible) about Japan's prewar relations with any of the East European countries. Later, Japanese ambitions were focused on South-East Asia, where colonies belonged either to the USA or to *Western* Europe.

Japan's Overseas Development Aid (ODA)

It is therefore not surprising that Japan's postwar overseas development assistance virtually omitted Eastern Europe. (This is based on Ministry of Foreign Affairs, *Japan's ODA 1988*, Tokyo, 1989.) Europe altogether comprised only a very small part of Japan's ODA. Totals of the years 1983–7 inclusive for the five countries listed in the source were: Cyprus (Loan Aid 0, Grant Aid 0, Technical Cooperation 0.01 (hundred million yen in each case)), 0.0 per cent; Greece (Loan Aid 0, Grant Aid 0, Technical Cooperation 0.29) 0.0 per cent; Malta (Loan Aid 0, Grant Aid 0, Technical Cooperation 0.05) 0.0 per cent; Portugal (Loan Aid 0, Grant Aid 0, Technical Cooperation 0.83) 0.0 per cent; former Yugoslavia (Loan Aid 19.25, Grant Aid 0.49, Technical Cooperation 4.37) 0.0 per cent. (The percentages relate to disbursements within Japan's total bilateral ODA.) The other figures are not stated to relate to disbursements. (These figures are on *ibid*. pp. 242–5; former Yugoslavia's alone on *ibid*., p. 245.) Thus Eastern Europe's share in Japan's ODA barely rose above zero. J. Wilczynski compiled voluminous information about foreign economic involvement from which some facts will be quoted here pertaining to Japan's economic involvement in postwar Eastern Europe during the Soviet era.

Credits

While development aid was negligible, with credits the situation was different. Various Japanese banks (Dai-ichi Kangyo, Fuji, Industrial Bank of Japan, Mitsui, Sanwa and Sumitomo) took part in 'Substantial Medium and Long-Term Credits Extended by Western Multinational Banks to Socialist Countries in the First Half of the 1970s'. The largest were Fuji (to the GDR, $300 mn, over 5 years, for industrial equipment) and Dai-ichi Kangyo (Hungary, $50 mn, over 12 years, for machinery and equipment). Eximbank was among the main government-owned institutions which granted credits to the East. The largest line of credit granted by any single bank to a socialist country was $1050 mn by Eximbank to the USSR. Credits to socialist countries from Western companies were at specially low interest rates, the Japanese moreover charging the lowest – 4 per cent.

Other Economic Involvement

Over the period 1972–4 the chairmen or presidents of the Bank of Tokyo, Fuji Bank, Hitachi, Ishikawajima Heavy Industries and Mitsubishi Chemical Industries visited one or more East European countries. Nisso-Iwai had representative offices or agencies in Bucharest, East Berlin and Warsaw.

Intergovernmental agreements on economic, industrial, scientific and technical co-operation were signed by Japan with all major East European countries. What resulted from these is generally not stated.

The largest industrial multinational corporations which were significantly involved in commercial dealings with socialist countries included the following Japanese ones: C. Itoh & Co., Marubeni-Ida, Matsushita Electric Industrial, Mitsubishi, Mitsui, and Nissho-Iwai. The branches included trading, chemicals (these two especially), engineering, electrical and electronic equipment, cables and food. All major East European countries were involved. Other multinationals significantly involved included Ataka & Co., Hitachi, Honda Motor, Kanebo, Kanematsu Gosho, Nissan Motor, Nippon Electric, Sony, Sumitomo Shoji Kaisha, Toyota Motor, Teijin, Tokyo Shibaura Electric.

Multinationals which had 'recently' completed or undertaken deals totalling in excess of $500 mn included Mitsubishi, Mitsui & Co., Sumitomo Shoji Kaisha, and Teijin. Also mentioned for deals under $500 mn were Ishikawajima-Harima, Kawasaki Steel, and Toray Industries. Communications equipment was supplied by Nippon Electric, Sony, and Tokyo Shibaura Electric.

During 1973–4 Ishikawajima-Harima Heavy Industries contracted to build large tankers for Poland and Yugoslavia. Large contracts for industrial plants completed or undertaken by Western multinationals in the first half of 1970s included Tokyo Boseki (a polyester fibre complex in Poland).

Czechoslovak, Hungarian, Polish, Soviet and Yugoslav metalworking machines and tools had been in use for years in Hitachi, Mitsubishi, and Toyota Motor. Technically advanced machinery and equipment was imported by Ishikawajima-Harima, Mitsubishi, Mitsui & Co. Other items were imported either for own use or for resale, such as by Marubeni-Ida, C.Itoh & Co., and Toyo Menka Kaisha. Tokyo Boeki handled East European metalworking machinery.

Licences sold by Western multinationals to socialist countries in the first half of the 1970s included Marubeni-Ida (synthetic yarns to Poland), Teijin (high tensile nylon thread to Czechoslovakia), Toyo Engineering (ethylene to Czechoslovakia). There was also some traffic in the other direction. A Bulgarian licence for electrolytic refining of copper at high current densities was purchased by Japanese firms among others. Japanese firms having multinationals which purchased socialist licences included Ataka & Co. (from the GDR), Mitsubishi (from Hungary) and Nissan Motor (from Czechoslovakia).

At an East–West Congress of Industrial Co-operation held in Warsaw in April 1974, Western multinationals included Nissho-Iwai from Japan.

Co-operation in early stages of industrial activities included an agreement by Tokyo Shibaura Electric with CKD Blansko (Czechoslovakia) in 1973 for development and design of turbines. Suntory (Japan) and Vinipex (Bulgaria) signed an agreement for provision of technology and construction of a malt factory in Bulgaria and the subsequent export of malt to Japan. Inter-enterprise industrial co-operation agreements in the first half of the 1970s included one by Sanyo Electric with Diora (Poland) for car electric parts.

Co-operative arrangements in delivering oil were agreed on several occasions since the late 1960s (because of the oil embargo).

Mitsubishi, Mitsui, and Nippon Mining and others were reported in 1973 to be negotiating for a copper mining project at Rudna (Poland) to cost $600 mn, repayable in copper deliveries to Japan. Japan was mentioned among joint venture partners in Hungary, Romania and Yugoslavia. To Japanese-Romanian ventures founded in 1974, Dai Nippon contributed 43 per cent and Sumitomo Shoji Kaisha 5 per cent (the rest by Romania). Another prominent Japanese multinational to enter into partnership was Teijin.

The Bank of Tokyo was mentioned among 50 largest multinational banks in the West having significant dealings with at least one socialist country. It was authorized to open permanent offices in Moscow. Certain other Japanese banks (Dai-Ichi Kangyo, Daiwa, Fuji, Industrial Bank of Japan, Mitsubishi, Sanwa, Sumitomo, Tokai) also had such dealings.

These details are not meant to be exhaustive, nor are they claimed to be novel – being based on Wilczynski (1976). Wilczynski too does not claim to report everything in entirety – thus his table I reports long-term co-operation agreements concluded by *selected* multinational corporations, a total of 60 fields of co-operation being listed (pp. 26–7), although this is by far the most comprehensive survey known to the author. Wilczynski's data show that a limited yet very significant Japanese economic involvement in Eastern Europe antedated the overthrow of communism.

More recent developments, which are more complex and widespread, are categorized below according to the East European country. Except that all the German entities are listed under Germany, the East European countries are listed in alphabetical order, this being the simplest sequence, and the other imaginable sequence – distance from Japan – being in this case too difficult to determine. In two country sections, Albania and Romania, rather extensive comparisons are included of non-economic as well as economic aspects, and in Bulgaria a somewhat less extensive comparison. These countries are chosen partly because they offer the best bases for such comparisons, but mainly because the writer is better acquainted with them than with the other East European countries. A longer than average comparison is also provided of Japan and Germany, in this case because Japan has more in common with Germany than with most East European (or any European) countries and due to the complicated and contradictory changes in the present century of the German frontiers and political and economic regimes.

4.2   JAPAN AND ALBANIA

4.2.1   Comparisons

Japan and Albania are extremely different, in area, population, population density, history, religion, language, economic system or economic development. In fact, apart from being both inhabited by human beings, they have virtually nothing in common! Such at least appears to be the dominant view not only of those who know nothing about either Japan or Albania, but of some who do know about one country or the other. When making a comparison, however, one needs to know about *both* sides. What I hope is a more balanced and informed comparison is now offered, but readers who are interested only in Japanese involvement in the Albanian *economy* should turn directly to section 4.2.2 'Relations' (and similarly in other country sections where a non-economic comparison is offered).

Although there *are* enormous (and also less enormous) differences between Japan and Albania, they do share certain similarities. However, to focus first on the differences, Japan is large in population and economically the most advanced country in Asia. Albania is small in population and economically the most backward country in Europe. Few Japanese desire to emigrate whereas it sometimes seems that the majority of Albanians want to do so. Japan is a power of global status, Albania a very minor one. Independent Japan must have a noteworthy future, whereas whether independent Albania has a future at all is perhaps debatable.

More verifiably, Japan is 12.9 times larger in area than Albania but has almost 40 times her population, so Japan's population density is three times that of Albania. (During Albania's communist period this difference was diminishing.) Japan consists of a group of islands, whereas Albania is within the Balkan peninsula, having one sole island of more than negligible size. Japan extends over a wider range of latitudes, being on the whole further south: her four main islands lie between latitudes 31°N and 46°N, Albania between latitudes 39°N and 43°N. Consequently Japan is warmer on average than Albania, and much more humid, although Albania is fairly well watered. In both countries (especially Japan) the seasons are clearly marked. Both Japan and Albania are mainly elongated north to south, in breadth being not too dissimilar. Across Japan's main island, Honshu, from Tokyo to Joetsu, the distance in a straight line (angled south-east to north-west) is about 220 km, Albania's biggest east-west distance (in the latitude of Korce) about 150 km.

Since Japan consists entirely of islands whereas Albania is continental, her neighbours having often encroached on or absorbed her territory, Japan's frontiers have been more stable than Albania's. (This does not take into account the Japanese conquests of Taiwan, at that time called Formosa, or of Korea or Manchuria, which are not considered part of Japan proper, Sakhalin (whole or part), or islands currently under dispute with Russia.)

Yet neither country's coastline has been absolutely stable. Apart from mythical changes, 'many extraordinary changes' are said to have taken place along the coast of Izumo and in the neighbourhood of the adjacent lake (Hearn, 1894, p. 181, n. 2). Certain changes took place in Albania's coastline between 1938 and 1993 (Hutchings, *forthcoming*; cf. Shehu, *c*.1997, pp. 27–30). (In both countries significant discharges from rivers may have been a main cause.)

Besides manmade disasters both countries have experienced natural ones, including earthquakes (more often and much more seriously in Japan). Both bestride seismically sensitive spots. Japan, but not Albania, suffers from typhoons and *tsunami*, and from cloudbursts and so on. There can be very heavy snowfalls in Albania, such as in the winter of 1985. A cutting-off of communications during winter, with the result that settlements in the northern mountains are isolated for up to five months, happens in Albania but not in Japan. Drought in late summer has become normal. Thus in Albania nature may be less catastrophic, but is regularly uncomfortable.

Both countries are in area about four-fifths mountainous or hilly, so only small proportions of their total areas are cultivable: in Japan about 18 per cent, or according to another source about 16 per cent (Reischauer, 1954, p. 261), in Albania 20 per cent. (In Romania this proportion is 42 per cent.) These small proportions have had profound influences upon both countries. Neither country has navigable rivers.

In both countries the present-day capitals were appointed not very long ago (Japan's in 1868, Albania's in 1920), and in both the present-day capital city lies further to the east than the earlier one (in Japan this earlier one having most recently been Kyoto; in Albania Shkoder was effectively the capital, though at that time no united territory existed). In Japan the compass direction even fixed the new name of the capital, Tokyo, that is Eastern Capital, while Tirana and Teheran, the capital of an oriental state, apparently have the same etymology. In both countries the present capital lies not far from the geographical centre, which contrasts with many countries, large and not so large. Both are divided into administrative districts, but each also has an alternative and more ancient terminology of regions (such as *Kanto* in Japan, *Laberia* in Albania).

Economically there is only very faint resemblance, Japan's Gross Domestic Product (GDP) being many times larger than Albania's, whether reckoned in total or per head, and altogether on a much higher technical level. Japan is highly industrialized, Albania much less so, though a build-up of industry did take place there during the communist period. Albania's endowment with raw materials is somewhat superior to Japan's, if reckoned per head. Japan is the biggest producer of industrial robots, Albania produces none. Among other sharp contrasts is the huge extent of advertising in Japan compared with its almost nonexistence in Albania under communist rule, and currently only slight extent. The two countries' transport systems are very different, Japan's being hugely superior.

Nevertheless even in their economies there *are* certain resemblances, some of which are important.

1. Both countries have been preoccupied with seeking to feed themselves: Albania by growing wheat, Japan by growing rice.
2. Both must rely on sizeable imports, though of contrasting type: Japan especially of foodstuffs, fuel and raw materials, Albania chiefly of machinery and equipment, plus some food. Japan can, whereas Albania cannot, finance these with her own exports.
3. Neither country earns much from international tourism.
4. Both countries generate a high proportion of electricity from hydropower.
5. Both have built railways recently.

The *types* of economic system of the two countries during the communist period in Albania were extremely different: in Albania full communism, in Japan capitalism though with some central regulation. Though one cannot always take 'isms' literally, the difference in this case was huge. A start having been made with privatization in Albania and generally with dismantling the state's hold over the economy, this difference is shrinking though it must for a long while remain wide. Following the socialists' election victory in Albania in June 1997, the difference will not go on shrinking.

Meanwhile, it has been in agriculture that convergence is most visible. Japan is traditionally a land of small farmers, in sharp contrast to the United States: about 1960 the average size of farms in Japan was one hectare, in the USA over 80 times as large (Hall, *c*.1962, p. 7). Whereas in Albania during the communist period, except right at the start, the goal was collectivization and there was continual pressure in that direction, Albanian farmers are now starting to become true owners of their land, and *their* farms, like Japanese ones, will be very small. At the time of writing it is not clear whether, following the Socialist victory that trend will continue.

As regards energy provision, Albania stands at an extreme point in that well over 80 per cent is hydro-generated; Japan too relies on hydropower, though not such a high proportion. Japan has coal as well. Albania, too, has coal (mostly lignite) and oil (viscous), but both countries have to import substantial fractions of their energy, which is a common weakness.

Neither economy has developed international tourism to any great extent, though for different reasons. Official Albania during its communist period viewed foreign tourism through an ideological prism: foreign visitors were not allowed full beards, were required to dress modestly, to travel in groups and so on. International visits were seen from a propagandist or utilitarian standpoint. Post-communist Albania wanted to expand tourism – former President Sali Berisha deemed this a national priority – but facilities must remain for some time quite insufficient. Japan has not harboured ideological objections, but is distant from countries from which most wealthy tourists set forth, and suffers from its reputation (not wholly deserved, but intensified by the rising yen) of being very expensive. It is also seen as unmanageable from a linguistic angle (though this barrier is also rather great in Albania) and for some potential tourists recalls unpleasant memories of the Second World War.

In both countries the pressure on food supplies already mentioned instigated efforts to remodel the landscape, largely by terracing. Concerning Japan, Hearn wrote of 'valleys between mountains with rice-fields ascending their slopes by successions of diked terraces which look like enormous green flights of steps' (Hearn, 1894, p. 120). (This relates to a journey from the Pacific coast to the Sea of Japan, approaching Izumo. The year is not given.) He mentions terraces elsewhere too (*ibid*., pp. 232, 330). Terraces in Japan are shallower than in Albania and the flat areas are much larger. In Albania, terracing is much more recent (chiefly between 1971 and 1978, Hutchings, 1996, p. 225) because demographic pressure is more recent and because from 1944 to 1985 the country was ruled by a regime which could, and did, demand from everyone unusual physical exertion. In Japan, terraces were created at various dates and not to any national plan.

Most Japanese and most Albanians are rather similar in physique. Both are normally slim, lightweight and muscular. The author believes he has never seen a fat Albanian; fat Japanese are rare. The Japanese language has even no adjective for 'fat' although it is, of course, possible to describe the condition, by saying in effect that one has got fat and is fat now (*futtote imasu*). The sumo wrestlers must be excepted. All Japanese have black hair (one has never seen or heard of any exception) while Albanians have dark hair as a rule. However, in that respect Japanese do not differ from Chinese nor do Albanians differ from the other Balkan peoples. Japanese hair is always straight but Albanian hair not always. The complexions of both races range from white to sallow, a rosy complexion being rare among Albanians and even rarer among Japanese (if present at all, in the Tokyo area).

Diets have changed and are changing, but at the time of writing remain widely dissimilar. There is a specific Japanese cuisine, but scarcely an Albanian one, which is Balkan albeit with special features: in particular, Albania is the only Balkan country where pork is not the meat chiefly eaten. (Albania is mainly Muslim, and eating pork is contrary to Islam.) If one can get it, lamb is the preferred meat. The bases of the Japanese diet are rice and fish, of the Albanian diet wheat, maize (corn) and pasta with, to some extent, vegetables and animal products. (Vegetarianism is practised in Japan, but hardly by intention in Albania.) The Japanese eat wheat but do not grow it, while Albanians eat rice but grows little of it. But each (like the English) adopts the name of the principal food to mean 'meal': in Japanese this is *gohan*, in Albanian *buke*. Also basic to the Albanian diet is macaroni, which in Japan is more exotic though available. Together with wheat in the Albanian case we may consider maize (corn); corn bread used to be preferred but has largely been supplanted. Albanians eat partly freshwater fish (from Lake Ohrid, if possible the speckled trout or *koran*), whereas almost all the fish eaten in Japan is sea fish. There is no Albanian parallel to Japan's love of seaweed. Milk is widely drunk in Albania (less than in Bulgaria, though yoghourt is found in Albania too). Fairly prominent now in the Japanese diet, milk is of relatively recent introduction, as witness its name, *miruku*, which is not of Japanese origin. The Albanian word for milk (*qumesht*) is indigenous. Processed foods are eaten vastly more in Japan than in Albania. Each country has a preferred alcoholic drink: in Japan *sake*, in Albania *raki*. The latter is coarser but the more potent. Beer and wine have gained popularity in Japan; both are available in Albania but in much narrower variety. Both countries produce wine, but more will be said about that in section 4.4

'Japan and Bulgaria'. Both grow fruit and practise sericulture (Japan on a bigger scale).

Given the big differences between the Albanian and the Japanese diets, the similarity of physique might suggest that diet has less importance than is often supposed. The similarity is more likely due to genetic factors, or to consuming relatively small *amounts*, and in Albania to an unavoidably energetic lifestyle (a lot of walking). Japanese, rarely commuting on foot, have a predilection for such energetic recreations as climbing Mount Fuji, or perhaps steps leading to Shinto shrines.

Japan is democratic, but with a hereditary emperor, while Albania has only very recently become democratic (in the Western sense) and never had an emperor. However, over centuries the Emperor of Japan was merely a figurehead, which narrows this gap, nor should one neglect the emergence in the present century of a self-proclaimed King of the Albanians (Zog) and then of a dictatorial ruler (Enver Hoxha). Within the past two centuries both countries have become more aware of the potential advantages of strong and legitimate central government, but have experienced revulsion against this, following defeat in 1945 (Japan) or the overthrow of the communist system in 1991 (Albania).

The two countries' histories have been fundamentally different: Japan never having been defeated until 1945, Albania almost continuously incorporated within other empires until 1912, and at certain periods thereafter. Thus Japan has almost always been independent, Albania rarely. The two countries' experiences of wars have correspondingly been very different. Japan, until 1944–5, hardly suffered from external wars; within the homeland these generated wealth and prestige. Albania's experience of wars has been generally defensive and painful and often disastrous.

On the other hand, the early histories of both countries are shrouded in mystery. Both histories are very long: Japan's dating legendarily from 660 BC, or in reality from some later but still early date, while Albanians (including their presumptive ancestors the Illyrians) have lived in the Balkans at least since 2000 BC, although their territory was severely compressed by Slav incursions beginning in the sixth century AD. During the past half-millenium both experienced internal conflicts; indeed, civil wars are characteristic of both countries, and in both a typical figure has been the provincial warlord. The Japanese *daimyo* is an exact translation of 'warlord'. (In the Albanian language 'warlord' would be *luftedashes*.) In either country over-mighty provincial chiefs in effect usurped national power; recent examples are Essad Toptani Pasha and King Zog (see Hutchings, 1996, pp. 231–3 and 256–7). Rulers, regional or national, often oppressed the domestic population. Though in Albania there has usually been no national power for them to subvert, foreign occupiers might occasionally be challenged, as in the early nineteenth century the Ottoman Empire was challenged by the domestic tyrant Ali Pasha Tepelene.

The modern histories of the two nations are centred around Japan's full independence (except 1945–51) but (since 1912) Albania's qualified independence, and around the fact that from 1944 Albania was ruled by an extreme communist government, whereas Japan's government – after full independence had been regained – became consistently Liberal Democratic. Consequently market capitalism was implanted in Japan and found there very fertile soil, in some respects more fertile than in countries where it had originated, whereas in Albania a nascent and corrupted capitalism eventually was transformed into a socialist economy, which since 1997 may be reworked.

In the Second World War Japan suffered the more spectacular devastation and may well have suffered more overall, yet according to official claims (which perhaps are exaggerated) Albania during the communist period was 'one of the countries that suffered the heaviest losses in men, and especially in material values' (New Albania Editorial Board, 1984, p. 63) in proportion to its population. The same source claimed that 21 per cent of houses were burned or destroyed, bridges, factories, workshops, mines, ports and means of communication either totally destroyed or heavily damaged (ibid.).

Both peoples speak languages which have been preserved despite being very different from those spoken by adjacent peoples. As a noted Hellenicist admitted, the Greek language although mastering other tongues, did not master Albanian (Bury, n.d., p. 6, n. 1). Neither language bears close resemblance to any spoken by *non-adjacent* peoples, yet neither is totally outside recognized language families: Albanian being Indo-European, Japanese (as rather recently recognized) Altaic, though in vocabulary scarcely resembling any Altaic language (Susumu, 1970, p. 144). Both use alphabets or, in the Japanese case, syllabaries (Japanese also uses characters) derived from other tongues: Japanese from Chinese, simplified to compose *hiragana* and *katakana*, Albanian from Latin. Both languages are scarcely used outside the homeland (though texts in Japanese outside Japan are starting to be seen). Both are difficult, but their areas of special difficulty are quite different. Albanian grammar is very complicated, while Japanese grammar is basically simple; on the other hand Albanian writing is simple but Japanese writing extremely complicated, and the Japanese language but not the Albanian one is able to express many degrees of politeness. Thus to a native of either country, the other's language offers both pleasant and unpleasant surprises.

If Japanese is an Altaic language, Albanian an Indo-European one, we might not expect to find resemblances between them, apart from accidental ones or words adopted from some third source. However, Altaic includes Turkic, Turkic includes Turkish, and a number of Turkish words have passed into modern Albanian. It therefore becomes theoretically possible that Japanese and Albanian might have individual words in common (with the above-mentioned qualifications). Are there in fact any? The author does not know Turkish or any other of the Turkic or Altaic languages, therefore cannot trace any intermediate link, but there are two pairs of words which have similar meanings and therefore *might* fall into this category. These pairs are (1) *shukin* (Japanese) and *shoqin* (Albanian), and (2) *iku* (Japanese) and *iki* (Albanian); *iku* in Albanian is past definite. Each is declined according to the normal rules of the respective languages. Since there is no phonological correspondence between the two languages it is almost certain that both pairs are coincidental, but it may be worth while keeping a lookout for others.

1. *Shukin* and *shoqin*: Both the Japanese and the Albanian words mean 'husband' though with different connotations. The Japanese word means literally 'master' but can be applied by a wife to her own husband (to someone else's husband it must be *go-shujin*). The Albanian word means literally 'comrade', can be applied to anyone's husband and is in the accusative case. Pronunciations are not identical, although if not clearly pronounced or heard one might be mistaken for the other.
2. *Iku* and *iki*: Both these words mean 'go' though the Albanian one more exactly 'go away' or sometimes 'go away as'.

In both Japan and Albania several religions are professed: in Japan, Buddhism (several variants, particularly Zen), Shinto (two variants) and, to a slight extent but persistently, Christianity. In Albania the religions are Islam and Christianity (two branches only of the latter, Orthodox and Catholic). All of Albania's religions have come from outside, whereas one of the Japanese religions (Shinto) is indigenous. But neither country is characterized by enmity between religions. In Albania religious dissensions have been much milder than in neighbouring former Yugoslavia or (at various times) Western Europe. In Japan, overt Christianity was stamped out, but in some degree survived underground. Religious wars are not characteristic of either country.

Both countries are mainly non-Christian. Albania used to be reckoned 30 per cent Christian (20 per cent Orthodox, 10 per cent Roman Catholic) but there must have been a wide diffusion of atheism or agnosticism during the communist period. What proportion of Albanians are now effectively Christian can only be guessed, but religion is reviving. In any case, in both countries Christians are a small minority. In Albania we do not find the phenomenon of Christianity having been preserved underground during more than two centuries as we do in Japan; this may be attributed to a keener religious sense of the Japanese, a greater persistence, or to the more tolerant attitude of the Ottomans than of the Shoguns. The Japanese evolved their own religion whereas the Albanians did not, the Bekteshism (a variant of Islam which also professes tenets from other religions) became widespread in Albania, which eventually housed its headquarters. In Japan, Shintoism and Buddhism eventually merged or coexisted, Buddhism, too, having evolved special forms in Japan.

Although the two countries' religions are different, popular attitudes towards them have something in common. In Japan, Buddhism and Shinto coexist, many Japanese embracing both and seeing no contradiction. This has happened too in Albania (or other Albanian-settled regions) with Islam and Christianity. Rose Wilder Lane tells about Kosovars (ethnic Albanians in Kosova, at present an involuntary part of Serbia) who went to the mosque by day and attended mass at night. In the northern mountains of Albania people did not make distinctions about religions: what mattered was to do what one thought was right (Lane, 1922, pp. 85–7). It is often said that 'the religion of Albanians is Albanianism'. Rather similarly, the Japanese used to be brought up to believe that their country had a divine origin, and, even though this is no longer believed by most people (though some terminology still reflects it), many Japanese or non-Japanese, certainly including this author, continue to think that there is something special about Japan.

Both nationalities are reputed for their warlike qualities. As remarked by Edward Gibbon, the Albanians and the British were probably the best warriors of the Roman Empire; Albanians subsequently among the best of the Ottoman Empire. The Japanese are more warlike than the Chinese or Russians, the Albanians more than the Greeks or Romanians (though not more than the Serbs). Yet neither people in antiquity carved out any empire. Albania has never ruled any empire, while the Japanese, apart from an earlier abortive expedition to Korea, began to build one only from the late nineteenth century onwards (only to lose it all in 1945). In classical times Albanians plundered but did not settle, while later on they settled (such as in Greece and southern Italy) but did not plunder. The Japanese at first settled but did not plunder, whereas more recently they plundered (and killed) but did not settle.

Japan (eventually) engaged in conquest: Albania did not. At home, both countries built castles, some of which withstood long sieges, but in Albania (as along the north-west frontier of India) these are supplemented by fortified homes (*kulla*) to which there is no parallel in Japan. One hears about Samurai homes (to be seen, for example, in Kanazawa) but not about Samurai castles. The difference is linked partly with the Code of Lek Dukagjini (in Albania individuals needed defence against the blood feud, as described below), partly with the far larger scale of the Japanese military, partly with Japan's stronger centralized government. More than a century ago Japan began to build a great navy; the Albanian navy has never been more than token.

Neither country can secure its own defence in the present-day world, though this conclusion assumes scenarios appropriate to each. Possible threats to Japan have been from China, North Korea and the USSR (now Russia), among which Russia, China and possibly North Korea possess nuclear weapons. Against these, only deterrence is possible and this is provided by the United States. Albania is not sheltered under any nuclear umbrella. The disintegration of Yugoslavia might have reduced the potential threat to Albania from that quarter, but Kosovo, with its Albanian majority under Serb oppression, remains a most serious unsolved problem. During the communist period, from 1978 onwards, hundreds of thousands of concrete pillboxes were built in Albania itself. In modern war most of these would probably be useless, but the combination of these defences, of difficult terrain, tough fighters and unpromising prospects from conquest has sufficed to deter aggression against Albania, and may well continue to do so, even apart from the unattractive prospect of attempting to rule a country where since early 1997 great numbers of small arms have been seized by civilians.

The two peoples more closely resemble one another in their attitude to honour. The extraordinary bravery in war, sometimes called fanaticism, of the Japanese was well attested during the Second World War by the *kamikaze* pilots and submariners, or by their fighting to the death in Okinawa and elsewhere. This is a more recent and more organized manifestation of the Samurai spirit, a better-known expression of which was ritual suicide through *harakiri* (ritual disembowelment) in circumstances when this was seen as the only way to preserve one's honour. Any offence, even accidental, had to be avenged. This code of behaviour, strikingly at variance with the Christian ideal (less often met in practice) of 'turning the other cheek', resembles, however, the cult of honour embodied in Albanian customary law, expounded in the Code of Lek Dukagjini. This has been explored in more detail by a Japanese scholar, Kazuhiko Yamamoto. According to his exposition, a theory proposed by Shinobu Orikuchi, a Japanese writer and folklorist, was found to solve the puzzle of the code's ethical structure. This draws attention to a guest-god (the code regards a guest as sacred) who confers divinity on his hosts and whose blood, if shed, would result in vengeance being wreaked on the whole community. Only the blood of the killer, who holds divinity himself, is equivalent to the god's blood and so is able to neutralize the shedding of the god's blood (Yamamoto, 1995, pp. 7–8).

The exposition is very interesting, but the religious backgrounds are largely different. The Christian attitude to suicide has always been hostile, whereas sacrifice (of oneself through martyrdom, most purely of Christ) is integral to Christianity. Similarly, Judaism featured burnt offerings, or Abraham's readiness to sacrifice his son. Islam places suicide beyond the pale. Shinto did not object to suicide, and Japanese Buddhism turned a blind eye to ritual suicide (Strauss *et al.*, 1991, p. 12). Thus *harakiri* did not conflict in Japan with the predominant religions, whereas suicide did conflict with Islam and Christianity. Suicide would also be at variance with the Albanian consciousness that they are less numerous than the peoples living around them, which makes them see their own population growth as a defensive weapon and suicide as counterproductive. The Japanese, much more numerous in relation to certain adjacent peoples as well as to peoples more distant from themselves, do not share those sentiments. *They* have been, over a longer period of time, more aware of domestic population pressure.

There are other differences. The Japanese code, Bushido, did not apply to the nation as a whole, only to its warrior (samurai) class. The warrior class was one of four into which the whole population was divided. The Albanian Code of Lek Dukagjini applied to the whole population living within a certain region (the northern mountains and adjacent areas) while similar though milder codes applied to the whole populations in *their* respective areas. Bushido was compatible with capital punishment (though the right to commit *harakiri* might be granted as an alternative, as to the 47 Ronin), whereas the Code of Lek Dukagjini did not include capital punishment (which would merely set off another blood feud). Again, as the last examples shows, Bushido did not require an equal number of victims on each side, whereas the Code of Lek Dukagjini did so require. Bushido amounted to behaviour adopted by a class controlled by (or controlling) the government, whereas the Code of Lek Dukagjini evolved in the absence of (and most probably *due* to the absence of) any supreme central government. Indeed, a rational explanation of Dukagjini Code is possible, if the code or something like it is seen as a necessary replacement for a non-existent supreme authority. This explains why it dominated within the northern mountains where no external authority, even that of the Ottomans, exercised effective sway. It explains, too, a similarity to the vendetta in southern Italy – another relatively lawless area. As for Japan, it explains why Bushido was most strongly present during epochs when the emperor's authority was in abeyance. However, a religious background, through its strong hold over popular consciousness, might reinforce its appeal.

Even if the explanations are not the same, there are important similarities between Bushido and the Albanian Code. Both primarily address males, and their sanctions target (above all or exclusively) males. Thus, loyalty is highly esteemed. A man must always have his weapon to hand, and only men who *are* armed may take part in certain gatherings. Honour is highly esteemed. Any hurt must be avenged. Certain hurts may be – or must be – avenged by death. Both emerged as coherent systems during the early Middle Ages and, apart from some gaps attenuations or exceptions, have lasted up to or almost up to the present day (to a later date in Albania than in Japan, which is congruent with Japan's faster economic, political and intellectual development). Thus we may conclude that the two peoples have been strongly affected by behavioural codes which, while by no means identical in nature or origin, do bear significant resemblances to one another. There are similar features in codes of behaviour in certain other parts of the world, for instance among the Bedouin a guest was under the host's special protection, but between Japan and Albania the resemblance is especially close. (The samurai spirit is sometimes likened to chivalry in Europe of the Middle Ages, but this seems unsound: see also Trevor P. Leggett in Hyoe and Richie, 1980, p. 170.) At any rate, both Japanese and Albanians evolved their own codes which differentiated them from their neighbours; whether the Albanians or the Japanese diverged the further is hard to judge.

Albanian and Japanese attitudes to honour and to behaviour in war must also be related to the propensity to behave cruelly towards enemies. That propensity would combine too with willingness to behave cruelly towards oneself (in the matter of *harakiri*). 'Cruel, but not treacherous' is a description sometimes applied to Albanians; at least the former adjective would apply to the Japanese, according to prisoners of war who fell into their hands in the Second World War. If one is intensely loyal to one's mates, one must be less unwilling to inflict cruelty upon their enemies. Also predisposing towards cruelty is the sensation of being menaced by powerful neighbours (see also section 4.11, 'Japan and Romania').

Being adjacent to larger and (at the relevant periods) more advanced nations, both Japan and Albania have been profoundly influenced over a long period of time by their neighbours. For Albania these have been the Roman Empire, the Ottoman Empire and Greece (probably in that order) while for Japan they have been China and Korea (in that order). Although Japan is so much bigger than Albania, external influences upon Japan have scarcely been weaker, due to the propinquity, and immensity of the ancient civilization of China. These influences have also been somewhat similar in nature. The *linguistic* influence is moderately strong, but affecting much more the written than the spoken tongue. The Japanese borrowed *kanji* from China, which are still integral to almost every phrase, whereas Japanese grammar and pronunciation are their own. The Albanians, too, acquired their alphabet from surrounding peoples although there were indigenous initiatives, and the Albanian alphabet was finally settled only within the past hundred years.

The *culinary* influence of China upon Japan was weaker than the corresponding Balkan influence upon Albania: as witness many Chinese restaurants in Japan today; but distinct 'Balkan' restaurants do not exist in Albania. A separate Albanian cuisine cannot be said to exist, though there are a few distinctive Albanian dishes (Elbasan lamb), whether there is a separate Japanese one is perhaps a matter of opinion. The author thinks so, but some (especially the Chinese) do not think so.

Chinese influence upon Japan was exercised over millennia, Chinese influence upon Albania during about a decade. In Japan, Chinese influence is visible wherever the language is written and via Confucianism. In Albania, Chinese influence can be observed in certain machinery and uniforms, scarcely anywhere else. Very few Albanians learned Chinese, and probably very few Chinese learned Albanian.

Both Japan and Albania have been, and to a considerable extent still are, male-dominated societies. Historically, in Japan male domination followed a period when female domination was the norm (information given by Kumiko Jesse) whereas in Albania there was no such prior period. Yet the end result was rather similar. In Albania, the blood fued excluded women, which lowered their mortality compared to males, making it safer, and so more normal, for them to travel to market from the northern mountains to Shkoder (this bias can still be observed).

Since men had to ensure their own survival they had to bear arms and be ready to use them, consequently heavy load-carrying became the women's task. On average, in the regions of blood feud, men lived shorter but more glorious and less laborious lives. There is no Albanian parallel to a man marrying into his wife's family (matrilinearity) (S. Trumbull in Hyoe and Richie (eds), 1980, pp. 88–9), nor can one readily visualize an Albanian wife verifying and regulating the sum in her husband's purse. According to Jacques Thiriet, since the Second World War, Japan has become 'a country in which the man's authority has gone down in inverse proportion to the rise in income and national wealth (ibid., p. 101). One reason for this must have been the equality of the sexes in marriage prescribed by the new constitution (Reischauer, 1954, p. 234). There is no parallel in Albania to today's dominant role in Japan of the wife in the household, and in dealings with the couple's children, particularly in regard to their education (which sometimes) results in excessive pressure on them, the 'exam hell'). Nor is there any parallel to the *geisha*. There are no parallels in Japan to the Albanian phenomena of 'house lord' (ruling an extended family) or of 'sworn virgin'. Male dominance in Albania would have been weakened during the period of communist rule, and probably before that during the reign of King Zog (Hutchings in Winnifrith, (ed.), 1992, p. 117), but despite the overthrow of both these regimes and the revival of religious institutions, including Muslim ones, and of the institution of 'sworn virgins' (see below), male dominance is not likely now to regain strength, given that Western feminism will become more influential in Albania.

Affecting, or affected by, this matter is the ratio between numbers of males and females. In modern Western societies females outnumber males, in older age-groups markedly, although more boys are born than girls. In Albania, on the contrary, statistics show an excess of males over females. At the end of 1983 the population was 51.6 per cent male (New Albania Editorial Board, 1984, p. 63). The reasons are not clear (foreigners have suggested various reasons, including even a dietetic one), but probably include a higher mortality of females in some areas or age-groups due to their more laborious lives (see above). On the other hand it has been claimed that the institution of 'sworn virgins' arose in response to a shortage of adult males (Young, 1995, p. 7; cf., concerning Greenland, Hoeg, 1994, p. 28). Clearly that would be an appropriate response – if it were appropriate – only as regards males in age-groups subject to the blood feud. Another reason, that some females would not be unwilling to make such a promise in return for being able to adopt (up to a point) a male lifestyle, can be imagined. The (rather slight) evidence is thus contradictory. Regarding Japan, in the last country (about 1878) an excess of males was noticed by Isabella Bird (1911, p. 103). She noted an excess of males over females in Tokyo of 36 000, and in the whole empire of nearly half a million. An apparently more recent persistence of a male minority in Albania than in Japan possibly confirms that male dominance has been more marked, or has continued longer, in the former country.

Turning to culture: the two countries do not have any type of music, the arts or architecture in common. On the other hand, in both countries unusual musical *instruments* are played: in Albania the *cifteli*, *sharkia* or *lahuta* (stringed instruments) and *gernete*, *gajdja* and *bishnica* (wind instruments); in Japan the *samisen* or *koto* (a 13-string harp). They have in common folk dancing though not the actual dances: for instance, the *Bon-odori* (Hearn, 1894, pp. 131–7, also Hyoe and Richie, 1980, pp. 28–9) has no counterpart in Albania. *No*, *kabuki* and *bunraku* have no parallel in Albanian arts, and nor do competitive swordsmanship (*kendo*), sumo or judo. So far we draw almost a blank. As regards crafts, Japan offers *cloisonné*, lacquer ware, doll-making, paper-folding, wood blocks, the folding fan and others; Albania not much more than copperware, certain musical instruments, rawhide moccasins, magnificent embroidery, and – by at least one talented individual – ceramics (see Christo, 1997–8).

Japanese literature is not a practicable subject for this author (very little having been translated). Some translations into English of Albanian literature have been made, such as of *The General of the Dead Army* by Ismail Kadare. To read Albanian is not so hugely difficult, but also a number of translations have been made by Robert V. Elsie. Albanian novels tend towards realism but Japanese ones towards lightness of touch (and often vagueness, which is a trait of the language). Comparison is more practicable in regard to poetry. Both languages can say much with few syllables. Albanian has a strong rhythm and metre. The poetic form especially developed in Japan is the *haiku*, which consists of seventeen syllables (usually divided into three sections of five-seven-five) with which the poet tries to express some thought which not only is beautiful (often though not necessarily in a visual sense) but also profound. The reasons for the popularity of poetry in both Japan and Albania are not altogether different. Both nationalities may have wanted, perhaps unconsciously, to exploit the unique possibilities of their unusual languages. For if Albanian and Japanese are difficult, this applies to above all to their poetic languages. The very unusually large proportion of poetry in total Albanian publishing – in Albania proper 40 per cent, in Serb-oppressed Kosovo the amazingly high 70 per cent (cf. Hutchings, 1996, pp. 151–2) – can be ascribed to censorship and political subjugation.

Both Japan and Albania seem to this author to be mainly monochrome, except in particular spheres or on special occasions. Most large and smooth surfaces are monochrome in Japan, such as houses, the almost universal dark business suit and white shirt, cars, or the robes of priests. Snow, the Moon, and Mount Fuji (all favourite poetic themes) are other illustrations. Albania has been mainly drab. One remembers a showery April (1989) when Tirana sprouted black umbrellas. The conical skull-cap or *qeleshe* worn by ethnic Albanians (or, if by other nationalities, only if these latter are demonstrating their attachment to things Albanian) is white or light cream, as three hundred years earlier but perhaps of squarer profile was the tall cap worn by the *haiku* poet Matsuo Basho. Against a monochrome background, occasional or seasonal splashes of colour stand out. This may be one basis for native delight at the cherry-tree blossom (*sakura*) in Japan, or gorgeous national costume, like that in which Lord Byron had himself painted, in Albania. Certainly, Japanese street stalls, or the shops and signs of Shinjuku (Tokyo), are as colourful as anywhere else. Though overwhelming they are, against the national background, exceptions. The same applies to festivals (Japanese: *matsuri*). Less common as festivals are in the Albanian context, one might recall King Zog's coronation day (Hutchings in Winnifrith (ed.), 1992, p. 117). Japanese *matsuri* are colourful due to the huge portable shrines, while Albanian festivals are colourful mainly due to costume.

Except to the extent that Western clothes are worn there is little resemblance between the two countries in dress. The Japanese *kimono* and *yukata* are much more flexible, thinner and lighter in weight than traditional Albanian dress, but both cultures evolved distinctive and comfortable footwear: in Japan *tabi* (one-toed socks) or *jikatabi* (workmen's rubber-soled footwear), in Albania *opinga* (rawhide moccasins).

There is virtually no resemblance in the media. Japanese newspapers are thicker, more numerous and more generally read than Albanian ones. Japanese TV has many channels, Albanian TV one single (state-controlled) channel. (Italian TV can be received, if not necessarily understood). Albania has no commercial radio. Recently new newspapers have begun to be published in Albania, but some may be falling foul of the authorities (*The European*, 16–22 Nov. 1995, p. 7). Since the communist period, Albanian newspapers have become more 'popular', but while Sharon Stone and other Hollywood glamour stars have made an appearance, *Manga* (adult comics) do not (as yet) circulate in Albania.

In the field of science and technology, both countries were very backward 150 years ago, but Japan imitated then innovated, while Albania is scarcely even within the first stage. Still, some quite substantial diffusion of technology during the communist period in Albania must be noted. Neither country has fielded many Nobel prizewinners. Although here the two countries belong to a different league, Japan, despite her wealth, modernity and widespread higher education, in this matter rates far below the USA, Britain or Germany. We have an explanation by an Albanian scholar: according to Dr Qevqep Kambo, the Japanese concentrated on applied rather than pure science. Whether that was not a good thing was debatable, but it did not produce Nobel prizewinners (*Bashkimi*, 22 July 1995, p. 6). Dr Kambo gave full marks to the Japanese for the hours spent on education, as well as for their persistence, discipline and big investments in science, but these in his eyes compounded the puzzle that there were not more prizewinners. Was he right that focus on applied science was the whole solution? Surely another reason has been linguistic: the works of Japanese scientists if written in their native tongue are scarcely accessible to foreigners. Albanian, too, would not be much more widely read.

Rather surprisingly, both countries are reported to have been destinations for foreign toxic waste. Apparently this is dumped in the northern region in each country. A British ship, the *Pacific Pintail*, loaded with 14 tonnes of plutonium waste, was due to reach Mutsu-Ogawara (Aomori prefecture) on 25 April 1995, having left France in February (*Daily News* (Sofia), 25 April 1995). Toxic waste has entered Albania via the northern railway from Montenegro. Both Japan and Albania have been superstitious lands, and to a degree still are. In both, examples (or alleged examples) have been quoted of interment of a living human being to ensure that a newly built structure stands firmly. In Albania the story concerns a young woman at Rozafa castle at Shkoder; in Japan there is also mention of a young woman and a castle (at Matsue), 'as a sacrifice to some forgotten gods' (Hearn, 1894, p. 163). Indeed, Hearn quoted the Albanian example. He mentioned too the burying alive of a man in the river-bed below the middle pillar of a bridge in the Matsue vicinity 'and thereafter the bridge remained immovable for three hundred years' (ibid., p. 149).

In Christian mythology the dragon symbolizes evil (St George's killing of one, for example). Dragon killings are found too in romances and medieval stories. This contrasts with China where the dragon is benevolent. As would be expected, the Japanese dragon (*ryuu*) is nearer to the Chinese one. The dragons on the gates of the shrine reached up stone steps from the first great temple at Kamakura are female (with mouth closed) and male (with mouth open) (Hearn, 1894, p. 65). Albanian myths, too, distinguish between a male dragon (*drangoni*) and a female one (*kulshedra*) (Durham, 1985, p. 213). Thus neither Japan nor Albania share the Christian symbolism. On the other hand, superstitions concerning foxes have been prevalent in Japan (Hearn, 1894, pp. 310–42), but not in Albania. Both countries developed a fantastic folklore, though the Japanese used to view certain elements of this as a genuine history of their nation in its earliest stages, which the Albanians did not. But Albanian folklore may form one basis for their system of customary law, which has no parallel in Japan.

The huge differences between the two countries' foreign policies are traceable to their contrasting sizes, military and economic capabilities and historical traditions. These differences reached their greatest contrast in the manner of their entries and exits from the Second World War. Yet one parallel did remain from their wartime experiences, in the two countries' relationships with former enemies. No peace treaty was signed between Japan and the USSR due to the Cold War, which had the consequence that the USSR was excluded from the peace process which culminated in the Treaty of San Francisco (1951). Greece and Albania remained technically in a state of war (which did not prevent mutual trade and diplomatic relations) until August 1987. Moreover, in each case the primary enemy became the chief postwar benefactor: the United States gaining huge influence, besides military bases, in Japan, while Germany (both Federal and reunited) has since 1987 emerged as Albania's chief trading partner, aid donor and diplomatic supporter. Germany did not lose time in becoming economically involved with post-communist Albania. Given the resemblances between the German and Japanese economies (see section 4.7 'Japan and Germany'), and fairly close contacts between those two countries' economists, the Japanese might decide not to lag far behind.

Regarding serious interest in each other, no Albanian experts on Japan are known to this author, although individual Albanians have written on specific Japanese themes (such as Nobel prizewinners, as mentioned above). Among Japanese experts on Albania, who are very few, is Kazuhiko Yamamoto, whose interest in Albania is recent but very keen and whose interpretation of the similarity between Japanese and Albanian attitudes to honour has already been described.

Both Japan and Albania have been secretive or very secretive countries: Japan, during her long period of seclusion and in the militaristic period before and during the Second World War; Albania especially during her communist period. Secrecy among great powers has tended to be more intense, the more easterly the nation (see Hutchings, 1987, pp. 225–9); Japan conformed to this rule. To Albania, not being a great power, it did not apply (the same book noted that Albania did not 'constitute a clear exception'): here the motives were mainly self-protection against what were (by no means wholly incorrectly) seen as hostile neighbours. Both countries were adjacent to (though at different distances from) Western powers (respectively the United States and Italy) where secrecy was much less intense, and this too exerted an influence. (The difference in principle is advantageous to the more secretive country.) After 1945 Japan became less secretive, as did Albania after 1992.

Thus although in important respects so unalike, Japan and Albania have in common a number of features or situations. Like those of Japan and Romania (see section 4.11, below), the common characteristics of Japan and Albania are to some extent those of peripheral states, which though greatly influenced by adjacent powers yet managed to invent or to preserve distinctive features.

More intangible and controversial factors may enter as well. Are Buddhism and Shinto inherently more beneficial to a country than Islam and Christianity? The influence in the Balkans generally of Islam has often been deplored; is not Japan well freed from it? More certainly, Albania has been handicapped by the blood feud. Japan, one might perhaps say, exemplifies what a larger, more populous, Albania might have been able to achieve, had it been better shielded, more independent for longer periods, less handicapped by religion or the blood feud, and ruled with more vision. That is another way of saying that, in most material and practical respects affecting life in the present day, Japan and Albania are indeed extremely different.

The two nations needed, however, to make contact with one another. Japan is adjacent to Russia, yet it took centuries for them to make contact (see Chapter 2). Albania is remote from Japan and historically there had been no connection. Albania's alliance relationships had tended to migrate in an eastwards direction: her allies were successively: Italy (or Austria), Yugoslavia, the USSR and China. (This easterly movement was noted first in Pipa, 1990, p. 37; see also Hutchings, 1996, p. 128.) Japan would be among the next most easterly. Pipa thought any further geographical continuation eastwards not possible, but he wrote before the overthrow of communism. An alliance with Japan would doubtless be favoured by Albania, but could hardly benefit Japan; an economic motive for Japan to make contact would also be needed.

4.2.2 Relations

The imperative for relations between the two countries is provided chiefly by the fact that Japan is an *importer* of certain raw materials, while Albania can *supply* certain raw materials. The composition of Albania's trade with Japan during the communist period is not given in Albanian statistics, but almost certainly Albania's imports were mainly machinery and equipment, her exports mainly raw materials. Direct economic relations between Japan and Albania during the communist period were nevertheless slight. Albania's exports to Japan as percentages of her total exports were: 0.6 per cent in 1980, 2.8 per cent in 1985, 1.8 per cent in 1988 (Cristofoli in Altmann (ed.) 1990, p. 245). Expressed in US dollars, total trade between the two countries was: 11 mn in 1983; 7 mn in 1984; 12 mn in 1985; 6 mn in 1986; 5 mn in 1987; 11 mn in 1988; (*ibid*, p. 239). The total, US$52 million, was slightly less than Albanian trade with the USA (US$60 mn), much less than her trade over the same period with China (US$145 mn), and vastly less than over the same period with Italy (US$308 mn). Not surprisingly, Albania's imports from Japan (US$44 mn) greatly exceeded her exports to that country (US$8 mn) (*ibid*., pp. 239 and 241).

Japan soon became aware of Albania's economic possibilities, and also of needs which Japan might help to supply. A small sum of money to the Japanese seems enormous in Albania. Thus a scene was being set for Japanese economic involvement. But before further involvement could take place, communist rule in Albania had to come to an end. Aid relations between the two countries commenced in Albania's post-communist period.

The first recorded event was an agreement for Japan to grant Albania 2.166 bn yen (about US$22 million) for 'regeneration of the agricultural sector', signed in Tokyo on 11 May 1994. This was from the Fund for External Co-operation of Japan (Anon., 1994d, p. 1 – RN=22232). This must have been for philanthropic motives, but no report has been seen of how this fairly substantial sum has been spent. The same Fund granted to the Albanian Electric Power Corporation (KESH) a credit (amount unstated) for rehabilitation of the cascade of the Drin river, according to an Albanian law dated 21 December 1995 (Anon., 1995a, p. 1176 – RN=24025). (The Drin has the biggest water flow of any Albanian river and is the chief generator of Albania's electricity.) Albania's People's Assembly on 5 September 1996 decided to ratify an Agreement on technical collaboration in the field of searching for minerals with the Japanese Agency for Metal Minerals (MMAJ) (Anon., 1996f, p. 814 – RN=24923).

Thus, a beginning has been made. But in the early months of 1997 extreme disorder erupted in Albania, which instigated limited foreign intervention, and in June 1997 a general election in Albania dismissed from power the Democratic Party (President: Sali Berisha), replacing it by the Socialist Party (President: Rexhep Meidani, Prime Minister Fatos Nano). Whether this opens a new chapter in Japan's economic involvement the future will show, but the Japanese are bound to be discouraged by the turmoil and by any subsequent reversion towards socialism which has damaging results.

4.3   JAPAN AND BOSNIA-HERCEGOVINA

Bosnia-Hercegovina has an area of 51 129 sq km and had a population (1991) of 4 365 639 (density 85.4 per sq km), but is fractured into mutually antagonistic statelets or 'entities'. Since June 1991 internecine war has caused great damage and loss of life. War crimes of great gravity have been committed. The three groups (Serbs, Croats, Muslims) all have different religious traditions which exacerbates their antagonism. To the extent that peace is now maintained following the Dayton Peace Accord, this is due to NATO (North Atlantic Treaty Organization) intervention and the close attention of the Great Powers. In these as well as in other respects Bosnia-Hercegovina has virtually nothing in common with Japan.

The economy is overwhelmingly agricultural, but there are iron and steel plants and, not surprisingly, arms manufacture is important. Since the internal war broke out there is naturally no tourism. There has been no sign of Japanese economic involvement. (See also section 4.15 'Japan and Former Yugoslavia'.)

4.4   JAPAN AND BULGARIA

4.4.1   Comparisons (Note: Including Some Non-Economic Comparisons)

It would be difficult to find any pair of countries of substantial size which are superficially less alike than Japan and Bulgaria:

Japan consists of islands, whereas Bulgaria is wholly continental. Japan is not located on any communications route, while Bulgaria bestrides the main land route from Europe to Asia Minor. Japan's area is 3.35 times that of Bulgaria, her population about 13.78 times larger, so the density of population in Japan is more than four times that of Bulgaria. (This is a bigger difference than between Japan and Albania.) Japan is well-watered, Bulgaria rather dry.

Japan is prone to natural disasters, which in Bulgaria are not of the same sort or so serious.

The ancestors of Japanese immigrated from somewhere (not known) to the south, those of the Bulgarians from a (known) place to the north. The Bulgarians (that is, their ancestors the Bulgars) abandoned their original language; the Japanese did not. The Bulgarian and Japanese languages have nothing in common (see below). Japan's religions are Shinto and Buddhism, Bulgaria's (predominantly) Orthodox Christianity and Islam.

Japan is invariably a food importer, Bulgaria in normal times a food exporter; Japan's diet does not favour dairy products or meat whereas Bulgaria's does; Japan is more advanced than Bulgaria industrially or as regards technology and science.

In the First World War Japan was on the Allied side, Bulgaria on the side of the Central Powers.

By all these reckonings, Japan and Bulgaria are totally dissimilar. Only a very few resemblances or parallels can be found:

In the Second World War both Japan and Bulgaria were allied with Germany and Italy; also Bulgaria would not fight against the Soviet Union, while Japan did so (under compulsion) only within the war's final days.

Both Japan and Bulgaria have concentrated on developing electronics (see below).

Other details were sought for which might confirm similarities between Bulgaria and Japan, but only trivia were found. Stowers Johnson (1964) relates his journey through Bulgaria, apparently about 1960, driving a red and white Dormobile. In Plovdiv he was invited to a Bulgarian meal: forks and spoons were laid, but no knives; however, one was specially brought for him, an Englishman, when his difficulties were realized (Johnson, 1964, p. 49). Much the same would happen in Japan, except that a fork, too, would need to be (and would be) brought instead of or as well as chopsticks. He mentions in the same home an alcove painted with exotic scenes of travel (p. 79); in a Japanese home such an alcove would be the *tokonoma* and would exhibit some artistic object. Apples, which are widely grown in both countries, have in either case a native name: in Bulgarian *yab'lka*, in Japanese *ringo*. Grapes are especially good in either country, though mainly used for different purposes: in Japan table grapes are excellent but in Bulgaria wine is the chief product.

This last difference reflects the very different histories of wine making in the two countries. Pamid wine dates in Bulgaria from the time of the ancient Thracians (Stanley, 1989, p. 447), other varieties such as Cabernet, Gamza, Mavrud, Melnik, Merlot, Otel (red) and Dimyat, Misket, Riesling, Rkatsitelli and Tamyanka (white) (*ibid.*) at much later dates, the industry having been banned during the very long period of Turkish (Muslim) overlordship (1396–1878). The industry did not restart in earnest until 1918 (Stevenson, 1997, p. 325) and thereafter still remained insular until after the Second World War (Richardson and Denton, 1988, p. 442). Wine made from grapes (as distinct from *saki* made from rice) in Japan has no long history but also (unlike Bulgaria, other Muslim-ruled lands, and also for a while the United States) has not been hindered by prohibitions. Some fine wines are now produced (Stevenson, 1997, p. 451). Japan began to brew beer in the late 1800s, the first brewer being a German (Bisignani, 1983, p. 117). Certain brands are now exported. Bulgaria brews beer, but exports are negligible. Beer is rarely mentioned in the Bulgarian national press; in 1982 output did not satisfy seasonal demand or certain other requirements, and was not rising (Tsvetkov *et al.*, 1982, p. 4 – RN=07141).

The two countries' traditions and experiences in war are seriously different. Bulgaria's experiences include several spectacularly horrible events. In 1014 a battle took place near the south-eastern corner of what is now Macedonia (FYROM) between the Bulgars and the Byzantines. The Byzantines were victorious; they took 14 000 prisoners. They blinded all of them except one in every hundred, who was left with just one eye so that these could shepherd the rest back to Ohrid. These others stumbled back, being met by the Bulgar king who died of shock. Four years later the Bulgar Empire collapsed. In 1876 the 'April Rising' against the Turks was drowned in blood, but it created martyrs who even now are freshly commemorated. Japan's military disasters have been more momentous – obviously the nuclear bombs being among the biggest single events – yet their impact on popular memory and lore has scarcely been greater. Much more is deliberately done by the Bulgarians to keep green the recollection of their nation's human tragedies. Indeed, few countries in the world pay more heed to their national history.

Architecture and Archaeology

Both countries now build in concrete, but Bulgaria used to build large structures in stone, Japan in wood. Correspondingly the Bulgarian style in building tends to be heavyweight, the Japanese one to be lightweight.

This results from Japan's much greater susceptibility to earthquakes, and because the Japanese had come from a warmer climate. 'Anthropologists feel that the basic style of Japanese houses, with thatched roofs and breezy air passages, points to an influence from a warm climate as found in the south seas' (Bisignani, 1983, p. 11). The Bulgarians came from homelands north the Black Sea, where the climate was colder, while trees were very sparse; probably their dwellings were of clay, or clay and wood. After the migration, during the period of the first Bulgarian state, 'probably the poor town and village population lived in dugouts or in small huts built of wood, clay, sticks and rarely of stone and clay mortar' (Stamov (ed.), 1972, p. 87). Larger structures were built of 'large stone blocks and mortar or of hewn stone and clay mortar. Brick was seldom used' (*ibid.*, p. 86). The first Bulgarian capital at Pliska was encircled by a stone wall 2.6 metres thick. 'Though little more than the foundations of the structure remain today, the impression they give is monumental' (*ibid.*, pp. 89, 91).

Attitudes to archaeology are dissimilar, almost contrasting. Though the Japanese attitude is drawing closer to the European one, excavations within Japan used to be regarded as impious, because implying doubt as to the divine origins of the Japanese people. This attitude has not entirely disappeared, for instance as reported in 1983 archaeologists had never been allowed to excavate the tomb of Emperor Nintoku in Osaka which was considered sacred (Bisignani, 1983, p. 13). In modern times the Bulgarians energetically excavate their ancient sites, retrieving and displaying the recovered artefacts in museums. Here they resemble other Europeans, but the Bulgarians have been specially active. According to the sumptuous book already quoted: 'The remains of Pliska are a valuable part of the stone annals of Bulgaria's distant past' (Stamov, 1972, p. 91). National pride imbued with historical sense, fostered by the communists among others, also most recently the desire to attract international tourism, have been the motives.

Location of Capital Cities

While Japan's capital was moved further to the east, a westerly site was chosen for Bulgaria's capital. This put the capital site farther from any possible Ottoman advance, but the chief aim was to choose a more central position within the greater Bulgaria promised by the Treaty of San Stefano (1878). This treaty did not come into effect, being replaced by the Treaty of Berlin which truncated Bulgarian territory on its western side, leaving the capital city offset to the west of the rump that remained.

This brought substantial economic disadvantages as compared with Varna (eastern Bulgaria) or Ruse (north-central) (John R. Lampe in Butler (ed.), 1976, p. 73). Tokyo's selection had been more rational, from an economic angle. This also illustrates the minor (and sometimes major) handicaps which afflicted the Balkan nations due to the intervention of the great powers, and which did not afflict Japan.

Language and Alphabet

Bulgarian is a Slavic language. This may be the occasion to say something about the Slavic languages, and how they differ from Japanese. They differ in virtually all respects! Each Slavic language has only one alphabet; Japanese has three. They have complicated grammars; Japanese grammar is basically simple. They have luxuriant verb forms; Japanese simple ones. They use prepositions; Japanese uses postpositions. They (except Bulgarian) make use of cases; Japanese does not. They have very wide vocabularies; the vocabulary of Japanese is much narrower. They do not distinguish between honorific and plain verb forms; Japanese does. They do not convert adjectives into verbs; Japanese does. They have relative pronouns; Japanese does not. The only resemblances that occur to this author is that both languages are phonetically spelled (with negligible exceptions), and that, like Japanese, most Slavic languages lack definite and indefinite articles.

Bulgarian does have a definite article; whether it also has an indefinite one is debatable, though most scholars consider not (see Victor A. Friedman in Butler (ed.), 1976, pp. 334–40). This puts Bulgarian slightly farther from Japanese than Russian is. On the other hand, Bulgarian grammar is simpler than Russian, which puts it nearer. Russian is a purer language than Bulgarian, in that the latter includes many more words of Turkish origin. Similarly, Japanese includes many words of Chinese origin. Thus, whether Russian or Bulgarian is farther from Japanese is unclear.

Economic Development

In level of economic development, GNP per head and virtually all other economic indices (omitting the very specific rose-growing, where Bulgaria sets the world standard) Japan far surpasses Bulgaria. This is a phenomenon mainly of the past quarter century. In 1970 Bulgaria's GNP per head amounted to $1375 as compared with Japan's $1898, i.e. Japan's was only 38 per cent larger (Cyril E. Black in Butler (ed.), 1976, p. 123). This gap has widened.

Black compares quantitative indices of modernization in Bulgaria and certain other countries including Japan. In many respects Bulgaria followed international norms, but between 1960 and 1968 Bulgaria's growth of industrial output was significantly higher than that of any other East European country except Romania, and of any other country except Japan. Bulgaria relied more on foreign trade than Japan did and ranked slightly below Japan in per capita energy consumption. Both countries had a low gross reproduction rate. Bulgaria has more physicians in proportion to population than Japan but much higher infant mortality. Total school enrolment in proportion to population was much below Japan's and Bulgaria ranked still further behind in scientific capacity as reflected in contributions to scientific journals. Bulgaria also ranked far behind Japan in telephones per 1000 of population and in availability of newspapers, radio and TV. One other major difference was the percentage of GNP devoted in 1965 to defence, which was 2.9 in Bulgaria, and 0.9 in Japan; this latter (among the lowest in the world) obviously reflecting Japan's inclusion under the US security umbrella (Butler (ed.), 1976, pp. 117–18 and 122–5).

Both Japan and Bulgaria have paid heed to development of electronics, though Japan on a much greater scale. Both have devoted heed to robotics and produce substantial amounts of mechanical handling equipment. As reported in 1984, in this production the Bulgarian firm Balkancar ranked first in the world, and third after the USA and Japan in total production volume (Lazarov, 1984, p. 4 – RN=10239). As mentioned in 1987, for more than a year the firm 'Vulna' had been turning out more than 150 types of reduction gear, which in quality or reliability were in no way inferior to American or Japanese (Gergova, 1987, p. 11 – RN=13189).

4.4.2 Relations

The extreme differences between Japan and Bulgaria can be said to favour mutual trade, which is much greater than between Japan and Albania (partly also because Bulgaria is much larger than Albania, and its manufacturing quality in some areas is acceptable). As early as October 1977 Japan and Bulgaria signed an agreement for deeper and wider economic and trade relations (Anon., 1977, p. 6 – RN=00614), and 15 months later an intergovernmental commission was set up to develop trade and economic relations between Bulgaria and Japan, including economic co-operation in third countries (*ibid.*, p. 3 – RN=02792). Enterprises in the two countries undertook some joint ventures even in advance of the overthrow of communism in Bulgaria. As reported in May 1984 the Japanese–Bulgarian Atlas Engineering Co., apparently the first Bulgarian–Japanese joint venture, included on the Japanese side Kobe Steel, Toshiba Electric, Mitsu (Bussan), and so on, and on the Bulgarian side Machinoexport and Technoimport (Totev, 1984, p. 17 – RN=9813). By April 1987 trade links had been expanding and joint activities had been undertaken in agrochemistry (Nikolov, 1987, p. 4 – RN=14109).

When Bulgaria entered its transition period, Japanese interest naturally grew. Early in 1993 Japan was offering Bulgaria 30-years loans: the Fund for External Economic Co-operation of Japan offered soft loans for the construction of a bridge over the River Danube, between Vidin and Calafat (long delays build up in crossing by the existing single road bridge near Ruse), for remodelling Plovdiv's non-ferrous metal works and utilizing the sulphur dioxide released in the processing of copper ore at Elisseyna Ltd. The 30-year loans would be released with periods of grace ranging from sever to ten years at 2.58 per cent interest (Anon., 1993, p. 4 – RN=20732). Evidently the Japanese side was envisaging long-term co-operation.

Bulgaria has at least one Japanese restaurant, which is in Sofia and (almost inevitably) is called 'Sakura' or 'cherry blossom' (*Daily News* (Sofia), 1995, p. 6). Its address is 100 James Bourchier Boulevard. There being little in common between Bulgarian and Japanese culinary tastes, this restaurant may well cater chiefly for resident Japanese or other foreigners. Japan probably has no Bulgarian restaurant. It was reported in January 1989 that the Mitsubishi Corporation would manage the Vitosha-New Otani Hotel in Sofia over a nine-year period. This would follow its radical renovation, to be carried out in two stages by Bulgarian and foreign firms, the first stage to be completed by 31 May 1989 (Nikolova, 1989, p. 2 – *ABSEES* B 1/89 (88)). Mitusbishi signed a contract in 1990 to manage the five-star hotel chain Vitosha-New Otani (Correspondent, *Sofiiski Vesti*, 3 January 1990, p. 3 – RN=16868). On 15 May 1996, representatives of the Industrial Bank of Japan conferred with the regulators of Mineralbank, which at the time was under special supervision. The visit was in connection with Mineralbank's obligation of 5000 mn Japanese yen (US$50 mn) for bonds sold on the Japanese securities market in 1989. The representatives of Industrial Bank of Japan were stated to have shown understanding, and gave an assurance that the debt might be reduced or exchanged for property. Meanwhile another Japanese company, Ebara, was to start a joint project with the metallurgical firm Technoimpex for the clearance of sulphur and nitrogen-oxide from

Maritza-Iztok (Maritsa East) power station. The project was worth US$7 mn. This article was headed 'Japan is present ever more strongly in the Bulgarian economy' (Todorov, 1996 – RN=24376). Without implying any huge presence one may agree generally with that assessment.

4.5 JAPAN AND (FORMER) CZECHOSLOVAKIA

4.5.1 Comparisons

Japan and (former) Czechoslovakia were in virtually all respects very different. Japan was on the perimeter of Asia, Czechoslovakia in the heart of Europe. Japan's capital city is located in the east of the country, Czechoslovakia's towards the west. Japan stretches mainly north to south, Czechoslovakia mainly west to east. Japan is much the more southerly. Japan has a long and continuing history, former Czechoslovakia's was short and now is concluded. Japan's population was about 7.75 times larger than Czechoslovakia's, her area 2.81 times larger, her population density therefore about 2.8 times greater. Japan fought as a state before and in both World Wars, Czechoslovakia never did. Czechoslovakia split into two – the Czech Republic and Slovakia – while Japan did not. In religion and language the two countries had nothing in common. On the other hand, both economies had been relatively advanced (Japan in a global perspective, Czechoslovakia in an Eastern European one) which might have stimulated Japanese business interest, but in this respect Czechoslovakia has fallen far short of Hungary.

4.5.2 Relations

Japan was not among the earliest investors in Czechoslovakia (Doleckova, 1992 – RN=19852). On the other hand, a US$150 mn credit was raised by Czechoslovakia from 15 West German, Austrian and Japanese banks (Anon., 1988, p. 3 – RN=15369); in 1991 Japan agreed to lend Czechoslovakia US$200 mn (Anon., 1991b, p. 2 – RN=17984). This was the result of the Czechoslovak government's request to industrially developed countries to grant Czechoslovakia about US$1 bn for the economic reform. This was generous and timely, but there are few other allusions to Japanese economic involvement. In February 1985 an interview was reported with the director of the Bratislava Musical Edition House, Opus, concerning pressing and contracts with the Japanese firm of Victor, part of the JVC concern, on digital compact discs (Fellegi, 1985, p. 5

– RN = 10700). No follow-up has been seen to this. In April 1991 Nomura (a Japanese firm) intervened in connection with the privatization of Pilsner breweries (Doleckova, 1992, p. 8 – RN = 19862). Nomura already had experience of Czechoslovakia: it served as adviser to the State Bank, and was acting as adviser to the Czechoslovak Ministry of Agriculture. Nomura could provide for Pilsner breweries all the credits it needed and rapidly. Nomura was aiming to enter Czechoslovakia via the Pilsner Urquell brewery. In July 1992 two Japanese firms, Fukuoka Jishi Co. and Miki Travel (the 'most significant Japanese travel company in Europe'), bought 40 per cent of the shares of Hotel Jalta in Prague. Built in 1958, the hotel was registered in 1991 as a protected building of special architectural interest; the new board was planning its wide-ranging reconstruction aimed at the individual business customer and at building a congress centre at the hotel, so that its large kitchen capacity be used more fully (Drabova, 1992, p. 4 – RN = 19873).

See also section 4.6 'Japan and the Czech Republic' and section 4.13 'Japan and Slovakia'.

4.6   JAPAN AND THE CZECH REPUBLIC

4.6.1   Comparisons

Comparisons of Japan and Czechoslovakia in several cases apply to Japan and the Czech Republic, but the density of population of the Czech Republic is higher than that of former Czechoslovakia, which among other things makes the Czech Republic less unlike Japan. The population of the Czech Republic is 15.52 million (1991), its area 78 864 sq km (Anon. (ed.), 1992d, p. 161), making its density of population 197 per sq km (Japan's being 322).

4.6.2   Relations

Relations between Japan and the Czech Republic have also been somewhat closer than between Japan and Slovakia but specific projects have not been numerous. A credit of DM 1.3 mn was obtained from the Japanese Eximbank by the glass company Egermann-Exbor, s.r.o. at New Bor, district Ceska Lipa. The company would use the borrowed funds for gradual reconstruction of Hantych glass works and of the glass finishing processes. According to the Director of the glass works, the financial co-operation of Japanese financial circles was the first with this type of glassworks in the Czech Republic. The former state enterprise was privatized by public auction in 1994. The works was producing a broad assortment of handmade non-lead 'Czech' glass. A world speciality was glazed glass, according to an invention by B. Egermann. In this unique glass technology, the greatest interest was found in Japan: up to 60 per cent of the company's production was exported. Despite a general decline in the production of utility and artistic glass, the company did not feel the recession. It had decided to enlarge production capacity (k(sa), 1994, p. 2 – RN=22551).

Reactions in the Czech Republic to advice or example from Japan have been mixed. Nomura's interest in Pilsner brewery has already been mentioned. On the negative side, a study by the Research Institute of the Banking House Homura, recommending or directly expecting a 20 per cent devaluation of the Czech currency, was heavily criticized. The need for devaluation had been caused by the deficit in the balance of payments current account. The background reason was, among other things, slowness in the reconstructing of Czech industry. A part from the technical point of view, this study, in the opinion of the Vice-Governor of the Czech Central Bank, was an example of a superficial approach by the analysts of various institutions. The macroeconomic situation of the Czech Republic was relatively unique (*sic*); there was low state debt, a balanced budget, an active foreign exchange balance, and so on. Earlier, it used to be argued that such a situation was impossible due to low unemployment; at present privatization is considered formal, permitting sound economic development, because of the state's share in banks. The old Latin tag '*ceteris paribus*' applied. If this were not taken into account, there would be a discrepancy between predictions and economic reality (Vit, 1996, p. 2 – RN=24051). But the Czechs also react sharply to criticisms from economists in other countries. After *The Economist* published an article claiming that the four big Czech banks are in poor financial health, *EKONOM* reprinted the main part of this article and gave the reaction of the representatives of the big four (Dostalova, 1997 – RN not yet known). On the other hand, Czech and Japanese investment institutes are to co-operate. Central Europe had not previously interested Japanese investors much, but the Japanese now increasingly felt that this region had progressed in market liberalization much further than other countries that were being transformed from a centrally planned to a free market system (Anon., 1994b, p. 2 – RN=22545). (Note that this refers to 'Central Europe' rather than to the Czech Republic explicitly: the Japanese tend to see the Hungarians as further advanced than the Czechs.) The Deputy of the General Director of

Czechinvest and the General Director of the Development Section of the Japanese Institute for Foreign Investment signed in Prague an agreement on co-operation by the two institutions. Czech sources admit that Japanese managerial and general economic experience are valuable guides. Thus, according to the Deputy Director of the Research Institute of Labour and Social Affairs, Milan Horacek, interviewed in October 1996, wise executives from the USA to Japan knew that they had to develop their human capital, invest in it and motivate it. Rates of unemployment and interest were not the only important factors (Polivka, 1996, pp. 11–13 – RN=24967). Firms like McDonald or Sony were bringing a new entrepreneurial culture. Future economic growth would be created by firms such as these (Klvacova, 1997, pp. 11–13 – RN=25876). Again similarly, another writer argued that those who six years earlier (that is, in 1991) had argued for foreign investment had proved to be right: together with capital from the West had come behavioural habits which, if acquired by Czech firms, would become very useful. In this connection, alluding to the Japanese, she writes:

> Important Japanese greenfield investment came to Plzen in 1996. Matsushita will build Panasonic TV sets from imported parts there. 350 workers are engaged in testing operations at present. By the end of 1997 the factory will start full operation and employ 1,200 workers in three shifts. Matsushita says that qualified labour was the reason for choosing Plzen. The instructions given to the workers are guided by the principles formulated by the founder of the firm in 1932. They emphasize discipline and good citizenship, as well as honesty, sincerity, respect and gratitude in interpersonal relations (Bautzova, 1997, pp. 35–9 – RN not yet known).

Perhaps, however, such a judgement does the Japanese a fraction more than justice, since in recent years 'all four of the country's leading securities firms have been disgraced by scandals' (Pitman, 1997).

Two other Czech commentators, considering how the trade deficit might be eliminated, rejected what they saw as a misunderstanding of Japanese experience. Having cited such 'myths' as shortages of capital and human resources being the responsible factors, or the solution being government support (a more generous pro-export policy), they pointed out that the oft-referred-to example of Japan showed a somewhat different reality. The plans of MITI (the Japanese Ministry of Trade and Industry) did not include supporting car production or Sony products, but in fact designated as key ones other industries (pharmaceutical), which had not turned out to be successful. The main factors of competitiveness rested within the firms themselves. The whole economy had to be prepared for international competition (Pernicky and Hybner, 1997, pp. 31–2 – RN=25266). The Japanese are helping the Czechs to learn this lesson.

4.7 JAPAN AND FYROM (MACEDONIA)

4.7.1 Comparisons and Relations

FYROM (area 25 713 sq km, population 2 033 964 in 1991, giving a population density of 79.1 per sq km, i.e. one quarter of Japan's) is extremely unlike Japan in virtually all respects. The economy of FYROM, already weak, suffered severely from the break-up of former Yugoslavia, and then from the Greek denial of the use of Thessaloniki, its only maritime outlet (Eftov, 1994, pp. 13–14 – RN=22030). There has been no report of Japanese economic involvement.

4.8 JAPAN AND GERMANY

4.8.1 Comparisons

Because of the unique sequence of Germany's truncation and division into West and East after the Second World War, and then of its reunification, this section is divided into four parts: (1) Introduction, (2) Pre-division Germany, (3) Federal Germany, and (4) the GDR; section 4.8.2 covers Japan's relations with the GDR and Germany post-reunification. See also in this connection Chapter 1.

Introduction

Japan's political relations with Germany have been of a different order of magnitude: the gamut from being enemies in the First World War, to having common enemies (though without being effectively allies) in the Second World War. At no time in these relations did *East* Germany have any special salience. Most recently, Japan and Germany (West Germany or, *a fortiori*, united Germany) have seen themselves (and are seen by others) as having much in common. Having been defeated in the Second

World War, both have since regained or (in the case of Japan) more than regained prosperity, although not their military dominance or (particularly in the case of Japan) their political influence.

In relation to Eastern Europe, Japan and Germany have much in common. Japan is second only to Germany as an investor in Eastern Europe. Both are wealthy, highly advanced and diversified market economies with wide financial networks. They offer somewhat similar things: capital, experience, technological and managerial expertise. Both have many scientists, technologists and designers. On the other hand, Japan has no common frontier with any part of Eastern Europe, nor has it reunited there with part of its prewar territory. Japan has never invaded Eastern Europe and has left no unfortunate memory there. there is no history either of Japanese migration into Eastern Europe (or vice versa), and nothing in common between the Japanese and the East European languages. We might therefore expect German policies towards Eastern Europe to be based on a mixture of economic, military political, social and cultural considerations, but Japanese policies to be based solely on economics. With some qualifications, this has on the whole been the case.

Pre-division Germany

During the approach to the Second World War and the wartime period itself, there were similarities between Nazi Germany and Imperial Japan. Both were nationalistic, militaristic and predatory states, now pursuing their national aims by military means. However, Nazi Germany existed for only twelve years in all and Germany had been unified for less than a century, whereas Japan had been unified for much longer. The extreme political subdivision of Germany over centuries had no Japanese parallel. In cultural matters, language and religion there was no likeness. In Nazi times the official ideologies appeared rather similar, but Japan's was more ancient and its mythical but supposedly historical origins were more firmly believed in by a less sophisticated populace. These differences stemmed essentially from the fact that Japan was isolated from other countries for a fairly large part of its history, whereas Germany was far from isolated. Germany was in the heart of Europe, Japan on the edge of Asia.

Federal Germany

Superficially, Japan and the two postwar German nations were not very dissimilar: in 1985 Japan had an area of 372 000 sq km and a population of 120.760 mn, Germany (West plus East, and including West Berlin) an area of 356 800 sq km and a population of 77.653 mn. Thus if then Germany = 1, Japan was 1.043 in area and 1.555 in population, and in density of population about 1.49. Japan did not suffer division, as Germany did, into East and West (plus the complication of West Berlin), though Okinawa was detached. The concern of this book being with Eastern Europe and Eurasia, all-Germany and the Federal Republic of Germany are not considered further.

The German Democratic Republic

The area of East Germany (the GDR) in 1985 was 108 300 sq km, its population 16 644 000. Thus, if East Germany = 1, Japan was 3.435 in area and 7.255 in population. Japan's density of population in relation to the GDR therefore about 2.1. Superficially, Japan and the whole of Germany, also had nothing, or extremely little, in common as regards geography, language or culture. If anything, however, Prussia's unity over a longer period of time, and more militaristic and paternalistic traditions than those of West Germany, had more in common with Japan than did the corresponding features of Germany as a whole, and at least geographically Prussia was the forerunner of the GDR, although the name of Prussia was no longer used. In practice, certain individuals and families or their successive generations lived or even flourished under both regimes. The economies of the two states were not too unlike, in that both were primarily industrial, with highly developed transport systems; both too were technically and scientifically advanced. On the other hand there was no parallel in East Germany to Japan's self-sufficiency in rice. A large fraction of the population of East Germany wanted to emigrate and had to be forcibly restrained, whereas few Japanese wished to emigrate, or if they did they encountered no artificial physical barriers. East Germany's compulsory inclusion within the Soviet bloc was not paralleled in Japan whose postwar directions of development had, however, been dominated by the American occupation and controlled by General MacArthur's Tokyo headquarters, or as the Japanese called it 'GHQ'.

4.8.2 Relations

The German Democratic Republic

Probably because of these similarities, the two countries' economic relations have been fairly strong and varied. Over a certain period contacts between the two countries which were reported in the journal *ABREES* (formerly *ABSEES*) straddled eight subdivisions, the most for any country of Eastern Europe or the former Soviet Union. The largest number were classified under 'Foreign Trade and Payments'. The GDR–Japan Economy Committee, meeting in Tokyo in January 1984, reported on mutual trade in 1983 (ADN, 1984, p. 1 – RN=09903). Trade turnover between the two countries had risen by 30 per cent in 1983 relative to the year before. The Leipzig Autumn Fair of 1985 was said to demonstrate the growing links between GDR and Japanese industry (Anon., 1985c, p. 3 – RN=11558). Economic and trading links between Japan and the GDR were set for expansion, *Neues Deutschland* claimed in December 1987 (Anon., 1987b, p. 27 – RN=14628).

Each country showed appreciation of the other's technology. As reported in March 1984, Japanese firms were exhibiting interest in buying equipment and know-how from certain branches of GDR industry. One successful exporter of both to the Japanese market was the Magdeburg enterprise, Edgar Andre (Anon., 1984, p. 27 – RN=09905). A year later the GDR was eagerly pursuing contacts with Japanese and Western manufacturers (Wessel, 1985, p. 3 – RN=11564). Two years after that, the Robotron Computer Combine in Dresden was emulating Japanese methods of zero defect production, though there were admitted to be problems of co-ordination (Marbach, 1987, p. 5 – RN=14191). The following year, several GDR machine tool manufacturers were exporting to Japan and simultaneously acquiring technological know-how (Kohler, 1988, p. 6 – RN=15009), but soon after this the GDR was urged to study *inter alia* Japanese methods of reaping commercial gain from technological innovation: unless the GDR became more effective in this, it would for ever be overshadowed by foreign producers (Peche and Steinitz, 1987 – RN=14192). On the other hand, in September 1989 the President of Japanese Toyo Engineering Corporation mentioned the GDR's 'high level of science and technology' (Pehlivanian, 1989, p. 4 – RN=16549). In March 1992 *Neues Deutschland* noted that while in the GDR patent applications had risen, Japan was leading decisively in microelectronics (17 108 registrations against the German 170 (dpa/ADN, 1992, p. 3 – RN=19581) – a ratio of a hundred to one. But well before that date the GDR as an independent entity was no more.

Germany Post-Reunification

German reunification was not followed by any immediate upsurge in Japanese interest. 'Right-wing excesses against foreigners' in certain German towns may have been viewed sensitively by some Japanese, although no Japanese citizens were affected. Nine Japanese middle-sized enterprises cancelled a visit to Eastern Germany unofficially for this reason, although explicitly due to 'wrong timing' (ADN/ND, 1992, p. 4 – RN=20483). Even by February 1993 Japanese investors were still cautious towards Eastern Germany; companies were waiting for the recovery of their own economy and for political and economic stabilization in Eastern Europe. This was the finding of a research group of the Free University of Berlin. However, stronger Japanese engagement in Eastern Germany could be expected in the medium or long term (ADN/ND, 1993, p. 4 – RN=20799). There had been Japanese investment in Brandenburg province, but Indian investment there had been larger (35 mn DM as compared with 20 mn) (ADN, 1992, p. 7 – RN=20208). Daimler-Benz (FRG) and IFA (GDR) wanted to include Mitsubishi in their existing joint venture manufacturing commercial vehicles in the GDR; Mitsubishi's President thought that a potential proposition (ADN/ND, 1990, p. 3), but apparently it has not been referred to since. Thuryngia was wanting Japanese investment, but a publicity tour of Japan by the province's Minister for Economy drew a virtual blank; several of his interlocutors had never heard of Thuryngia (one of the least prosperous provinces of Germany), and investors had so far been interested in low-risk investment, like tourism. What had been thought to be a binding engagement by Sony to establish a production unit in Jena turned out to be merely a non-obligatory declaration of intent (Frost, 1991, p. 6 – RN=19279). On the other hand, as regards types of cars bought by East Germans, by November 1992 Japan had already become the chief foreign supplier (the most favoured firm Mitsubishi with 18 206 cars); Japan had succeeded in forcing France into second place (ADN, 1991, p. 8 – RN=19301).

Takata (Tokyo) is the first Japanese company investing in Saxony (adjacent to Thuryngia). Takata manufactures car accessories; at Elterlein in the Erzgebirge (mountain range between Saxony and Bohemia) the foundation stone was laid for a factory in which air bags and seat belts would be made, as from December 1997, and Takata Sachsen GmbH would be registered. The company employed 11 000 workers globally. The executive Director of Takata (Europe) GmbH in Cologne, when asked about public money support for the Takata investment, answered that they would hope to obtain the maximum amount of 35 per cent. There would soon be about 200 people employed at Elterlein. The Director said that Takata had ambitious plans, but it would be premature to speak about long-term business development; he also did not mention the planned turnover. Takata did not want to arouse too high an expectation in this high unemployment region; the possible subcontractors had first to provide quality certificates. Takata combine, one of the leading companies in its field of associated automobile products, had a turnover of about DM 2.5 bn in 1994; it exported mainly to Asia and the USA. Its international activities had increased in recent years. Takata intended to invest DM 50 mn in Saxony (him, 1995, p. 22 – RN = 23490).

Privatization has created certain opportunities, but little has so far been reported about Japanese participation. In September 1996 the Federal Institution for Reunion-Conditioned Special Tasks was soon intending to complete privatization of the chemical industry in Bitterfeld. A final decision about production of chlorine would be taken slightly later. An international consortium, led by the Norwegian concern Norsk Hydro a.s. in Oslo, was producing chlorine with companies of 60–70 workers. Other participants in this consortium included the Japanese firm Mitsui (him, 1996, p. 21 – RN not yet known).

German and Japanese economists have kept in fairly close touch (the author remembers seeing the lengthy c.v. of a German economist clatter out from his Japanese host's fax machine) and collaborative work has been carried out. Views have been exchanged on how best to assist countries in their economic transition. A German–Japanese conference of economists evoked a German view that Japan, beside increasing capital investment, had to send technicians to teach and lead in quality control and information technology (IT). 'If these conditions were met, Japan could make a successful contribution to the economic restructuring of Eastern Europe' (Hax *et al.*, 1995, p. 77). The prerequisite for developing IT was a stable electricity supply. Specifics of Japan's investment in Eastern Europe are not covered in the above-mentioned book. There is much discussion of German reunification and its effects in central and Eastern Europe, and some interesting discussion of transferring managerial and organization methods to Eastern Europe, with allusion to 'high context culture' and 'low context culture'. It is pointed out that both Germany and Japan could find less stressful economic conditions in Eastern Europe than in America or East Asia for expanding exports, as competition from outside was less. Germany had contributed the largest portion of aid to Eastern Europe.

4.9   JAPAN AND HUNGARY

4.9.1   Comparisons

Japan consists of islands mainly stretching north-east to south-west: Hungary is landlocked and angled west to east. Japan is largely mountainous, Hungary mostly plains. Japan has four times Hungary's area but twelve times Hungary's population, so three times her population density. Japan is situated in more southerly latitudes and subject to natural disasters of types which Hungary is not. Japan's people immigrated at least a thousand years earlier than Hungary's is largely Christian, Japan almost entirely non-Christian. Their languages have nothing in common, apart from the peculiarity of being unlike any language spoken by adjacent peoples. Historically, there has been little contact and above all no antagonism. Literature which links Japan and Hungary is extremely scant: the only prewar item known to the author is mentioned below (see also bibliographical note at the end of this section).

4.9.2 Relations

Despite these fundamental differences, there does seem to be a certain high-level affinity between these nations. Perhaps each sympathized with the other's loss of an empire? In the music world, warm relations have been established. Ken-ichiro Kobayashi, who is a Professor at the Tokyo College of Music and been permanent conductor of the Tokyo Metropolitan Symphony Orchestra and has held other musical posts in Japan, burst onto the Hungarian music scene in 1974 when he won first prize at Hungarian Television's first International Conductors' Competition. In 1987 he was appointed Principal Conductor of the Hungarian Symphony Orchestra. He has made recordings with this Orchestra and with Budapest Philharmonic Orchestra. The author saw him in action – an amazing sight – at Fairfield Halls in Croydon, England, in November 1996.

More relevantly, though prosaically, there is an affinity from business standpoints. Uegaki points out that the Hungarian way of privatization was similar to that of the Zaibatsu Dissolution in Japan. It was carried out in a spontaneous way, preserving some of the institutions of the *ancien regime* in power, and took the form of institutional cross-ownership (Uegaki, 1993, p. 37). The Japanese – quite correctly – perceive Hungary as having been in the van of economic reforms in Eastern Europe. For investors, Hungary also offers low labour costs, a geographical situation in the heart of Europe with well developed infrastructure, and good rail and road connections to the European market (Ellingstad, 1997, p. 11). At any rate, among all the countries of Eastern Europe or successor states to the former USSR, with the exception of the vastly larger Russia, by far the greatest economic involvement with Japan is recorded by Hungary. This found reflection in the journal

ABREES (formerly *ABSEES*), edited since 1980 by the present writers, which over a certain period include 45 mentions of contacts between Japan and Hungary, as compared with 99 mentions of all contacts between Japan and the whole of Eastern Europe and the former USSR. Thus Hungary recorded nearly half that total. These also covered a broad range of topics: finance, foreign trade and payments, industry and construction, labour and wages, management, tourism and transport and communications – seven subdivisions. Over the same period Germany recorded contacts with Japan in eight subdivisions, no other country in more than three. Much the largest number of Hungarian contacts related to foreign trade and payments: a total of 35. What is the background here?

Two of these foreign trade and payments contacts – as well as two within the category of tourism – related to tourism. In 1985 an agreement was reported on importing Mitsubishi cars for part of the convertible currencies spent by Japanese tourists in Hungary (Anon., 1985a – RN = 12048). From 1989 onwards an Austria car dealer would start to export (Japanese) Subaru cars to Hungary (MTI, 1988b, p. 6 – RN = 15813), and then, following an easing of customs regulations regarding car imports, an Austro-Hungarian mixed company was to be set up to sell Subaru cars and their components from Japan. The 4-wheel-drive cars would sell for foreign currency. Presumably this would be either to tourists who were already in Hungary, or to others who possessed such currency (Anon., 1989c, p. 10 – RN=H 4/89 (89)). Agreement was reached on increasing the number of Japanese tourists to Hungary (Anon., 1985b – RN = 12073). (Within the Soviet bloc, agreements on exchange of precise numbers of tourists by countries were normal.) Some years later, charter flights would start between the two countries, these being intended mainly for workers at the Esztergom plant (see below) and for Japanese tourists to Hungary. A single IL-62 airliner was expected to be sufficient (R.Zs., 1991a, p. 5 – RN = 18720). In October 1993 the Hungarian National Tourist Authority was considering how to attract more Japanese tourists. Dr T. Teglassy, its chairman, told the reporter that instead of concentrating on Germany or other Western countries which were closer both geographically and traditionally, experts were about to deviate from the 'normal priorities' and to emphasize the importance of the Japanese tourist market. He explained that, considering the annual number of guests (20 mn, or, including transient ones, some 30 mn), Hungary was the world's fifth major power. (This is a little hard to believe, but that is what he said.) However, as regards spending within the country, Hungary lagged far behind – it was placed 45th. The aim of Dr Teglassy's forthcoming visit to Japan was to talk about a connection between the two countries. Apart from the currently operating charter flights the Japanese would allocate landing rights to Hungarian aircraft at the new Osaka Airport which would open next autumn, while Hungary would reciprocate *vis-à-vis* a Japanese partner company at the Ferihegy Airport of Budapest. The abolition of visas was being discussed diplomatically, and a positive solution would certainly add to the mutual exchange of visitors. (Szego, 1993, p. 13 – RN=21725). Hungarian bonds were floated in Japan (MTI, 1992, p. 1 – RN=20526), although later the Japanese assigned then a lower rating (MTI, 1993, p. 5 – RN= 21720). (For continuation, see later subsection.) Further items have concerned Hungarian exports to Japan, Japanese exports to Hungary, and other spheres.

Mutual Trade

The bilateral trade situation, as reported in 1978 from the Hungarian viewpoint, was far from satisfactory: in 1977 the value of exports was less than $10 mn while imports were some $65 mn. Ways had to be found for a more balanced exchange of goods (Anon., 1978a, p. 21 – RN=02442). This aspiration has possibly been the springboard for an announcement that as from 1 April 1978 Japan would lower some import duties; the report discussed the improved chances of Hungarian exporters, particularly those of the food industry (Anon., 1978b, p. 7 – RN=01580). The Hungarians paid heed to food exports. Hungarian participation in 'Foodex', the most important exhibition and fair of the Far East, first held in Japan in 1986, became (from some date presumably in the late 1980s but not precisely known to the author) 'traditional'. Although only two Hungarian companies took part in 1991, ten Hungarian companies (out of some 1000 exhibitors from 40 countries) were to present their products in 1993. The Hungarian Ministry of Agriculture stressed that the Japanese market was very demanding, though if a product did get accepted the Japanese were reliable and faithful clients. (Szalay, 1993, p. 11 – RN=20852). It seems that only slight success had been achieved, since by March 1992 only one Hungarian food item had gained recognition in Japan, which was sour cherries in brandy – certainly a narrow base for satisfaction – as well as two non-food items: Tungsram's halogen headlights and Rabatex's handkerchieves (B., 1992, p. 5 – RN=19617).

Both countries continued to take action to benefit trade. In September 1985 the Hungarian Prime Minister, at the conclusion of his four-day official visit to Japan, spoke about a possible increase in economic co-operation between the two countries (Bossanyi, 1985, p. 1 – RN=11614). A Hungarian delegation led by Ferenc Havasi visited China and Japan (Gal, 1987, p. 4 – RN=13300). In January 1990 Toshiki Kaifu, the Japanese Prime Minister, visited Budapest, and Tokyo reported on Japanese credits to Hungary (MTI, 1990a, pp. 1, 3 – RN=16981). Matsushita Electric Industrial Co., Japan's twentieth largest company, was to open a Budapest bureau; its task was to open up the market for domestic appliances in Hungary (Anon., 1990a, p. 9). Mitsubishi's chairman was interviewed about the Japanese interest in East-Central Europe. He noted that 250 Japanese were now living in Poland, and 160 in Czechoslovakia, but 500 in Hungary. This was closely connected with the fact that Hungary was the first to start along the reforming road (Trom, 1991, p. 3 – RN=19320). Among other action to promote Hungarian exports to Japan was the announcement by the Japanese foreign trading organization JETRO (founded in 1958 as a non-profit entity close to the government) that Hungarian companies which wanted to get into the Japanese market might apply by tender for an office in one of Tokyo's business centres for a period of two weeks to two months, and pay only for the office services (B., 1992, p. 6 – RN=19617). JETRO opened its office in Budapest (date not stated) as the first one in central Europe (HV, 1993a, p. 18 and 1993b, p. 2 – RN=21141).

Joint or Co-operative Projects

These began remarkably early. By October 1980 Hungarian co-operation was reported with the Japanese 'C. Itoh' among other capitalist industrial companies (Anon., 1980a – RN=05314). By July 1986 the first Hungaro-Japanese mixed industrial plant was inaugurated in Budapest: a plastic processing plant was operating on Japanese engineering equipment (MTI, 1986, p. 3 – RN=12848). Suzuki has set up a car manufacturing plant at Esztergom, as is mentioned below in more detail. A thousand years ago the nation's political capital, but hitherto mainly known as the site of a large (if curiously unmoving) Roman Catholic cathedral, Esztergom remains Hungary's ecclesiastical capital. Lying 55 km north-west of Budapest, Esztergom can be reached from the capital by land or water. It faces across to present-day Slovakia (formerly Czechoslovakia); there is a cross-Danube ferry which during the communist period might be used only by Hungarian and Slovak citizens. Esztergom's geographical situation is good and evidently was judged by Suzuki to be satisfactory. The town already had textile and engineering manufactures. The population in 1962 amounted to 23 000; any increase since then may be chiefly ascribed to Magyar Suzuki.

Hungary also produced on the basis of foreign, including Japanese, licences. In May 1980 the first agreement on licences and co-operation in the machine tool industry between Hungarian and Japanese firms was signed (Anon., 1980b, p. 9 – RN=04826). Hungary exhibited at EMO '81, the world exhibition of machine tools at Hanover, some of them based on Japanese licences. There was Hungarian interest in Japanese technology and management (MTI, 1984, p. 4 – RN=10332). A Hungarian pharmaceutical company was in touch with the researchers of two Japanese companies, Takeda and Kowa (R.Zs., 1993b, p. 5 – RN=20541). In a report on the Professor Shiba awards, it was noted that Japanese quality improvements had been applied so far by 700 employers of 18 companies (Magos, 1989, p. 5 – RN=16215). Later, there were proposals for young Hungarians to receive work training in leading Japanese enterprises (Bereczki, 1992, p. 2 – RN=19622), although in this department not everything went smoothly (see below).

The inauguration of Suzuki's plant at Esztergom, which took place in May 1993 was attended and addressed by Osamu Suzuki, Chairman of Suzuki Motor Corporation. In his view, Magyar Suzuki shareholding companys technological basis was fit for achieving a series (total envisaged output of the chosen type) of 200 000, which was currently internationally considered to be economical. Increased production depended on market requirements. By the end of the year a capacity of 50 000 could be achieved by two shifts; with three shifts, without any additional investment, 120 000 cars could be built annually. The site of the Esztergom factory could be doubled, and next to it was a former Soviet exercise ground which also could be used. Following exhausting (or perhaps the original would mean, exhaustive) marketing work, production of motorcycles could also commence. As regards the demand for motor cars, Mr Suzuki believed that as soon as the ratio of Hungarian subdeliveries exceeded 50 per cent, in parallel with an increased series, the profitability could improve. There would be no impediment to supplying West European customers with cars made in Hungary. (However, in this connection see also later paragraphs.) Osamu Suzuki also announced that the building of sedan-type cars had begun (cf. the author's description in a later paragraph) and such could already be ordered from the factory's 60 contractual dealers. The 1300cc variant's price was 1 090 000 forints (Hungarian currency). the factory had already so far manufactured 40 000 'Swift' type cars and, following initial hiccups, waiting times (probably meaning, in delivery to customers) had already been overcome.

Bela Kadar, Minister for Foreign Economic Relations (of Hungary), told the correspondent that out of $5 bn direct foreign and actually working investment the Japanese part totalled 2 per cent. Half of this $100 mn was brought in by Suzuki as an advance (R., 1993d, pp. 1, 5 – RN=21134). By April 1996 Suzuki had increased its capital participation in the consortium Magyar Suzuki to 80 per cent. It was hoping that its Hungarian company would be in first place among (Hungarian) domestic exporters. On attaining the planned turnover of US$330 mn it would become one of the ten largest companies in Hungary. If it exported 38 000 cars in 1996, Suzuki would be the largest Hungarian exporter, announced the president of the Japanese concern. Following a slump in 1994 – in the fiscal year 1996–97 only 23 000 cars were manufactured – production in the 1995–96 fiscal year was expected to rise to 40 000 cars, attaining full production capacity since production started in October 1992, and in 1996–97 to 50 000 (Anon., 1995c, p. 26 – RN=24111).

In fact, the Hungarian internal market for cars proved much more limited than has been expected. The Hungarian economy had been severely depressed. It consequently became necessary to rely more on exports. Istvan Lepsenyi, Director-General of the Hungarian Suzuki shareholding company, announced that in the second half of 1993 the export of Hungarian Swifts would start to the former Soviet Union. The first deliveries would be to Russia and Ukraine, but there was great interest in the Baltic states and the Central Asian republics. In Lepsenyi's view, exports could be expanded to the Central-Eastern European region as well. The Japanese had already created a good trading network in the Czech Republic and Poland. Actually, Suzuki in 1995 exported 23 870 cars to the value of US$154 mn, while over 12 000 cars were sold in Hungary. The export result of Japanese cars in general was helped by a doubling of exports to the EU countries of the Subaru Justy model (*ibid.*). In the last five year, Suzuki had deficits. In January 1996 Suzuki sold more than Opel and had become the most sold trade mark in Hungary (CTK, 1996b, p. 6 – RH=24527). In the first quarter of 1996 the internal market for sales of private cars in Hungary stabilized. Korean and Japanese manufacturers had the biggest shares of the market, including 20.5 per cent for Suzuki and 5.4 per cent for the combined totals of Nissan, Mitsubishi and Honda. The proportion of cars from the former USSR fell (Anon., 1997a, p. V – RN=25601). As regards car manufacture in Hungary, however, Japan – let alone Magyar Suzuki – was not the only active nation. In 1995, investments by Ford, Volkswagen (Audi) and Suzuki would exceed US$1.5 bn. Because of the investments of so many world car giants, Hungary was becoming more involved with making cars, whereas it had formerly specialised on making trucks and buses (Fedorov, 1997, p. VI – RN not yet known).

The special problem of exporting to EU countries was noted earlier. The Suzuki Swift, a boxy five-door compact (the authors' description) should be economical and versatile enough, also not competing with too many other sorts, to find a ready market in Central or Eastern Europe or in successor states of the former Soviet Union. It is rarely seen in Britain (the author has seen just one in his home town of Croydon), doubtless in part because here, as in other EU countries, the market is already saturated with cars of this general sort, nor does the Swift offer unique features. But additionally, exporting to the EU necessitates meeting content requirements set by the EU, yet Magyar Suzuki could not, as its European-based rivals do, import components from the EU duty-free. The Chairman of Suzuki said in May 1933 that currently 37 domestic (Hungarian) companies were supplying parts to Esztergom, making the Hungarian manufacturing ratio 32 per cent (R., 1993d, pp. 1, 5 – RN=21134). Asahi Shimbun (Japanese newspaper) in or before February 1993 had already expressed anxiety about this aspect, but the more optimistic view was then expressed that 'Hungarian industry, having recovered from the recession, would be able to manufacture parts even of Japanese technical perfection; or if not, subdeliveries could be obtained from former socialist countries associated with the EU or from Eastern European manufacturers' (R., 1993c, p. 5 – RN=20853). In any case, Magyar Suzuki confronted this problem. By October 1992 20 domestic contractual suppliers were working for the Suzuki plant, while many more firms would shortly be involved in selling, servicing and part-time supplying of the Suzuki Swift (Anon., 1992a, p. 1 – RN=20264). As reported shortly after the February 1993 report, Suzuki would create a joint company for production of clutches together with one of it biggest suppliers, Daikin, the Japanese department store Itochu, and Bakersz Kft belonging to the Bakany Works at Tatabanye (north-west Hungary). The Japanese would take part as entrepreneurs, as well as handing over the licence. Following the transfer of equipment, the initial capital would be increased – probably in June or July 1993 – to the planned 115 mn yen, of which Daikin would subscribe 50 per cent, Bakersz 40 per cent and Itochu 10 per cent. Initially the casing and all parts of the clutch would come from Japan. Within two years Hungarian companies should manufacture these components. A considerable volume of items would necessarily come from Japan. According to a tripartite contract signed in March 1992, the Esztergom plant would annually get 1300–1400 containers by sea and 700–800 tonnes of products by air. (It is presumed, though not definitely revealed, that these should include other items beside clutches.) Since no warehouses had been built at Esztergom, Suzuki would rely on continuous maritime and air deliveries. (Reliance on continuous deliveries is not uncommon within Japan, but would seem risky over such a distance and with possible international complications.) The aim was to get the necessary components within three days from the Hamaku plant in Japan to the assembly plant at Esztergom (Anon., 1992b, p. 5 – RN=19614). Production would start in summer, and from October 1933 Hungarian-assembled clutches would be fitted into the Esztergom Swifts. As from the second year of operation, the joint venture's sales might amount to 160–200 mn yen. Via the Japanese marketing network, exports (of clutches, apparently) was also possible (R., 1993a, p. 5 – RN=20854; cf. Ellingstad, 1997, p. 12).

These were not the only problems. Some Hungarians being trained for cadre posts found being sent for instruction and discipline under Suzuki in Japan too demanding. (Kovacs, 1991, pp. 1, 5 – RN=19330, 19332). (One may perhaps sympathize with them as regards food, the Japanese and Hungarian cuisines being quite unlike). Others included a rumour of bankruptcy. Istvan Lepsenyi denied that the company was to go bankrupt – that news had spread following a misinterpretation of a Finance Ministry submission by a government spokesman. Lepsenyi gave a remainder that the board of directors had already that summer decided to increase the original capital. Undeniably, the contrasting value of the Japanese and Hungarian currencies unfavourably influenced the refunding of the investment; there was, however, no danger of bankruptcy. The liquidity of Hungarian Suzuki was documented by the more than 2 bn forints bank deposit. The 1.3 bn forints state guarantee was necessary in order to keep the Hungarian ownership within the original capital at a size which allowed a veto concerning important decisions. There were also some adverse reactions from the workforce. Ever since September 1993 (as reported in November of that year) there had been lengthy and numerous conflicts. The workforce complained about low wages, the lack of social amenities in the factory (such amenities of a basic sort were normal in the socialist days), the extraordinary conditions of commuting. If the talks failed, the workers were prepared to go on strike (MTI, 1993c, p. 5 – RN=21712). But actually no strike took place. A pre-Christmas report (23 December 1993), brought relief to the workforce. In January 1994 talks could start about the collective contact. (The report previously identified mention of this pre-Christmas report, dated later than the item mainly abstracted.)

Early in February 1997 Magyar Suzuki announced that it would post its first profit in 1996. Pre-tax earnings would be 750 mn forints, on revenue of 55 bn forints. The company produced 51 000 cars in 1996 (slightly more than anticipated in 1996–97 – see above). compared with 36 000 in 1995 (42 per cent more). Projections for 1997/98 were for 55 000 vehicles, 60 bn forints revenue and a slight rise in profits (EIU, 1997, p. 30).

As regards production of buses, the chief Hungarian producers, Ikarus, has been in difficulties for years, and incurred very serious indebtedness, reaching apparently by October 1996 132 billion forints (US$ 80 million), as much as its basic capital, and bankruptcy became a possibility. Suzuki had earlier showed some interest – its first technology agreement with the Ikarus components factory of Mor was signed in 1991 (R., 1991b, p. 5 – RN=18708), but there seems to have been no concrete follow-up (Lubczyk, 1996, p. 12 – RN=25008). Hungarian co-operation in manufacture of articulated buses, as reported much earlier (Anon., p. 3 – RN=03905) also apparently came to nothing. New articulated trolleybuses, 'looking rather like the old Hungarian Ikarus buses' were in operation in Tashkent (the capital of Uzbekistan) in October 1994, but these were built by a Russian concern in Engels; it had been agreed that the vehicles might be assembled in Tashkent (Kucherenko, 1994a, p. 3 – RN=23121). Thus, apparently, a Russian firm had displaced or forestalled a Japanese one.

T. Inoguchi mentions a transfer of Nissan diesel engine technology to the 'Laba' Railway (1993, p. 86). The author has no details of this transfer and Inoguchi does not provide any. There is, in any case, a complicated misnaming here. 'Laba' should be 'Raba': Inoguchi overcompensates for the Japanese alphabet's lack of an 'L'. Secondly, Raba is the German name; Gyor is the Hungarian one. Gyor, 109 km west-north-west of Budapest, is an industrial town, which during the communist period manufactured textiles, and also did flour milling and distilling. Like Esztergom, it is a river port. Here, too, the German firm Audi has set up an automobile factory, the city having been selected by Audi from more than 100 European cities (Anon., 1993e, p. 1 – RN=21133; be, 1994, p. 26 – RN=22632).

Sony's 'Global Localization'

Sony, the globally important telecommunications enterprise, is acquiring a stake in Hungary. Sony opened an independent representative office in Budapest. The Japanese company would supply its products direct to Hungarian customers. P. Ramocsa, the office's representative, explained that Sony's commercial activity was characterized by 'global localization'. This meant that following its arrival in a particular country, the company would establish all its activities – from planning through manufacturing to marketing – locally. Sony intended to set foot in Hungary in three stages: first, it would create its network of services in every big town; second, the supply of components would be secured by establishing an independent storehouse; and third, it would set up a subsidiary for marketing and servicing, owned by the company. The representative did not exclude the possibility that, like other telecommunication firms, Sony would bring its production to Hungary. Hajime Murano, commercial director, added that in the previous year Sony had a turnover of 24–25 mn marks in the Hungarian market, which substantiated the more active commercial policy. Whereas earlier Sony had sold its products with the help of dealers, this year (1993) it was starting to sell with no outside help. The opening of the Hungarian office, as distinct from Western companies' practice, was not going to become a bridgehead towards the East European markets. The substance of global localization was that Sony always concentrated on the internal markets of the individual countries. The previous year agencies had been opened in Moscow, Prague and Sofia; in Poland the marketing and servicing subsidiary was already operating. Soon Eastern Europe would enter 'as a member with full rights' into the company's worldwide network (O., 1993a, p. 5 – RN=21135).

More recently it has been announced that Sony will establish its first plant in central and eastern Europe in the Hungarian town of Godollo, which is 30 km north-east of Budapest and hitherto has been mainly known as the seat of the former Hungarian summer residence of the Habsburgs. Purchase of 20 000 square metres (sq m) of land will cost DM30 mn. The plant will initially employ 200, later 700. It will manufacture audiovisual products, and production will start in 1997. The products will be marketed in European countries (CTK, 1996a, p. 20 – RN not yet known).

Japanese Imports into Hungary

JETRO is a worldwide import development company of Japan. As reported in February 1993 its 79th branch was set up in Budapest, its director in Hungary being Hayato Taguchi. The Budapest bureau was the first one to be set up in the East European countries in order to participate through Hungary in the so-called 'Speed programme' of Japan in the region. It concentrated on processed food products. Its activity has been manifold: seminars, exchange of experts, exhibitions. 'Foodex' is the most important exhibition and fair of the Far East, and probably of the entire world, first arranged in Japan in 1976. In 1993 the event was to take place in Makuhari, 40 km from Tokyo, on a covered space of 54 000 sq m, with some one thousand exhibitors from 40 countries taking part. With the financial support of JETRO, ten Hungarian companies (Agroman, Hungarofruct, Inter-Trade, Mirelite, Monimpex, Szilasfood, Zwack and others) would present their products (Szalay, 1993, p. 11 – RN=20852).

The Yen in Hungary and Exchange Rates

The national currency of Hungary is the forint (Ft), but other currencies including in particular the German DM play some role. The balance of payments and interest payments data for 1992 was published in dollars (MTI, 1993b, p. 5 – RN=20839). Helmut Schlesinger, president of the German Bundesbank, in a lecture in 1993 at the Budapest University of Economic Sciences, suggested that the exchange rate of the forint should be adjusted to that of the German currency. He remarked that it would not be against their principles, the mark being a hard currency, and thus the decisive factor for economic stability. Asked about this idea, Dr F Hershegyi, the Vice-Chairman of the central bank, said it had already been considered the previous year to change, within the basket of foreign currencies, the ECU for the German mark. This would be useful since half of Hungarian exports was accounted in marks or in currencies related to them. Dismissing the anxiety that this step could be risky, he pointed out that the announcement by the head of the German central bank suggested that he considered the Hungarian economy fit for the step. It also indicated that the monetary policy of the Hungarian National Bank during the past three years was being recognized abroad as well. To adjust the exchange rate of the forint to the mark required a joint decision of the central bank and the government (M.M., 1993, p. 5 – RN=20847). Despite this qualified approbation, the change was not in fact made.

An increasing role is played in Hungary by the Japanese yen. Unlike the DM and the yen, the forint is an internal currency only; within Hungary a forint is worth slightly more than a yen. In the first quarter of 1993 the yen – forint rate went up from around 68 to nearly 80 forints for 100 yen (Anon., 1993f – RN=20848). The rising yen affected the Hungarian state debt, a sizeable part (believed to be under 50 per cent) of the foreign composition of which comprised yen. The view was expressed in some

Hungarian circles that Japan was to some extent responsible for Hungary's debt burden. Dr. Harshegyi described as 'cynical, economically unsubstantiated and even false' this view – which had been voiced on a governmental level as well. The fact was that 34 per cent of foreign credits, that is $7.4 bn, came from the financial institutes of the Far Eastern major power, and of their repayment half would become due to Japan in the next 4–5 years. (The above is quoted from the Japan supplement of the *Vilaggazdasag* newspaper introducing a report by Andras Trom in *Nepszabadsag* of 2 April 1993.) Dr Frigyes Harshegyi, the guardian of Hungary's foreign exchange till, dismissed the quoted view as politically inspired and far from economic and professional realities.

Without credits, Hungary would have collapsed just like Poland did in 1981. He dismissed the argument, that the burden of debts hampered the recovery from the dismantling of the economy, as a completely false assumption. The deteriorating of the standard of living was not due to the external debt but the concomitant of the change of regime. 'If the country had not a single filler [one-hundredth of a forint, hence a microscopic amount] of debt, loss-making industrial branches like metallurgy and steel production would have to be cut down anyway', he claimed. In his view it was 'directly fantastic that Japan chose just Hungary' from this region to place her surplus finances.

Loans and Aid

Foreign trade and payments includes loans and aid, some of which relates to Hungary's communist period. A 16.1 billion yen (some $70 million) credit was granted by Japanese banks in 1983 to the Hungarian National Bank for financing agricultural and energy programmes (MTI, 1983, p. 8 – RN=09504). A new $400 mn credit was raised by this Bank from a US–Japanese banking group (MTI, 1985 – RN=12045). Then followed a long interval; perhaps the Japanese were waiting to see how *perestroika* would develop. At the beginning of 1989 a $60 million loan was accorded to Hungary by the Japanese Export-Import Bank (Anon., 1989b, p. 5 – RN=15798). Japan's increasing role in Hungarian credit deals was noted in March 1989 (Trom, 1989b, pp. 1, 2 – RN=16204). In May 1989 the Japanese Export-Import Bank and another six leading Japanese financial institutions accorded a $60 million credit to the Hungarian National Bank for a period of 14 years; no strings were attached (MTI, 1989, p. 1 – RN=H 5/89(89)). Later that year, according to a Nihon Keisai Shimbun report, the Japanese government reiterated their intention to accord $80 million support for Poland and Hungary in 1989: half in food supplied for Poland, the other half for revitalizing both countries' economies (Trom, 1989a, p. 2 – RN=H 10/89(90)). In April 1990 Yohai Sasakawa, Chairman of the Japanese Shipbuilding Industry Foundation (Sasakawa is a noted philanthropic institution) handed a letter promising $1 million grant to the President of the Hungarian Academy of Sciences for further education of researchers below the age of 35 (MTI, 1990b, p. 8 – RN=H 4/90(92)). In April 1993 Japanese Start-Credit, 'like its German companion', mainly wanted to assist the creation of small and medium-sized companies, though certain occupations were disapproved, apparently taking into account moral or ethical considerations (see below). Seven financial institutions in Hungary were commissioned to liquidate the credit approved by the Japanese Eximbank amounting to nearly 8 bn forints. To get the credit the applicant had to have 30 per cent private resources, an acceptable business project and a guarantee cover. The rate of interest was always 75 per cent of the central bank's base rate plus 2 per cent commercial bank interest yield. Expiry was between one and 15 years at most with five years' grace. The borrowers might not engage in the arms industry, ecologically harmful output, property agencies or in running nightclubs. (Among these, 'property agencies' seems the odd man out; they must have acquired a shady reputation.) The credit's financial resources were still far from being exhausted: the bank so far had signed refinancing agreements for only 400 mn forints by mid-June (B.V.J., 1993, p. 5 – RN=21127). In May 1993 the Chairman of the Hungarian National Bank visited Tokyo, together with its Vice-Chairman, who made the following summing-up: since 1987 the Bank had received credits from Japan 14 times, and these together with 400 bn yen worth of Samurai bonds totalled US$3.5 bn (MTI, 1993a, p. 3 – RN=21130).

Other Projects

An unusual joint venture was announced in April 1996. The Hungarian company Dermo Print was intending to found a joint venture company for production and distribution of its systems of identification of persons on the basis of fingerprints with the Japanese company Nippon LSI Card Tento. The joint venture would trade as Nippon Dermo: there would be equal share participation of both partners and basic capital of US$900 000. The plant should be completed within four months in the Japanese town of Matsubara. The Dermo group expected its product, which allegedly permits far safer and simpler identification, to be widely used, for example as door keys, starting car engines, telephone use, drawing money from banking counters, or starting computer pro-grammes. Several thousand of these Dermo identification products had been sold in Switzerland and it was expected that several hundred would be sold in Japan. A similar joint venture arrangement was being pre-pared by Dermo with a Canadian company, and co-operation was being considered with Microsoft, whose experts were said to be seriously inter-ested in the technology (Reuter, 1996, p. 20 – RN=24521).

Japanese Participation in International Aid and Consultations

Japanese individuals and institutions have also taken part in international aid and consultations relating to Hungary. The Hungarian National Bank signed a US$200 mn credit agreement with a group of banks, including the Bank of Tokyo and the Industrial Bank of Japan, for an eight-year period (MTI, 1988b, p. 6 – RN=H 6/88 (86)). In March 1989 Japan's increasing role in Hungarian credit deals was noted (Trom, 1989b, pp. 1, 2 – RN=16204). In June 1989 Dr Saburo Okita, a former Japanese Minister of Foreign Affairs, became economic consultant to the Hungarian government (Anon., 1989a).

Hungarian Bonds on Tokyo Stock Exchange

Hungary has made many launches of bonds on Tokyo stock exchange. As reported in January 1993, since the Hungarian National Bank launched 40 bn yen worth of so-called Samurai bonds on the Tokyo Stock Exchange, it would be the 13th time that sales of Hungarian securities were sold in Japan. Their run of five years would yield an annual interest of 5 per cent. Originally it was contemplated to issue bonds worth 30 bn yen, but the great interest in them induced the central bank to add another 10 bn. Their buyers were mainly small, entrepreneurial and private investors. The Hungarian bonds were very popular in Japan since in-vestors considered the risk acceptable, apart from the rate of interest which was higher than the customary one. Hungary was seen as a reliable debtor (O.Sz.A., 1993b – RN=20842). According to a subsequent report, debated 11 March, the Hungarians launched another 50 bn yen worth of Samurai bonds on the Japanese stock market. Their rate of interest during the run of seven years would be 6.45 per cent. The Vice-Chairman of (Hungary's) central bank announced that during the past two and a half months it had issued bonds worth US$1.3 bn. He assessed the country's annual credit requirement at 2 bn. The central bank would acquire $1.5 bn – the remainder should come as target credits of international financial institutions or from commercial banks. Dr Harshegyi pointed out that the very fact that the financing of the debt was solved, while foreign exchange reserves amounted to $4.5–5.5 bn, offered economic policies a perspective of at least 18 months. The credit funds agreed between the central bank and the Japanese Eximbank were already available for Hungarian businessmen employing not more than 200 people for developing their companies. With a run of 15 years, the loans' interest rate was 15 per cent. (The source also recommends looking at *Nepszabadsag*, 20 April 1993, p. 5, which was not accessible to the author.)

Concluding Remarks

Vignettes (later in this paragraph) showed how the Hungarians saw themselves in relation to Japan, or how the Japanese viewed Hungary. Japan's deputy minister for international economic questions welcomed the Hungarian government's intention to institute a stock exchange (Trom, 1987, p. 2 – RN=H 12/87 (85)). A Japanese newspaper expressed a Hungarian politician's view regarding Hungary's place in Central Europe (Trom, 1990, p. 32 – RN=16979). As noted, Hungary was seen as a reliable debtor. This positive view has been more than reciprocated in Hungary. As early as 1979 a Hungarian source quoted – implying approval – a Lyons (France) newspaper to the effect that it was the Hungarians' ambition to become 'the Japanese of Europe' (Gati, 1979 – RN=3907). Presumably the meaning was that the Hungarians should be equally enterprising, innovative and successful. It can be said that a start has been made, though there remains a long way to go.

4.10   JAPAN AND POLAND

4.10.1   Historical Background

Official relations between the two states were curtailed by the fact that during Japan's Meiji Era (1868–1912), when at last Japan emerged from its isolation, Poland had not regained independent status. Polish patriots were, however, active before 1918, and in 1904, when Japan was at war with Tsarist Russia, some contacts occurred between these and the Japanese government. In the summer of 1904 two Poles, Pilsudski and Dmowski, travelled to Tokyo independently, were at first unaware of each other's presence, and presented opposing points of view. Pilsudski was 'the revolutionary minded leader of the PPS; while Dmowski was 'chief spokesman for the National League, the Polish nationalist movement'. Pilsudski proposed that the Poles should commit acts of sabotage and supply information, while the Japanese would send weapons, ammunition and money. Dmowski agreed that there was a quantity of inflammable material, but feared the consequences of an uprising which, in his view, Russia would easily and brutally crush. The Japanese showed some interest in gaining Polish support, but did not take up the Polish offers. The reasons are not clear, though evidently the Japanese thought the complications would outweigh the benefits. The two parties had different objectives, in that each wanted Russian forces to be tied down nearer to the other adversary. The international statuses of the two parties were very different. The fact that the Poles did not speak with a united voice must have weakened their impact further; and the fact that Japan was a conservative authoritarian state, which would be supporting the Polish Socialist Party if they gave support to Poland, must also have been a deterrent. It is also possible that Britain, an ally of Japan, warned against involvement, because a Polish uprising would bring Russia and Germany closer together, which was not in the British interest. Both Poles and Japanese might have benefitted from an alliance which would have put pressure on Russia at each end of its immensely long territory. In the end, however, these contacts came to nothing (Thackeray, 1992, pp. 52–67).

Polish–Japanese official relations between the two wars can be glimpsed through the prism of Polish–Soviet relations. These latter commenced with war, ding-dong retreats and advances which ultimately secured for reborn Poland a swathe of territory belonging formerly to Tsarist Russia and inhabited by many who were not ethnic Poles. The USSR and Poland made peace but did not become friendly. Given the clashes between Soviet and Japanese forces during the 1930s, Polish–Japanese relations are unlikely to have been antagonistic. However, as Japan and Nazi Germany drew closer together, while Poland emerged as the next Nazi target, Japan would not have expressed or intended any support for Poland. Japanese sights were fixed on the United States and on European colonies in South-East Asia, which had nothing to do with Poland, while Poland was engrossed with the threat from Germany, and subsequently with defeat and occupation by Germany and the Soviet Union. In consequence Poles, who experienced German brutality in the Second World War, and also the Soviet Katyn murders, but did not experience Japanese brutality, do not have negative views about the Japanese. Each lies on the periphery of Russia (or the former USSR), and each has fought against the Russian Federation's predecessor state. The Soviet invasion of Polish territory in 1939 ended the active land war immediately to the west of Soviet territory, and their invasion of Japanese territory (Manchuria) in 1945, in conjunction with US atomic bombs, concluded the war in the east.

On the whole, the Polish view of Japan has been more favourable than the Japanese view of Poland. According to Takashi Inoguchi, 'in Poland Japan is ranked at the top of all nations in the world in terms of its favorable image' (Inoguchi, 1993, p. 86). Postwar Japan, at first amenable to US governance and then to its influence, belonged in effect to the anti-Soviet bloc of NATO, and also had espoused the capitalist system of economy which the USSR anathematized. The Japanese therefore took note of Soviet policy towards Poland, the largest and most populous of the East European states, and this on occasion had the effect of modifying their policy towards the USSR. One such occasion was the proclamation of martial law in Poland on 13 December 1981, which 'again strained Japanese-Soviet relations'. Japan did not at once adopt any economic sanctions against the Soviet Union but eventually decided on four comparatively mild steps (Daniels and Drifte (eds), 1986, p. 75).

4.10.2 Comparisons

Postwar Poland is not far from being as large in area as Japan (84 per cent) though its population is less than one-third as large, making Japan's population density about 2.7 times greater. Poland is continental, more northerly, colder and drier, has a well-developed transport network and (together with Hungary, the Czech Republic and Slovakia) is in a favourable location for delivering goods to north-central Europe. On the other hand, Poland's telecommunications are not satisfactory. In most economic spheres Poland is well behind Japan, and in certain spheres especially so. Consumption of medicaments has been US$16 per head annually in Poland and US$412 per head annually (26 times more) in Japan (Krauss, 1995, p. 5 – RN=24156). Where, as in production of tractors or shipbuilding, the Polish economy is quite strong, the Japanese economy is stronger still. Thus on general grounds the potential for Polish–Japanese trade and economic relations does not seem high.

4.10.3 Relations

And in fact, during the communist period, such relations were correspondingly slender. For several years Polish–Japanese trade remained roughly stable at US$380 to 400 mn yearly, but Poland had a large passive balance. In 1989 the Japanese government reiterated their intention to accord $80 mn support for Poland and Hungary, as described in section 4.9.2 (Trom, 1989a, p. 2 – RN=H 10/89(90)). Something like three-quarters of this support was destined for Poland. Between 1991 and 1993 the volume of exchanges fell from US$500 mn to US$250 mn with Japanese exports consistently the larger. In 1994 the Polish deficit was US$306 mn.

In 1973, during the Soviet period, Mitsubishi, Mitsui and Nippon Mining and others were already reported to be negotiating for a copper mining project at Rudna (Poland) to cost $600 mn, to be repayable in copper deliveries to Japan, but nothing further was heard about this. In January 1987 the Japanese Premier had visited Warsaw, and there were hopes of greater bilateral co-operation (K.P., 1987, p. 13 – RN=13374), but it is not clear that anything concrete resulted. The overthrow of communism – in which the Poles took the lead – could only stimulate Japanese interest, and in 1990 it had already been announced that the Polish sector of the Trans-European motorway (north–south) would be completed in 2005, with 80 per cent of the cost to be financed by the Japanese under favourable conditions (TOMS, 1990, p. 1 – RN=17439). Japanese technical assistance must already have commenced, since in June 1991, in the course of a visit to Japan by Polish Prime Minister, the Japanese Prime Minister confirmed that such assistance would continue. The Polish Prime Minister met representatives of Japanese economic circles and Parliament in Tokyo, but it transpired that Japan, while supporting the changes in Poland, was refusing any further reduction in Polish debt (PAP, 1991, p. 1 – RN=18743).

More positive Japanese attitudes were signalled in mid-1994. A correspondent, reporting on a two-day session of the Japan–Poland and Poland–Japan Economic Committees, regretted that these had not attracted much attention from Polish businessmen. Poland had perhaps lost a large part of its opportunities to enter the Japanese market. (The lecturers' colleagues reserved their opinion.) According to the Japanese, Poland was the fastest developing Central European and East European country, and they continually stressed that opinion. Both sides might think about the future with optimism. The Japanese Minister of Trade and Industry did not exclude a return of Japanese governmental guarantee on trade and investment in Poland. Japanese businessmen were waiting for this question to be precisely defined. Many who had arrived in Poland for the first time did not hide their interest in investment by Matsushita. Success in this joint venture would give a green light for other investors. The Japanese Chairman of the Japan–Poland Economic Committee told the Polish Prime Minister that he would urge the

Japanese government to a greater engagement in the Polish economy (JAC, 1994, p. 4 – RN = 22335).

Seventeen months later a less favourable view was being expressed. Poland did not have a good reputation in Japan since it asked the Paris Club for partial amortization of its debt. In Japanese eyes this was a sign of dishonesty. Poland was also considered in Japan to be a country of high investment risk (Kryst, 1995, p. 5 – RN = 24586). But now the Poles were becoming more enthusiastic. As far as the Polish President was concerned, Poland had to become the second Japan, co-operating closely with that country. From 1995 onwards there have been stronger indications of Polish interest in securing economic co-operation with Japan. The new Polish President had this as one of his projects. In October 1995 a Polish government delegation, including the Minister for Overseas Economic Co-operation, visited Tokyo. Before it arrived there had been meetings of businessmen of both countries, promotional activity, seminars and visits to Japanese industrial companies. These would have been needed, since Poland's reputation in Japanese business circles was not high. Around that time there were only traces of Japanese investment in Poland, amounting to about US$10 mn. The largest was Toyota Motor Poland, a spare parts depot. Following his return, the Minister for Overseas Economic Co-operation expressed the wish that before the end of 1995 a major Japanese firm would start to invest in Poland. During the previous visit of the former Polish President to Japan, the Japanese Prime Minister confirmed officially that Poland had to fulfil three conditions before the government would support businessmen who invested in Poland. In September 1995 the Poles, in their own view, had fulfilled the third and last condition by repaying the first instalment of capital to the London and Paris Clubs. Yet up to 1 November 1995 it was not known if guarantees would be unblocked (Wasilewski, 1995, p. 4 – RN = 24585).

According to the state agency for foreign investment, in a report dated August 1996, foreign capital invested in Poland came from five countries: the USA, Germany, Italy, Holland and France. Firms from Japan were not among the great investors; the largest investment was by Matsushita, but only US$13 million (Mikinski, 1995, p. 9 – RN = 23254). This is actually the Japanese company Philips Matsushita Poland, which built a factory at Gniezdno, exporting 80 per cent of its production of batteries to Western Europe. Its head, Mr Kobayashi, made speeches as a 'guru' and promoted investment in Poland (Wasilewski, 1995, p. 4 – RN = 24585). Overall, Poland still does not receive a huge amount of foreign investment. Spain, a country similar to Poland in many respects, has received a much larger total. As reported in December 1995 by the United Nations Conference on Trade and Development (UNCTAD), during the last ten years US$10 bn had been invested in Spain by foreign investors, as compared with about US$2.5 bn in Poland. Over 800 foreign businessmen were asked by Poland's State Specialized Agency for Foreign Investment to assess the Polish position. Poland was found to be attractive from the point of view of workforce, size of market and perspectives of growth. However, the investment conditions were worse; there were no preferences, taxes were high, as were customs duties (JAC, 1995, p. 4 – RN=24146). The Japanese doubtless took note of these disadvantages.

Customs duties are surely one reason why the Japanese-American company Isuzu is interested in the Katowice Special Economic Zone (south-east Poland) which includes land at Tychy. Here, Isuzu has been intending to build a plant to manufacture diesel engines, but there are problems because the land contains some old buildings, and Isuzu will buy only if the land is clear of obstacles. (This is just one illustration of problems encountered in this zone connected with land.) (Szot, 1997, p. 10 – RN=25335.) About 80 investors, mainly foreign, were reported to be interested in this zone.

Japan has figured in other economic spheres too. In April 1996 the (Polish) Economic Committee of the Council of Ministers advised the government to adopt several important proposals. One concerned the Minister of Finance and related to concluding an agreement with the World Bank. The subject-matter of the agreement would be exploitation of an offer by the Japanese government of non-repayable assistance amounting to 53 mn yen, equalling 0.5 mn zloty; it was designated for the activities of the Communal Development Agency. (The implied zloty – yen exchange rate does not match the author's information; the yen total is assumed here to be authoritative.) The Agency's chairman clarified that the Japanese donation would be used to work out a project of investment for local municipal administrations (Sieradzinski, 1996, p. 5 – RN=24576).

In various business respects, Polish and Japanese views or interests do not coincide. For instance, Polish policy for fairs differs from that of the Japanese (see also section 4.11 'Japan and Romania'), in that the Poles have tended to prefer fairs of general scope, the Japanese much more specialized ones, such as 'Foodex' in Japan (cf. Syzdek, 1995, p. 14 – RN=23851). This Polish preference is inherited from Soviet times. More generally, Japanese activity in Poland must now mesh in with tasks and priorities set by the European Union. In connection with the arrival in Poland in late April 1996 of Neil Kinnock, the EU Commissioner for Transport, discussions were to be held about the development of the

Polish economy, including that of transport, in connection with the Polish application for membership of the EU. The Polish Minister of Transport has since declared that work on adjusting Polish transport to the requirements of the EU has considerably advanced. Commissioned by Poland at the request of the Polish Minister of Transport, the Japanese (no mention of which firms or individuals) had elaborated a general plan for the Polish transport system while an EU consultant company prepared a document discussing the possibility of Polish adherence to the EU. The government on this basis completed a document 'Transport Policy' which would soon be discussed in parliament (Wodz, 1996, p. 5 – RN=24605).

While the EU now dominates in the fixing of Polish standards and in Polish economic policy generally, Korean interest too dilutes Japanese economic involvement. This is clearly illustrated in projects for automobile manufacture. In recent negotiations relating to large-scale deals in this sphere, the Japanese were not the first to become involved: Fiat of Italy were. This is relevant because one of the Poles' main preoccupations has been to make their automobile industry more competitive. From 1983, the Polish car producer FSO began discussions with foreign car producers with the aim of modernization. A Japanese consortium – Daihatsu, Itochu and Sumitomo – became a potential competitor. This project was first reported in March 1984, and over several years negotiations continued. Visits by Prime Minister Nakasone to Poland in January 1987, and of the Polish President Jaruzelski to Japan in August 1987, were influential. However, in September 1988 it was announced that the contract had been awarded to Fiat. Apart from Fiat's long history of involvement in car manufacture in Poland – going back as far as 1921, with post-Second World War manufacture commencing in 1950 – certain other considerations apparently carried some weight. Daihatsu is said to have demanded a very strict system of quality control which was not enforceable in Poland (as reported in December 1986). More broadly, adaptation of Japanese work methods and style to Poland might be a problem. The Japanese companies were unable to come up with the necessary financing. They seemed not particularly enthusiastic about investing on such a large scale in Poland. Fourthly, the Poles made a request for renegotiation of already agreed interest rates, which the Japanese immediately rejected. Fifth, Fiat and the Italian government showed much greater unity than was shown on the Japanese side. Thus, apparently, a number of circumstances swayed or determined the result.

Although, given equal starting points, Daihatsu might have vanquished Fiat, it lost out to another firm from the Pacific rim. The eventual

Polish choice of Fiat was quickly followed by a decision to stop medium-sized car production. But then negotiations were conducted with Daewoo, with which a contract was signed in October 1995. In the next six years Daewoo would invest US$1121 million in FSO; the contract was the largest in the history of the Polish economy. There was, incidentally, resentment against Britain because via the British subsidiary of Daewoo it had allowed the entry of Asian competition, Korean as well as Japanese (Walewska, 1996, p. 7 – RN=25332). But these allusions to Daewoo take us away from Japan (see *inter alia* Mikinski, 1995, p. 9 – RN=23254). According to the most recent report which seems to equate the two countries, Japan and South Korea are new sources of investment in Poland (Ershov, 1997 – RN not yet known).

One may conclude that Japan's economic involvement in Poland has been moderately variegated and well-intentioned, but that the two sides have not always seen eye to eye, their enthusiasms have often not been synchronized, other countries have become more deeply engaged, and as a result Japanese involvement has been hesitant and on the whole rather limited.

4.11   JAPAN AND ROMANIA: A COMPARISON OF PERIPHERAL SITUATIONS

4.11.1   Comparisons (Note: Including Non-Economic Comparisons)

It might seem that Japan and Romania are in all respects so different that no meaningful comparison could be possible.

Indeed, there *are* huge differences between them. For a start, the eastern seaboard of Japan faces the world's greatest ocean, Romania's the virtually landlocked Black Sea. Japan is elongated, Romania almost circular. Japan consists of islands – Romania does not. The population of Japan is more than five times that of Romania, her population density about three and a half times greater. Japan is a world leader in a number of aspects of industry and technology, while Romania is backward in most (though not all) economic directions. Consequently Japan has a high standard of living, Romania one of the lowest in Europe (perhaps the lowest apart from Albania). Japan has been for some 40 years a political democracy, Romania is just becoming one. Japan is inhabited by virtually a single race (the Ainu – Koreans and Burimin hardly count here), whereas Romania has been multiethnic (though becoming more homogenous following the post-Ceausescu departure of almost all of the

Saxons). The Japanese and Romanian languages are unrelated. Japan has always been independent, whereas Romania, during most of her history, has been incorporated within one or more much larger empires. There is no Japanese parallel in recent times to Romania's recent confused political history. Romania has never had an emperor, unless at some time Nicolae Ceausescu could have labelled the first one – in 1974 he ascended a higher pedestal, as President, but in 1989 was executed – though it has had a King and might have one again; it is Christian (in one denomination or another) which Japan generally is not, and while the Japanese tend to have a fairly high opinion of themselves. Romanians tend to be self-deprecatory.

Some of these differences might be epitomized. Several guidebooks to Japan contain a story about a songbird which was given as a present but which would not sing. Three of Japan's sixteenth-century rulers were asked what to do about it. Nobunaga declared 'I'll make it sing.' Hideyoshi wanted to try a different approach: 'I'll persuade it to sing,' while Leyasu announced 'I'll wait till it sings.' There is a slightly analogous Romanian story: Christ had been crucified, and the problem put to his followers, supposedly consisting of Hungarians, Saxons and Romanians was how to recover the body. The Hungarians replied at once: 'We'll fight for it!' But it was thought that they might not be able to kill all the guards, so the same question was put to the Saxons. Their solution was 'We'll bargain for it.' But it was feared that not enough could be offered for a treasure of such value. So the Romanians were asked, and their reply was 'We'll wait until after nightfall, and then steal it!' The two stories illustrate the universal human dilemma that, in order to gain something, one may try either more, or less, forceful or cunning approaches. But they also show or suggest fundamental differences between Romania and Japan, such as, that the different approaches which in Japan are ascribed to different emperors, are ascribed in Romania to the different nationalities.

The list of differences between the two countries could be extended, but these seem to suffice. Given all these differences, can there possibly be similarities? Perhaps surprisingly, there are. Some similarities are doubtless coincidental, and/or will apply to other pairs of countries; still, it appears not without interest to draw attention to them here.

In both countries monks have lived in quite large numbers in monasteries or abbeys which have had – and in some cases still have – great prestige. In Romania monks and nuns belong to the Orthodox Christian Church, in Japan to Shintoism or Buddhism – especially Zen Buddhism. Their belief systems are not the same, but the modes of life of monks (and in Romania also nuns) are not very different: dwelling within hierarchical communities not inside city limits, celibate, living frugally (that applies in Romania to the rank and file, perhaps less so to the upper hierarchy), dressing modestly, engaging in physical labour, prayer and meditation, or other religious acts, respected by the circumjacent populations.

Both countries are subject to earthquakes, although Japan more often and far more seriously. Yet the problem is gaining increasing attention in Romania. An article in October 1995 provided a map of seismic zones in Romania, reckoning from A (highest intensity) to F (lowest). The zone of highest intensity is a narrow strip to the north of Bucharest, extending from near Ploesti north-eastwards, that is at the bend of the Carpathians. Bucharest itself is in zone C, as are certain small areas near the border with former Yugoslavia. The whole north-west of Romania and most of the centre, also the Dobrudja, are zones of relatively low intensity. Still, it is thought that 25 000 buildings in course of construction could be at risk. Between 1 January and 30 September of 1995, various measures were taken: building work was stopped in 645 cases, rebuilding done in 2384 cases and consolidation in 342. Fines totalling 857 010 lei were imposed. To consolidate and rebuilt 172 schools would cost 250 bn lei at 1994 prices, while 240 bn lei were needed to consolidate 10 500 apartments in category 1 of urgency. In 1995 it was envisaged examining 15 800 apartments which had structural faults. Global experience (Kobe and Tokyo in Japan being prominently mentioned here) was cited to illustrate the costs of earthquakes (Radulescu, 1995b, p. 16 – RN=23868). The author, when preparing to lead a tour party to Romania in 1990, heard about tourists' fear of earthquakes; one individual opined that the tour ought to be cancelled. But it went ahead and the only earthquake damage actually seen – in King Carol's palace at Sinaia – was one cracked mirror (Cf. Radulescu, 1995a, p. 5). It might have been worse. A Romanian scientist, Loan Sandalescu, has claimed to be able to predict earthquakes with a ten-minute error, and up to about seven months in advance. Sandalescu's 'The Energy of Earth Movements' was presented at Lisbon in November 1988 within the framework of a United Nations seminar. A footnote pointedly stated that the newspaper did not guarantee the quality of the ideas presented (Petcu, 1995, p. 5 – RN=23567). One presumes that the Japanese would be interested in these if there is anything in them, but no evidence for or against is available. Nevertheless, the Japanese have recognized the Romanian's problem, as is shown by the fact that their government assigned certain funds for the rehabilitation of Romanian schools affected by earthquakes (see section 4.11.2).

The above paragraphs may already have made headway against any assumption that the two countries have nothing in common, but before continuing, some other general considerations must be made. The author has visited both Japan and Romania within the last three years, which helped to direct his attention towards this pair, as did an apparent partial parallel between Japanese and Romanian policies towards villages.

On the other hand, the Japanese seem eager to emphasize their own differences from other nationalities – even their uniqueness. Thus, comparison with another country may be not welcomed. Or, if there is to be comparison, should this not be with a country that one might respect: with the United States perhaps, or maybe with Britain. But with Romania? If that might seem inappropriate or even insulting, it is appropriate to point out that, here, *situations* are compared more than countries. Secondly: there really are certain similarities between Japan and Romania.

The Romanians, too, tend to think of themselves as exceptional – though some people think of them simply as exceptionally bad (as another commonly heard story illustrates). But this is the language of their detractors. There is much ignorance, too, about both countries, which the British media does not combat sufficiently. Here is one illustration: 'Around the World' in the *Daily Telegraph* gives temperature readings in many cities. Only one city – Tokyo – is listed for Japan, and not even one for Romania, although Bucharest exceeds Prague and Belgrade, both of which *are* listed, in size of population.

Certainly, in offering an unorthodox comparison, one needs what has been felicitously called a 'central organizing hypothesis'. Apart from the general framework of the current book, this is outlined in the subtitle of this section: 'A Comparison of Peripheral Situations'. The concepts of 'centrality' and 'peripherality' have wide application in international affairs – they are at the heart of the current issue in Britain of how far and fast to go in European integration. Especially, though not exclusively, there are examined here features of Japan and Romania which can be ascribed to their being situated on the periphery of adjacent, larger and (in some respects) more powerful countries. It will be supposed that certain modes of behaviour are characteristic of peripheral situations, while opposite or complementary modes are characteristic of central situations. Peripheral behaviour can include special modes of behaviour towards a militarily or culturally stronger central country.

Of course, in its own eyes every country is at the centre of things. This might be formally more justified in, say, China, Russia or the United States, because of their huge size, but is also true in Britain, New Zealand or Albania. When in Moscow it is difficult not to think oneself at the node of global events. An atlas for Albanian schoolchildren places Albania first and foremost. But this does not eradicate typical traits of behaviour.

One may focus on aspects of a country's history or on characteristics which stem primarily from its relations to other countries in relation to which it is peripheral, as will be done here in regard to Japan and Romania. The country or countries in relation to which they are peripheral might differ for a given pair of countries or they might (probably to a more limited extent) be the same.

Japan and Romania both lie on the periphery of the former Soviet Union (currently the Commonwealth of Independent States (CIS); more exactly Russia, and the Ukraine and Moldova, are adjacent to Japan and Romania respectively). The other larger states to which they are on the periphery are not common to both, but in each case there are, or have been, two: in respect of Japan, China and the United States; in respect of Romania – considered historically – Austria-Hungary and Turkey. To focus especially on the neighbour they have had in common, the former Soviet Union: geographically they were at opposite ends of that country: Japan on its east, Romania on its south-west.

A peripheral country may consist of one or more islands. That is Britain's situation in relation to the continent of Europe. Japan comprises numerous islands though only four are large, whereas (except within the Danube delta) Romania possesses only one (tiny) island. In contrast to Japan, Romania is a continental country. However – something that is not visible from small-scale maps – she has mainly *water* frontiers. Japan has 100 per cent water frontiers, while Romania has 66 per cent. One has in mind here, apart from the short Black Sea coastline (7.7 per cent of the total frontier length) the Danube and its tributary the Pruth, which make up 58.3 per cent of the total. The Danube – some 600 metres wide on average, relatively fast-flowing, deep, not lacking lethal obstacles such as passing vessels and the Iron Gates dam, and polluted – has to be reckoned impassable to any except the strongest, most daring and most committed swimmer; during the Ceausescu period its northern bank was also patrolled by armed guards (as the writer has seen through binoculars) who were probably ordered to shoot to kill, and there were no boats. Consequently, most Romanians were confined within the national territory, not only by human obstacles (wire, guards) but to some extent by natural ones. So that, although not from a physical geographical viewpoint an island, from a human geographical angle Romania came near to having some of the physical characteristics of one. As regards the 34 per cent of land frontiers, with the partial exception of former Yugoslavia, Romanians were not welcome in the adjoining countries.

Most non-Romanians do not think of that country as having mainly water frontiers; but that may be their mistake. It is almost necessary to visit the country to become aware of the fact; however, two centuries ago Edward Gibbon, when writing of Dacia in Roman times, pointed out that its natural boundaries were 'the Dniester, the Theiss or Tibiscus, the Lower Danube, and the Euxine Sea '(1980 [1776–8], p. 32). While this places present-day Romania too far to the east – the Pruth must now be substituted for the Dniester – the other water barriers (Theiss or Tibiscus being the modern Tisza, and the Euxine Sea being the Black Sea) approximately hold good. The Tisza remains a significant boundary is proximity to its confluence with the Danube, while the Danube now has more abundant traffic and hydro-electric works.

As if to emphasize its quasi-maritime situation, Romania built a navy, including even frigates, during the Ceausescu period. This was not of the dimensions of the Imperial Japanese Navy or of the present-day Self-Defence Forces, but large enough to be burdensome to the national budget. (Per man, a navy is far dearer than an army.) It presented a puzzle to Western analysts as to what this navy was to be used for; one theory – not disproved by events – was that it was to enable the Ceausescus to escape in the case of a national uprising.

A peripheral country, if sundered from the continental mass, may very possibly not possess adequate raw material or fuel resources. In any event it is likely to be concerned to obtain sufficient supplies. This was a major determinant of Japanese national policy in 1941 and it remains an important one. Romania, much smaller and weaker but relatively better endowed with natural resources, has never gone to war to obtain raw materials, but has shown concern for obtaining materials from abroad and for conserving her own stocks. Although Romania has deposits of iron ore, the iron and steel combine at Galati processed entirely ore imported from the former USSR. Romania is 26 per cent forested, has one of the finest sylvan landscapes in Europe, yet her forests were ordered to be conserved by President Ceausescu until the year 2010; consequently her furniture industry had to consume imported timber. Growing reliance on imported materials and fuel has become an increasingly important influence on Romanian policy.

A peripheral country, if (as is probable) it is less populous than the continental mass, may need to make up for that by other qualities: militarism, a higher degree of centralism, more intense mobilization, unusual or quasi-magical means. The two countries under comparison both exhibit certain of these characteristics, even if in unequal degrees.

Centralism was exhibited very early in Japanese history. During lengthy periods, when Japan was not at risk from foreign attack, this weakened, or, if it was revived, it was for aggressive rather than defensive purposes.

Romanians look back 2000 years to the days of Burebista, who ruled over a territory not much smaller than that of present-day Romania, but at that remote epoch centralism could not mean what it does today. Yet throughout the intervening millennia the unification of all Romanian lands, on which basis a powerful central authority could be founded, was a guiding objective of Romanian patriots. This is another way of saying that until relatively recently (except for a short while within the year 1600, under Michael the Brave) it was not attained. Coincidentally also in 1600, resulting from the battle of Sekigahara, unification was in effect completed in Japan. Centralism was personified in Romania during the present century by Carol II's royal dictatorship and then by the Ceausescu regime. One expression of centralism is the large size of Bucharest (population about 1.8 million) by comparison with the next largest city (Brasov, under 350 000).

Militarism is exemplified in Japan in the second half of the nineteenth century and the first half of the present one, the Meiji and part of the Showa periods, although not since then, thanks to very different circumstances: the introduction of political democracy and the alliance with the United States.

Great Britain too exhibited militarism, although in an unfamiliar and usually unrecognized form: though having only a small (but professional) army, Britain in recent centuries had until this one by far the largest and most powerful navy. This was also partly recruited by selective conscription (the press-gang, or impressment), which though in abeyance is still legal.

A peripheral situation confers some freedom of action about whether or not to enter continental wars. In both the First and the Second World Wars Great Britain declared war on Germany, not the other way about. Romania and Japan also entered both world wars voluntarily. Both performed useful services to the Allied cause in the Great War but their territorial gains were large in proportion to those services. Japan gained the Caroline, Marshall and some other islands in the Pacific, while Romania gained Transylvania and Bessarabia and retained southern Dobrudja. Both Japan and Romania also entered the Second World War voluntarily, and again on the same side (the opposite one to the First World War), though probably neither was very conscious of the other's actions.

Divine, Devilish, Terroristic or Magical Weapons

A feature which may be regarded as characteristic of peripheral states is a propensity to resort to, or to imagine or report being aided by, unusual, especially horrible, divine or quasi-magical weapons. The Old Testament offers an example in the history of the Israelites: their escape through the parting of the Red Sea which drowned the pursuing Egyptians.

The prime example of supposedly divine intervention in Japanese history is the repulse of the Mongol invasion in 1281 by the 'Divine World' or Kamikaze. If this was not really divine intervention, it did look like it. Moreover, this had been the second such instance. In English history, one thinks in such a connection of the storm that scattered the Spanish invasion fleet in 1588. There are other near-parallels in this sphere, such as that both Japan and Britain placed great reliance on their navies and particularly their battlefleets. Each dreamed of bringing the potential enemy to battle in one decisive encounter, when during the present century Japan would have relied especially on her super-battleships *Musashi* and *Yamato*. 'Yamato' was the kingdom which began the Imperial Japanese state, that is a semi-mythical name. That hope of victory proved to be a pipe-dream. But the comparison needs to be brought back to Japan and Romania.

Romania exudes less of an aura of military prowess than Japan, and among the peoples of south-east Europe the Romanians are probably less warlike than the Serbs. Yet Romanian warriors, at that time called Dacians or Geto-Dacians, under Decebal (Decebalus, *c*.100 AD) fought bravely and for some time not without success against the mighty Roman Empire. Though not favoured by divine intervention or other special boons, the Dacians were buoyed up by belief in their god Zalmoxis, and expected immortality if dying in battle for the Zalmoxian state (Treptow, 1992, p. 15).

On the subject of militarism one other Romanian phenomenon needs to be mentioned, which is the Legion of the Archangel Michael, or as it was more commonly known in Britain, the Iron Guard. During the 1930s the Iron-Guard was the Romanian form of fascism which, however, exhibited two features which distinguished it from other contemporary fascist movements. One was its religious name and atmosphere: it supported, and was supported by, the Orthodox Church to which most Romanians belonged, and still belong. But more significantly in the present context was its cult of death. In her novel *Fortunes of War*, based to some extent on actual experiences, Olivia Manning describes how, when the Iron Guard came to power, funeral processions, attended by numerous priests, were constantly being held. In former centuries Japan could count on the Samurai virtues and mystique and on superior sword blades. Contempt for death was a feature of the Samurai code. Perhaps there is no East European country where the ritual suicide of Yukio Mishima could have taken place, but if there were one this might well have been Romania, by a member of the Iron Guard.

We jump forward fourteen hundred years in Romanian history after Decebal, or five hundred years backward from the Legion of the Archangel Michael, to discover a phenomenon which is devilish rather than divine. This was the technique of terror practised by Vlad the Impaler (Dracula) who ruled Wallachia (the southern plain) between (chiefly) 1456 and 1462. His prisoners were executed in peculiarly horrible ways, the best-known being impalement, which was the fate of captured Turks in particular. The higher-ranking the victim, the longer or thicker was the stake. The impaled person was sure to die, but slowly. In the so-called 'forest of the impaled, some 60 miles north of Dracula's capital Tirgoviste, 'thousands of stakes of various heights held the remaining carcasses of some 20 000 Turkish captives; their bodies were in a state of complete decomposition', and so on. This was in 1462, an unusually hot summer. So appalling was the sight and stench that Mehmet II, who had conquered Constantinople nine years before, the next day gave orders to retreat. 'In his eyes, Dracula's country was not worth the price of victory' (Florescu and McNally, 1989, pp. 147–8).

Japan, too, has a bad reputation in the United Kingdom for harsh treatment of prisoners, but those who complain most vociferously of this have probably never read a history of the Balkans. The horrors or the civil war in the former Yugoslavia are a current illustration. In general, one has to allow for foreigners' – and, in this connection, especially *Western* – ignorance. (For example, few people outside Romania know about the great defensive battle in 1917 at Marasesti which has the same connotation to Romanians as Verdun has to the French.) Dracula also practised a scorched earth policy: he poisoned wells, diverted rivers to create marshes, and so on. His own people were concealed from the invaders in dense forest, where also pits were dug to trap camels, horses, and so on. The castle of Bran, which is often associated with Dracula, can be found by tourists to be a disappointment, but one feature that comes up to expectation is its ornate well-head. This actually contained poisoned water, the true well being hidden inside the structure. One of the counties of Wallachia is named Teleorman, which is not a Romanian world. 'Orman' means 'forest' in Turkish while 'Telef' in Turkish means ruin, loss or death. The complete name apparently refers to the traps and perils awaiting whoever penetrated it.

Magical or allegedly magical weapons are not unknown in other contexts, especially in defence against expected heavy odds. Britons of the author's generation would remember rumours during the Second World War that an invasion of Britain had been attempted by Hitler but had been routed by our setting ablaze the invasion fleet. In fact, no invasion was attempted. An analogous but even more bizarre rumour circulated in Romania, soon after the invasion of Czechoslovakia in 1968 by Soviet forces plus those of several East European states (not including Romania). There was much apprehension at the time among Romanians that Romania would be the next victim, and his public declaration that invasion would be resisted brought Nicolae Ceausescu wide popularity not only within his own country. Actually Romania was not invaded, just as Britain in 1940 was not. But in Romania it was rumoured that Soviet forces *had* invaded the extreme north but were repulsed by the Romanians using secret weapons and with the help also of the British Royal Air Force! This sounds and is ridiculous, but British tourist parties in Romania never encountered any trouble at Customs, and so on, with the authorities, and the author was told quite seriously that this was due to the RAF's help in 1968. Apparently there is a reserve of credulity in Romania which wants to believe in quasi-miraculous help at hand at a time of need. And the same may be true of Denmark, which is peripheral in regard to Germany: Holger Danske – a historical personage but now a stone figure in the basement of Elsinore Castle – would come to the country's aid in time of need. However, the fact that he did not stir in April 1940, when Denmark was invaded by Germany, shook some people's belief!

Romania under Ceausescu, when under threat of invasion, resorted to other unusual expedients, such as the formation of the Patriotic Guard and proclamation of the principle that any order to the national forces to surrender would be illegal. Several major constructions during the Ceausescu period concerned water, and while irrigation or navigation were the chief motives, a subsidiary motive was possibly to create water barriers in order to check an invading (Soviet) army.

Towards the end of the Second World War, the Japanese leaders were apparently willing to put their faith in extraordinary events or achievements, such as the Kamikaze pilots and the one-way expedition of the *Yamato* super-battleship – without enough fuel to return – which was to have sacrificed herself in assaulting Okinawa.

Japan was defeated in the Second World War by a device (atom bombs) never before employed in history. She promptly surrendered. Romania was confronted by imminent invasion by the Red Army. What on earth can one do when faced by the inexorable advance of an enemy? One might change sides. So at 4 a.m. on 23 August 1944 the Romanians stopped fighting on the side of the Germans and started fighting against them. The *volte-face* was masterminded by King Michael, with the collaboration of the main parties including the Communists. It achieved complete surprise and had the result that the German front in Romania collapsed, and the Red Army, now assisted by the Romanian army, was able to advance swiftly across into Hungary. This shortened the war by a significant span. Thus both countries extricated themselves.

Loss of Territory

Another major influence of a central power upon those on its periphery is territorial. This has been a major influence of the former USSR or its successor state upon both countries. The former Soviet Union (FSU) absorbed, encroached upon or irrupted into the territories of all European states adjacent to it, from Finland to Romania. Along the southern frontier, too, this happened in the form of a lengthy incursion from 1979 onwards into Afghanistan, and in the Far East encroachment applied to Japan. Thus, loss of territory to the former USSR is a common factor in that country's relations to Japan and to all of the East European states, including Romania.

Yet neither for Romania nor for Japan did this happen as a direct result of military operations by the FSU. Bessarabia, which the Soviet Union took back in 1940, had been Romanian between 1918 and 1940. In a secret annex to the Nazi–Soviet non-aggression pact of 23 August 1939 the Soviet side stated its interest in Bessarabia, while Germany denied any political interests in that area. This left the way open for Soviet annexation (Romanian resistance could be discounted, the British 'guarantee' could not be operative and other states were uninterested) at any convenient moment, which proved to be 28 June 1940. There was no resistance. A year later Romania entered the war on Germany's side, but when the tide eventually turned and the Red Army reoccupied Bessarabia in 1944, this amounted merely to recovering what had been decided by the Nazi-Soviet pact. As regards Japan, the former Soviet Union entered the war almost as its very end, after the first atomic bomb had been dropped and only the day before the second would be, which means that, for its annexation of southern Sakhalin and four Kurile Islands, the USSR was mainly indebted to other powers' warlike exertions.

Again, neither Romania nor Japan has so far succeeded in taking back any lost territory. As regards Romania there has taken place a proclamation of independence by Moldova, in place of the former Soviet Republic of Moldavia. Moldova conceivably may eventually join Romania, but this is not on the current agenda. Romania in 1991 signed a treaty of friendship with Moscow which made no mention of the Moldovans, a treaty which excited some criticism elsewhere in Eastern Europe. Japan has so far had no success in inducing either the USSR, or its principal successor state, the Russian Federation, to relinquish the 'northern territories'.

Romania was not the target of any atomic bomb, but Romania under Ceausescu was the only East European country where anti-nuclear demonstrations (officially orchestrated, no doubt) could be held under the communist regime, and also was the only one where atomic-bomb proof shelters were built, as part of the House of the Republic construction at the western end of the Boulevard of the Victory of Socialism in the rebuilt heart of Bucharest. Ceausescu evidently did not believe that the former USSR would protect Romania, and probably he saw the former USSR as the most likely attacker. Japan, which *had* been a victim, built neither a deterrent nor bomb shelters, and this difference was symptomatic of a major divergence in the two countries' policies following the Second World War: Japan continued to act as an ally of the United States and under her military protection, whereas Romania under Ceausescu started to act more as an independent power. Japan started to behave like a peripheral power and went on doing so, whereas in some directions (though unrealistically) Romania stopped behaving like one. To put it another way: Japan was still capable of behaving like a central power (although now supported by economic rather than military power) but did not; Romania was not capable of behaving like a central power but tried to do so. This was shown in both the domestic and the foreign policies of the Ceausescu regime, such as in its extravagant policies – though only partially carried out – of building and demolition in Bucharest and in villages, and its quasi-independent foreign policies, e.g. in regard to Israel or the 1984 Olympic Games, which in the West attracted both praise and blame: praise at first and blame later. Romania tried to exert a political role which was not buttressed by adequate economic or military strength, whereas Japan declined to exert a political role which would have been supported by economic strength. Each could have learned from the other.

Cultural and Economic Issues

The Japanese and Romanian languages are unrelated. Japanese is an Altaic language. Romanian predominantly a Romance language – one of the versions of Latin today – although with admixtures from many other tongues. The accepted proportion is 70 per cent Romance; the remaining 30 per cent comes from various sources, Japanese not being one of them. However, two languages – like two people – can have features in common even if they are unrelated. In this case they have. Romanian uses the Latin alphabet with certain modifications: except in foreign words there is no k, w or x but four letters – a, i, s and t – may be either accented or unaccented. The details are not relevant here. Romanian is spelled phonetically and its sounds are perfectly matched to the existing alphabet. However, up to 1862 Romanian made use of the Cyrillic alphabet (in use now by Russian, Ukrainian and various other languages). The changeover to the Latin alphabet was made over several years, ending in 1862 in Wallachia and Moldavia which had been joined to become Romania in 1859, but in the former Soviet Moldavia, slightly larger than the current Moldova, has been made only within the last few years. On both occasions the changeover to the Latin alphabet had political resonance, since Romanian thus spelled is much more visibly a Romance language.

The Japanese, too, considered switching to a Latin alphabet, but apart from adopting Romaji (for teaching Japanese more quickly to foreigners) did not make such a switch. Both countries, at any rate, had been dissatisfied with their previous system of writing. Some Japanese remain dissatisfied with their own enormously complex script, though most adults see the disadvantages of changing over to an alphabetical system as exceeding the advantages. The point here is that a peripheral country does not create its own alphabet, and this can engender long-lasting drawbacks.

There are certain minor similarities between the Japanese and Romanian languages. Both prefer 'r' to 'l', Japanese having no 'l', sound, while Romanian tends to alter 'l' to 'r', as in *popor* (people). At first sight there seems to be no equivalent in Romanian to the Japanese *kanji*, and certainly there *is* none to their enormous number and complexity. Yet one very embryonic and now outdated equivalent is the pictorial symbolism of the Orthodox Church (see later paragraph). A peripheral situation promotes importation of symbols, for instance new road signs are adopted in Britain from Continental practice.

One other similarity is the presence in each language of 'respect language', though in Japanese this is integral, but in Romanian marginal. While in English 'thou' has fallen out of use, leaving 'you' for virtually all purposes, most Continental languages retain both, but Romanian has three versions: one normal, one intimate and one ceremonial, *Dumneavoastra*. The ceremonial one has always to be used in meeting somebody for the first time. *Fortunes of War* points out that even a waiter had to be addressed as 'lord'. This similarity is surely connected with the fact that in both Japan and Romania the history of both countries is in substantial part the history of great families – in Japan Taira, Minamoto, Tokugawa…in Romania Cantacuzino, Mavrocordat, Brancoveanu, Bratianu – although in Japan these held real power, whereas in Romania that was subject to Turkish suzereignty. Similarly, in the Russia of the last century, one used forms of address such as 'your honour' (*vashe blagorodiye*), and so on, which fell into disuse during the Soviet period. And this is still the case in Spanish (*usted*). One might speculate, too, that the longer great families are in power and the greater their power, the more 'respect language' becomes ingrained. Unlike Greece, Albania, Serbia or Bulgaria, Romania was never divided into *pashaliks* during the period of Ottoman domination: the native provinces remained and over a considerable period Romania was ruled indirectly, via rulers of its own nationality, rather than by Turkish pashas. This in turn was directly related to the fact that Romania was on the periphery of the Ottoman Empire, being the farthest subjugated country, within Europe, from Istanbul.

In Romania, another sort of imported symbolism was the Byzantine system of dating, according to which the world was created in the year 5508 or 5509 BC reckoned by our system. Up to about 1790 AD this system was used in Romanian inscriptions with special symbols for individual thousand, hundred, ten and one digits (after which one would deduct 5508 or 5509 to arrive at the AD year). A peripheral country imports such symbols from another centre, in the Romanian case from Constantinople. Analogously, in Japan *Western* notation is always used to represent years, so Europeans learning Japanese do not have to learn a new system. Thus the Japanese practice is simpler than the one previously in use in Romania and is currently in general use, although dating based on the emperors' reigns survives also.

Japan is perhaps moving towards adopting a central position in symbolism, as may be seen by the emergence of Japanese symbols into Western cities or shopping centres (such as 'Galleria', Hatfield, England). Knowledge of the most frequently used *kanji* will presumably become an ornament to humanistic education in the West.

In large part there is no resemblance between the Japanese and Romanian economies. The discussion here assumes that the serious problems currently exhibited in the Japanese economy will be overcome (this is written in December 1997). On the whole the Japanese economy has been efficient, productive and highly automated, the Romanian economy none of these. Japan's enormous strength in microelectronics has no parallel in Romania. Yet in some directions the Japanese economy has not been particularly efficient (see Woronoff, 1990).

In both countries very attractive handicrafts can be bought, or if their quality level is higher in Japan the price, too, is much higher. Although each country has its own specialities, which in Japan would include things made from paper, and in Romania icons painted on glass, in both countries textiles and articles made from wood are especially sought after. The latter are both small and large, even including the world's largest all-wooden building, at Nara in Japan, which the author had the opportunity of visiting, as well as the world's oldest one. There is, therefore, no wooden building of such a size in Romania, though Maramures region has a church with a very tall all-wooden spire. Also characteristic of that region, especially of Romania, are elaborately carved wooden gates, and gables, spires or domes built upon ordinary cottages. These were being erected in Romania even during the period when the Western press was reporting only demolition of villages. One finds in each country a rare phenomenon – wooden fences topped by their own roofs. Identical fences of this type can be seen in the Village Museum in Bucharest and encircling Sento Gosho Palace in Kyoto. While on the subject of villages, it is too tempting not to notice that the Romanian world for village is *sat*, while one of the Japanese words for village is *sato*.

But is building and carving in wood a peripheral feature? One precondition is adequate supplies of timber, which usually requires that the population density is not high; people cut down trees. In Romania the county with the highest proportion of its area forested is Suceava, along the northern border with the former USSR, and remote from Bucharest. Whether a high proportion of forest land is characteristic of a peripheral country is less clear. Romania, relatively highly forested, is adjacent to the mainly treeless Ukraine. Japan is less forested than Siberia, which, however, may make Siberia peripheral to Japan, rather than the other way about, which indeed is probably true (as already illustrated in Chapter 2). The result is that both Japanese and Romanians are specially skilled in woodworking. Among literary materials which are illustrative of this as regards Romania may be noted *Monumente be Arhitectura in Lemn din Tinutui Sucevei* (Architectural Monuments in Wood of the Suceava Region), which includes numerous diagrams, drawings and photographs.

As regards borrowing (or not) of living habits from the former Soviet Union: Soviet-style architecture was run up in Romania as well, but concrete blocks of flats in Romania tended to be a shade more decorated, whether in towns or new rural settlements. Regarding vernacular architecture there seems to have been no borrowing. Right up to the frontier between Romania and the former USSR (now that of Ukraine) one sees no influences of the Ukraine upon Romania. Romanian styles of cottage building are quite unlike the Russian peasant cottage or *izba*. In either country one can judge one's location correctly solely by looking at the cottage exteriors (and in Romania, as a rule, whether cottages were built by Romanians, Hungarians or Saxons). Musical instruments, too, are different (for example, pan-pipes rather than balalaika). Styles of folk dancing are certainly different, and festive clothes markedly so. Japanese popular culture also has not apparently adopted any Russian customs. Both countries drink tea but only one has evolved the tea ceremony! Evidently neither Romanians nor Japanese are attracted by Russian models, which contrasts with the obvious Romanian adoption of models derived from other influences, chiefly 'Oriental', as they call it (actually Turkish) influences in architecture, clothing (up to the last century), coffee-drinking, food, and so on. In previous centuries the Japanese have adopted models showing Chinese, or perhaps South Sea, influences (in styles of houses), and more recently Western (especially American) influences. If in these spheres Japan or Romania are peripheral, it is in relation to some non-Russian civilisation (or civilisations).

Summing-up

To sum up. There are resemblances between Japan and Romania in symbolism, human isolation, concern with supply of raw materials, destruction of invaders, manner of entrance into and exit from world wars, loss of territory, and in certain cultural aspects. Several of these can be subsumed under peripherality of behaviour *vis-à-vis* an adjacent continent or continental power, but whereas recently Japan has kept up a peripheral mode of behaviour though having some of the attributes of a central power, Romania in the later stages of the Ceausescu period behaved contrarily. This contrast (and others) has been reflected in the two countries' very different fortunes in economic life as well as in international relations.

The above may be (it is hoped) of general interest or perhaps of interest chiefly from international relations or cultural angles. Has it relevance to Japan's economic involvement in Romania? It is at any rate arguable that Japan's involvement in Romania has been greater than might have been expected. That involvement is now examined.

4.11.2   Relations

Reasons why the Japanese would be expected to prefer Hungary to
Romania, as regards economic involvement, have already been
mentioned. Yet Romania is second in amount of Japanese involvement within Eastern Europe, thus leading Poland. Romania has big
resources, potentially a big market, and under Ceausescu had a diversified economy. For example, it produced cars and all-terrain (Land
Rover type) vehicles, aircraft (under British Aircraft Corporation
licence) and at another extreme musical instruments, including even
grand pianos.

Although the Japanese may have been on the whole slow in discover-
ing Romania's economic potential, this is also true of other foreign
states. Moreover, one exception has been 'Rulement' ball-bearings
firm in Alexandria. 'Rulement' ('rulement' means 'bearing' in Romanian) received from the Japanese government foreign exchange valued
at US$12.5 mn. The credit would be reimbursed with 2.5 per cent inter-
est as the bearings were sold. Other known details included that Rulement had started work in three shifts – this at a time when in the whole
country 25 000 engineers were out of work. Achieving growth in 1995,
relative to the year before, of 9.4 per cent, Rulement had been unaf-
fected by the vicissitudes of transition because it retailed abroad (in 42
countries). Quality of production and labour productivity assured good
earnings. Net profit in 1994 was 3.8 bn lei, and in the first half of 1995 it
was 3.6 bn. Investments in 1995 (as reported on 18 September 1995)
had been 1.9 bn lei, imports of tools $4 mn and of primary materials
$2.9 mn. Monthly sales abroad were 2.5 mn ball-bearings, on the inter-
nal market 350 000, but these latter were being paid for with difficulty.
The value of modern utilized equipment exceeded 5 mn DM. Within
what is, all-told, an agricultural town (Alexandria is on the Wallachian
plain, south-west of Bucharest) work in this enterprise was going on
according to Western parameters, stimulated by the market economy.
Rulement was described as a 'rare flower' in the Romanian economy
(Marcovici, 1995, p. 4 – RN=23867). It contrasts with a completed but
idle factory west of Suceava, viewed from outside by tourists including
the author in 1987 and 1988, which had been negligently created without a source of power!

The month of May 1996 was a climactic time for Japanese economic
involvement in Romania. As reported on 9 May, an agreement was completed for Romania to borrow US$495 million on the Japanese capital
market (Anon., 1996e, p. 1). Commenting on this on 17 May, Vasilescu

described the Japanese loan as the biggest emission of shares in the history of Romania. In the capital market, it had never happened that a flow of 52 billion yen (half a billion dollars) should be aimed at Romania. This was in conditions considered to be most unusual. The annual interest rate was 5.2 per cent: 'not very small, but not much'. There were two types of public obligations, of 100 000 yen and 1 000 000 yen. In the subscription, managed by Nomura, great Japanese corporations and banks had taken part, besides numerous small investors. 'We in our turn are awaiting the money. It is a real oxygen cylinder for us.' (This is a common expression in Romanian for something that is very helpful.) (Vasilescu, 1996, p. 4.) The Ninth Session of the Mixed Romano-Japanese Economic Committee was held in Bucharest (Anon., 1986, p. 1 – RN = 12511). Later that same month, in relations with Romania, the Japanese authorities had decided to pass from co-operation involving assistance and expertise to a more direct form of collaboration, the Romanian Minister for External Affairs, Teodor Melescanu, learned in Tokyo. The Japanese government had decided to contribute $50 mn by way of a loan accorded to Romania. Two other concrete projects to be launched soon envisaging Japanese participation were a plan for modernizing the national energy system (Renel as the beneficiary) in the value of $45 mn, and a credit towards modernizing the container port of Constantza. The Romanian diplomatic chief also remarked the interest shown by the Japanese in re-equipping the steel combine Sidex at Galati (Anon., 1996d, p. 24 – RN = 24622). The amount of the Japanese government credit for modernizing the container port of Constantza has since been defined as $175 mn, the yearly throughput to reach one million containers (Morinos, 1997, p. 1).

A further subscription to Samurai bonds was made known, the document being signed on 20 September 1996. This was put out on the Japanese capital market for the National Bank of Romania (BNR). The chief manager, Nomura Securities, confirmed that the issue was in excess demand. In consequence, growth was being sought of the allocated portion. The banking syndicate through which the placement has been effected was made up of the following financial companies: Nomura Securities, Daiwa, Nikko, Yamaichi, Kokusai, Merrill Lynch, Kankaku, LTCBS, New Japan. Purchase of bonds would be made between 25 September and 8 October. Money would be transferred to the BNR on 9 October. This emission of 30 bn yen would earn interest of 5.05 per cent (5.2 per cent in May), with maturity in five years' time (on 9 October 2001), whereas the previous emission had a three years' maturity. The 5.05 per cent rate of interest was favourable also because it was fixed, and would not fluctuate according to conditions of the Japanese capital market. Interest would be paid at six-monthly intervals, on 9 April and 9 October (Nicolescu, 1996, p. 4).

Not everything went smoothly, however. An important delegation of Japanese businessmen learned about Romania on 8 – 9 October 1996. Their journey, organized by the Chamber of Commerce and Industry of Osaka, had as its main objective to visit TIB '96 (evidently a trade fair). The programme included an appointment with George Cojocaru, President of the Chamber of Commerce and Industry of Romania. The meeting was hardly a success. Both Cojocaru's proposals to the Japanese – to set up a trade representation with permanent status at Bucharest and Osaka with the aim of tracking down opportunities for business deals, and for organizing fairs under the title 'Economic Days' at Bucharest and Osaka and the reciprocal allocation of free space of these occasions – were refused. The motives were that the Japanese were at present in receipt of numerous applications from Asian countries and had difficulty in satisfying them. Also, the Japanese said, TIB was too general: that system had not been in use in Japan for more than a decade. Any fair now was specialized. This article was headed 'Japanese from Osaka are not charmed' (Ceausescu, 1996, p. 4 – RN=25355). ('Economic Days' was a common appellation of foreign economic exhibitions in the former Soviet Union.)

In Victoria Palace (Bucharest) on 14 January 1997 an accord was signed of non-reimbursable assistance by the Fund for Political Development and Humanitarian Resources of the Government of Japan, administered by the IBRD (International Bank for Research and Development). The documents referred to projects which would be beneficiaries of financing from the World Bank: a project following a loan, that for rehabilitation of schools affected by earthquakes, and the project for stocking and commercial trading of cereals. Japanese aid for the first project, which envisaged support for recently privatized companies, amounted to $686 100; for the second to $131 000; for the third to $647 710, this last for making studies of variants of development of port infrastructure, for elaborating a programme of improvement of commercial practices, and for starting to privatize units with state capital which specialized in cereals stocking (A.St., 1997, p. 8 – RN=25353).

A renewed drive to extend relations appeared to be signalled by an official visit to Romania in June 1997 of Masahiko Komura, Secretary of State at the Japanese Ministry of Foreign Affairs, at the invitation of the Romanian Minister of Foreign Affairs (MAE), Adrian Severin. A press conference at MAE described the visit as representing an important moment in the evolution of bilateral relations, which would give a new impulse to political, economic and cultural-scientific collaboration (Terenche, 1997, p. 4 – RN not yet known).

Representatives of 65 Japanese firms were to visit Romania at the start of December 1997 with the aim of identifying potential suppliers of spare parts for Japanese industry, especially for the electronics and electrotechnical branches and for finishing apparatus. The report claimed that this was first large-scale Japanese delegation to visit Romania since 1989 with such a definite intention. 'In the conditions of integration of Hong Kong under Chinese jurisdiction and the instability which has begun to manifest itself in the sub-Asian markets (Malaysia, Thailand etc.) Japanese firms are looking at other possible partners in Central and Eastern Europe', according to Toru Suehiro, the Bucharest director of JETRO. 'The visit this year to Japan of a delegation from Romania led by President Emil Constantinescu could not come at a more favourable moment'. Romania should profit from this favourable conjuncture by providing as many samples and documents as possible (Radulescu, 1997, p. 9 – RN not yet known). Thus the new economic situation in South-East Asia might react favourably upon Romanian–Japanese economic relations.

It is interesting that the first reaction of the Japanese firms to the new situation was to envisage Romanian firms as spare parts suppliers; this had also been the bias of Albanian manufacturing industry in the later stages of the communist era there.

As regards the effects of restructuring of the Japanese economy, these are not yet clear and it is too early to foresee their consequences which, however, might include stimulation of Japanese investments in Europe.

Japanese Marketing in Romania

Japanese corporations have pursued their interests to some extent independently of the official negotiations. Matsushita has been in the lead. On 27 May 1991 at 10.30 a.m. six pairs of scissors cut the inauguration ribbon of the exhibition and shop of Panasonic-Technics, situated at 12 Stefan cel Mare (Stephen the Great) Street in Bucharest. The shop belonged to the mixed capital company Electronica International (Romania and Japan), SRL. It was the result of collaboration between Societatea Comerciala Electronics SA and Matsushita Electric International. Its directors – one Japanese and one Romanian – stated that apart from the Bucharest shop there were subsidiaries in Sinaia, Constantza, Pitesti, Eforie Sud and Miercuria Ciuc, and soon would be in other towns of Romania. (The named cities are all of medium size, except Constantza which is Romania's chief port and third largest city, and Sinaia which is below medium size but a prime tourist resort). 'Electronics International' would promote and sell in Romania large consumption electronic goods such as colour TV sets, video cameras, video recorders, various audio equipment, household goods, and other highly modern apparatus manufactured by Matsushita. According to Matsushita's Director for Europe and Africa, the Bucharest shop was the first step. Currently it was important to establish a distribution network in Romania; conclusions from the experience would led to co-operation with Romanian manufactures (Papadiuc, 1991, p. 5 – RN = 18766). That sounded promising, but no follow-up report has been seen.

It is announced that as from 8 September 1997 Honda and Susuki will take part in the Giurgiu Free Economic Zone (Anon., 1997c – RN not yet known).

Attitudes

Romanian business observers react sensitively to foreign evaluations of Romania; thus, signs of approval attract attention. One illustration was the rating of BB+ accorded to the BNR (National Bank of Romania) by the Japanese Samurai agency. The correspondent of *Romania libera* commented that although according to the IMF the Romanian economy had reached a critical point, the BNR evidently kept credibility on the external front. (Lazar, 1996, p. 20 – RN = 25067). Commenting on an assignment to Romania of the same rating, BB+, by the 'Japan Credit Rating Agency', Vasilescu wrote that although not AAA, AA or even BBB, this was much better than B, CCC or CC. The rating meant that the Japanese could believe in us: if loans were made, the Romanians had the capacity to reimburse and would not be bad payers (1996, p. 4). As reported in September 1996, Japan Credit Rating had reactivated the rating BB+ accorded to the BNR in the spring of 1996, though other ratings of which Japanese investors had taken account were BB (Standard & Poors) and BAZ (Moody's – this refers to Moody's Investors Service in the USA (*Heti vilaggazdasag*, 27 September 1990) – (Nicolescu, 1996, p. 4).

FIMAN and CIMP (managerial associations: FIMAN stands for Fundatia Internationala pentru Management din Bucuresti: that is, International Foundation for Management of Bucharest) organized a two-day seminar on 'How to do Business with Japan' on the occasion of the presence in Romania of Yoshimichi Miki and Junichi Hyakuya, respectively Executive Director and Director of the Daiwa Institute of Research in London. Two subjects, described as important, were approached: the Japanese economy and its characteristics, and how to effect direct foreign investment. Topics included: the Japanese style of management and strategies adopted by Japanese car manufacturers. Romanian managers were shown how to make contacts (or contracts) with Japanese firms, including mention of the risks involved.

The Japanese also learned something. Two days were evidently not enough but they were able to see that the image of Romania was much worse than the reality. For example, the two guests had the impression that Romania had an energetic nuclear policy, which is not the case considering the introduction of the CANDU system at Cernavoda – work which was quite unknown to the Japanese. Daiwa's report 'Romania – Renaissance of an Economy', published In January 1996, is on balance favourable to Romania, but this – the Romanian reporter noted – was not enough. For potential investors, and especially for Japanese, the problem consisted in whether there was social stability, a good infrastructure, and a good legislative system from the viewpoint of economic performance. The two guests could affirm that Romanians were 'very kind, rational, capable and pleasant interlocutors', but not more than that. Daiwa was attempting to seek to create a fund, gathering money from businessmen for investing in Romanian firms. At present they were in a 'minus situation', which was regrettable given that Daiwa had a long tradition of introducing new concepts into the internal capital market, and might become a good friend of the Romanians (Radulescu, 1996, p. 4). This sounds fine, though Daiwa and other leading securities firms have subsequently acquired reputations for dishonesty in Japan itself: Daiwa's headquarters were raided by public prosecutors (Pitman, 1997, p. 54).

Outstanding Japanese achievements in science and technology are publicized: for example, Romanians were informed that Tsukuba (the Japanese science city) had announced the world's most powerful computer, the CP-PACS (*Romania libera*, 23 May 1996, p. 8). While interested Romanians are informed about Japan's technical and economic advances, at the popular level and even in business advertisements it is Japan's exoticism that largely impinges. For instance, Minolta's copiers EP 1050 and EP 70 are advertised as 'MORIKO and MITSUKO – your office geishas' (*Romania libera*, 19 February 1996, p. 21). Altogether, mentions of Japan in the Romanian press may be termed reasonably numerous (cf. *Romania libera*, 28 April 1995, pp. 8, 9, etc.).

4.12   JAPAN AND SERBIA / MONTENEGRO

4.12.1   Comparisons and Relations

Serbia and Montenegro are examined together here as they now call themselves the Federal Republic of Yugoslavia (FRY), though that term is not used in this book to avoid confusion with the former Yugoslavia. The language of Montenegrins, other than ethnic minorities, is Serbian.

Serbia has an area of 87 314 sq km (23.5 per cent of Japan's) and a population of 9 721 177 (March 1991), 7.8 per cent of Japan's, making Japan's density of population three times that of Serbia. The area of Montenegro is 13 818 sq km and its population 616 327 (1991) giving a density of population of 44.6 per sq km and making Japan's density of population 7.5 times that of Montenegro. Serbia is mainly mountainous except in the north (the Vojvodina), while Montenegro is ruggedly mountainous. Serbia has a strategic stance along and across the Danube, and has some industry, mineral deposits and substantial agriculture, while Montenegro is almost entirely pastoral. Before the Yugoslav war, tourism in Montenegro was developing (the picturesque diminutive former capital of independent Montenegro, Cetinje, being more of a magnet than Titograd), but since then has virtually disappeared. The economies of both countries suffered severely from that war and from UN sanctions.

The Japanese as a nation have little collective knowledge of the Balkans and no personal acquaintance with Serbia/Montenegro, and therefore no experience of the wartime atrocities; they may find Serb strength and firmness attractive. However, while the situation may change following the lifting of UN sanctions, so far there has been no report of any Japanese economic involvement in Serbia/Montenegro.

4.13   JAPAN AND SLOVAKIA

4.13.1   Comparisons

Comparisons of Japan and Czechoslovakia in several cases apply to Japan and Slovakia, but Slovakia has a lower density of population than the Czech Republic (107 per sq km, deriving from population 5.27 million, area 49 035 sq km) which makes it more unlike Japan.

4.13.2   Relations

As reported in January 1995 the Japanese Eximbank, under agreement with the Slovak National Bank, was to open a credit of 4.219 bn yen (US$42 mn) for assistance to and development of the private sector in Slovakia. Small enterprises up to 150 employees and middle-sized ones of up to 600 employees were eligible. Accepted projects had to be on the territory of Slovakia and the credit could not exceed 69 per cent of the project costs. Eligible were new projects for modernization, renovation or reconstruction which increased the productivity or effectiveness of such enterprises, or strengthened their working capital. The CSOB (Ces-koslovenska Obchodni Banka) was one of the six commercial banks authorized by the Slovak National Bank, and agreed upon by the (Japanese) Eximbank, to act as intermediaries for the credit purposes to be granted to the final users. The Eximbank's funds might be drawn on in Slovak currency, on the basis of an application, in the case of projects of type B until 6 August 1996, or for projects of type A until 5 February 1997. Projects of type A, following assessment of the project by the Slovak National Bank, might obtain a credit of up to 65 mn yen (approximately 20 mn Slovak crowns, or US$650 000); those of type B would have to be approved by the Eximbank and subsequently would be financed by even higher amounts of credit. The interest rate charged was fixed in the agreement of the SNB and the Eximbank, depending on the current discount rate, which at that time was around 16.75 per cent. The applicant had to comply with the standard conditions of the credit process of the CSOB (Anon., 1995e, p. 5 – RN = 23357).

The Japanese are interested in privatization (both in principle and in order to profit from it) and in one case its postponement was said to threaten the entry of Japanese capital. The (Japanese) Yazaki concern had made it a condition for its entry into Tesla Prievidza state enterprise that this would be constituted as a limited liability company by the privatization process; so far this had not happened. Yazaki was intending to start production of cables for automobiles as from January 1994 (Anon., 1993d, p. 4 – RN = 21879).

4.14   JAPAN AND SLOVENIA

4.14.1   Comparisons

Slovenia, the northernmost republic of former Yugoslavia, became independent in 1991 following a short successful struggle against the

Yugoslav National Army and with the aid of EU diplomatic intervention, and has been at peace since then. Slovenia's area is 20 256 sq km (5.4 per cent of Japan's), its population 2 020 000 (1.6 per cent) so the country is small on both counts. Both Japan and Slovenia are mountainous, sunny and well-watered and have only very small minorities (Slovenia's being Hungarians, at 0.5 per cent and Italians at 0.1 per cent). Industry provides 55 per cent of Slovenia's GDP, tourism 2.5 per cent (Natek *et al.* 1992, pp. 38, 122) (with regard to tourism, see also below). Slovenia, which claims a unique location at the crossroads of Roman, Germanic and Slavonic cultures (Herman, 1993, p. 18 – RN = 21314) has nothing in common with Japan in history, culture or religion. One may, however, find in both economies attractive consumer goods (see below).

4.14.2   Relations

Since the internal war broke out in former Yugoslavia, only Slovenia – unitary and much more advanced economically than any other part of former Yugoslavia, mainly speaking a single locally known language (Slovene, a Slav language but not mutually comprehensible with Russian) but able to manage with a more widely known one (German) – would be expected to have significant economic relations with Japan. Slovenia has even been reckoned to have the best prospects among all the East European economies now in transition to promote co-operation with Japan.

However, as described in June 1993, trade between Slovenia and Japan had so far been unbalanced, being characterized by the greater share of Japanese products in the Slovene market than vice versa. In Slovenia's car imports Japan's share was about 27 per cent (Japan had, by the way, the same proportion of car sales in Latvia), in computers and related equipment 19 per cent. Slovenia also imported from Japan electrical machinery and appliances, chemical products and some other items. Its exports to Japan consisted mostly of sports accessories (including probably a special design of skis, manufactured at Begunje, near Bled) and equipment, jewellery, pharmaceuticals, wine, and so on. At the meeting of a joint committee, Japanese representatives showed especially great interest in promoting co-operation in tourism (Slovenia had a splendid tourist industry, at the time largely idle due to the continuing Yugoslav war which no longer impinged on Slovenia, but many potential tourists feared that it did, and easily accessible to international magnets such as Venice.) The Japanese also showed special interest in joint actions in third markets, and generally in a greater presence of Slovene firms in Japan. Slovenia had a sound monetary system, convertible national currency, controlled inflation, and relatively big hard currency reserves, as well as an open market economy. GNP per capita was around $6000 (this was, however, well below the pre-Yugoslav-war level – Gerdina and Baskar (eds), 1993, p. 44) and the labour force well qualified thanks to a very good educational system. Besides, Slovenia was a member of the World Bank and the IMF which reduced the risks of investing into the country. Japan was trying to stimulate exports from Slovenia to reduce its existing trade deficit with Japan. On the Slovene side there was great interest in all forms of co-operation with Japan, especially in technology and technical and scientific co-operation (Herman, 1993, p. 18 – RN=21314). All this sounded promising, but no follow-up reports have been seen. For what it is worth, the author saw no signs of Japanese economic involvement while holidaying in Slovenia in 1993, 1994 and 1996.

4.15 JAPAN AND FORMER YUGOSLAVIA

4.15.1 Comparisons

Japan and former Yugoslavia differed not so greatly in area (Japan 372 000 sq km, Yugoslavia 255 800) but much more in population (Japan 120 million, Yugoslavia 23 million – 1984 data), making Japan's density of population 3.6 times greater. In almost all other respects the two countries were extremely different. Japan was ancient, with a unified history: the Yugoslav state modern (1918 onwards), the earlier history of the territory and of its inhabitants being fragmented. Japan had a single language with three alphabets, former Yugoslavia several languages also with three alphabets. Both countries had two religions, but while Shinto and Buddhism were friendly to one another, Christianity and Islam were antagonistic. Former Yugoslavia also had two mutually opposed divisions even of Christianity: Roman Catholicism and Orthodox Christianity. Economically, or as regards technology, Japan was highly advanced, former Yugoslavia on the whole backward, but the degree of advancement and the standard of living declined sharply from north to south. The types of economic system were also unlike, though under Tito a distinctive form of more moderate socialism was being evolved. Since 1991 Japan's history has been peaceful and continuing, former Yugoslavia's contentious and bloody, and now to all appearances and probability is terminated.

Former Yugoslavia had no experts on Japan as far as the author knows. Japan's recognized experts on the Balkans are few, and there seems now to be only one recognized expert on Albania (see 'Japan and Albania'). (This lack enabled the present writer to lecture about Albania and the Balkans generally at three universities in Japan in May 1995.) This lack of expertise supplied no basis upon which to appoint Akashi as UN representative in Bosnia, and his judgements there resting apparently on suppositions that the warring parties should be given the benefit of any doubt, and that the outside world should intervene as little as possible and not with military means, appeared shaky at the time and since then have been thoroughly discredited. His replacement was eventually followed by the Dayton Peace Accord although, this being the Balkans, many unsolved problems and enmities remain. This book in any case assumes that the former Yugoslavia will not be reconstituted.

4.15.2   Relations

Even while Yugoslavia remained a unified state, its economic relations with Japan were slight and uneventful. The only available reports relate to the republic of Croatia. In January 1991 it was announced that cars up to 2000cc. might now be imported duty-free by Croatian residents. Ominously, though not surprisingly, small Japanese cars were cheaper than the Yugoslav-made Zastava, though it seems that the main motivation of the Croatian government was to retaliate for the imposition by the Serbian government of a system of obligatory deposits for purchases outside Serbia, which amounted to import duties on Croatian and Slovene goods. The main loser was the federal budget; as the correspondent noted, nobody was caring much about that in those days (Anon., 1991a, p. 6 – RN=18247). Already the diverging constituent parts of former Yugoslavia were hitting one another's economies. More surprisingly, plans to redevelop the old centre of Dubrovnik with Japanese money encountered resistance in the town itself (Anon., 1987a, pp. 6–7 – RN=13920). Perhaps its residents already foresaw that the future would hold destruction for their historic city, making redevelopment at that moment futile? If so, how right they were!

BIBLIOGRAPHICAL NOTE

The only pre-Second World War item relating to both Japan and Hungary that is known to the author is: *Hungaro-Japanese Relations in 1935*

(Budapest: Royal Hungarian University Printing Office, 1935), reprinted from *Far East*, vol. 1, nos 1–3. This is listed in the School of Oriental and African Studies Library (London) but could not be found. It seems likely that political relations were its focus. From 1977 onwards *ABSEES* (later *ABREES*) has published abstracts *inter alia* about Hungarian–Japanese economic and business relationships. Section 4.9 is based largely upon these; thanks are due especially to the late Erwin Soos and to Professor Vladimir Dolezil. Others, including the author, contribute about other countries. *ABREES* in fact supplies material about all the states dealt with in this book, though in uneven detail and not necessarily in every issue. The Economist Intelligence Unit (EIU) quarterly and annual reports also allude to the topic. Iliana Zloch-Christy (ed.), *Privatization and Foreign Investments in Eastern Europe* (Westport, Conn.: Praeger, 1995) contains important articles about Japanese investments in Eastern Europe by Ken Morita ('Japan's Foreign Direct Investment in East European Countries') and Gabor Bakos ('Magyar Suzuki: Case Study of Japanese Investment'). Also useful is Marc Ellingstad, 'The Maquiladora Syndrome: Central European Prospects', *Europe-Asia Studies*, vol. 49, no. 1, 1997. Among Japanese sources, note A. Uegaki, 'Japan's Postwar Economic Reform and Transformation of Socialist System Today' in *The Economic Review of the Seinan Gakuin University*, March 1993.

5 Concluding Remarks

Japan's economic involvement is by far the largest in total and most diverse in Russia, but on a per head or per area basis appears to be much the largest in Hungary. As reported by Morita (see Zloch-Christy, 1995), at the end of 1991 the stock value of Japan's direct investment in East European countries amounted to: Hungary US$221 mn, Romania US$9 mn, Poland US$5 mn, Bulgaria US$1 million. Thus of this total, Hungary had received over 90 per cent (93.6 per cent). In 1990 Hungary had received US$29 mn and in 1991 US$181 mn. This increase came principally from Magyar Suzuki (car production of the Japanese Suzuki Motor Corporation with a Hungarian partner) (Zloch-Christy, 1995, p. 184). This very high proportion devoted to Hungary hardly holds good any more but Hungary remains easily in the lead in Eastern Europe. Germany (the former GDR), Romania and Poland probably figure among the next three Central or East European states. Among the non-Russian successor states of the former USSR, Kazakstan rates highest, with promising possibilities for Uzbekistan and Turkmenistan. In many of the formerly 28 (now 27) countries, both Asian and European, Japan's involvement is negligible or nil. Some notes follow about larger regions and then other remarks, including especially a discussion of the reasons why certain countries or regions are preferred, and which institutions are most active.

5.1   RUSSIA

Japan's economic involvement in Russia has certain distinguishing features by comparison with her involvement in non-Russian successor states of the former Soviet Union or by comparison with her involvement in Eastern Europe.

1. A particular zone of Russia – the Far East – is much more important than its economic strength would lead one to expect, which is apparently for three reasons: Japan's demand for timber which Russia's Far East has in abundance, nearness to Japan, and Japan's promotion of political objectives. Russia goes along with this because it is far more convenient to draw equipment, machinery, and so on, from Japan than to despatch it from European Russia, and because Russia

does not have the capital to develop fully or in the near future these extensive, remote (from Europe) and climatically rigorous regions.

2. Russia is *at present* the only country among those examined in this book that supplies Japan with a raw material – timber – that it really needs.

3. Only Russia offers a direct overland transit route from Japan to the non-Russian successor states of the former Soviet Union or to Eastern Europe.

More exactly, the characteristics of Japan's economic involvement in Russia are the following:

- Russia's provision of timber.
- The entanglement of political with economic relations.
- Certain regions of Russia are importantly affected by the Japanese trading situation.
- The Japanese supply certain items in large quantity – tyres, rails.
- The Japanese build telecommunications.
- The fishing agreement with Russia.
- The advantage to peripheral states of being permitted to send goods across Russia overland or by air.

5.2   NON-RUSSIAN SUCCESSOR STATES OF THE FORMER SOVIET UNION AND EASTERN EUROPE

Viewed in more detail, the characteristics of Japan's economic involvement with the non-Russian successor states of the former USSR and with Eastern Europe are the following:

Only certain states are involved at all: not Tajikistan, Azerbaydzhan, Georgia, Armenia, Moldova, Estonia, Latvia or Lithuania and scarcely Kyrgyzstan, Ukraine or Belarus (despite the last two being of substantial size). In only Kazakstan and Uzbekistan is there significant involvement, yet even the latter appears to be more involved with Germany and the Republic of Korea. Turkmenistan might have some importance in the future, when too Uzbekistan might gain more importance.

The populations of the above are: Tajikistan 4.648 mn, Azerbaydzhan 7.137 mn, Georgia 5.464 mn, Armenia 3.362 mn, Moldova 4.147 mn, Estonia 1.542 mn, Latvia 2.622 mn, Lithuania 3.603 mn, Kyrgyzstan 4.051 mn, Ukraine 50.994 mn, Belarus 10.008 mn, Kazakstan 16.028 mn, Uzbekistan 18.487 mn, Turkmenistan 3.270 mn. By Spearman's correlation coefficient, population and involvement are positively correlated at 0.7125, when 1.0 would mean perfect positive correlation. Apparently size of population is a significant indicator of Japanese economic involvement. Other motives or obstacles are considered later in this chapter.

5.3   EASTERN EUROPE

Japan's economic involvement in Eastern Europe has been selective, as regards the countries preferred, the branches chosen, and also the time period. Japan's involvement antedated the overthrow of communism in these countries, but this involvement was mainly in the forms of trading and credits – the latter at advantageous rates – plus intergovernmental agreements of unclear scope, and while there were purchases of licences plus certain joint ventures, only since the demise of communism (or occasionally in its final *perestroika* stage) has it been permitted to make any direct entry into the manufacturing sphere. Trade, joint ventures, plus the activities within Eastern Europe of Japanese firms, now are most often mentioned, other spheres being only occasionally mentioned or even not at all. (Transport is mentioned more often, but chiefly in relation to the FSU.) Regarding manufacturing industry, in only one country – Hungary – has Japan's entry been on any sizeable scale. Hungary has been favoured apparently for several reasons – among them good geographical situation, more advanced financial arrangements, and having been among the first to break free of the communist system. Poland has been favoured perhaps less than might have been expected, Romania if anything more. The Japanese, like others, prefer to invest where the circumstances are peaceful. Slovenia, unified and peaceful, is perhaps heading to where one would expect. Certain countries, including the rest of former Yugoslavia, are still hardly touched. Even more limited are the branches involved. Obviously in the lead is the automobile industry, not only in Hungary but (as was intended) in Poland, where there are also, as in East Germany, motor vehicle parts depots. Economics – not more nebulous political, strategic or humanitarian considerations – have become the chief motor. The Japanese government has set exacting requirements for official support. The Japanese try to insert their own managerial methods. If in competition with other leading firms, Japanese firms do not necessarily succeed, and even if they succeed, may not find it plain sailing. Yet their involvement is increasing. Already, the Japanese have made a substantial entry into the economic arrangements of

Eastern Europe – for the first time in the history either of Eastern Europe or of Japan.

This means substantially more complex Japanese economic arrangements. Even if only certain countries are affected, these countries are generally unfamiliar to the Japanese, and extremely varied in size and level of economic development, as well as in historical experience, religion and culture. One may set against this increased complexity a simplification resulting from the elimination of Soviet influence. Japan, if she wishes, can involve herself in the economic arrangements of Eastern Europe (or of Europe overall) in new circumstances, and having in mind different objectives, which can be solely economic rather than also political or strategic. While in regard to the Russian Federation political objectives still remain, a certain simplification is apparent here too.

5.4 SPHERES OF ACTIVITY AND TYPES OF PARTICIPATING INSTITUTIONS

Aid, loans, other financial or foreign exchange aspects, trade, joint ventures, and investments including manufacturing investments, have all played a part. The chief post-transformation innovation is manufacturing investment, which is still quite limited as regards both field and country. Passenger car assembly is the favourite. Eastern Europe is car-hungry and will doubtless commit most of the same mistakes in this sphere as Western Europe, perhaps in accentuated degree. The Japanese will help them outstrip to an even greater extent than before the available driver skills, repair facilities, filling stations, roads and parking. One comparative statistic is available for Japanese penetration of the passenger car market in Greece, which in 1970 was 14.5 per cent, in 1975 was 10.8 per cent, in 1980 was 49.4 per cent (Strange, 1993). The 1970 and 1980 percentages were highest among the countries listed, but in 1990 Norway, Ireland and Finland were above 40 per cent (for that year Greece not being given). As mentioned, the Japanese proportion of the passenger car market was over 27 per cent in Latvia in 1996, in Slovenia too (year not stated) about 27 per cent. Thus, in certain East European countries Japanese penetration of the car market approaches that in certain other European countries having small populations and no domestic car production, some of which are not remote from Eastern Europe (or in a geographical sense are within it), but which have had different political and economic histories.

A second preferred sphere is electronics, to which much the same applies: the Japanese can make it and the East Europeans want it. This, by the way, also happened to Greece earlier: in October 1978 Hitachi established a joint venture in Greece to import and assemble CTV (colour television) parts (Strange, 1993, p. 198). Eastern Europe, especially Poland, can supply certain raw materials but this aspect in Japanese priorities apparently does not rate so high as manufacturing.

So much is true of Eastern Europe. Not so much has been reported from non-Russian successor states of the former USSR, yet clearly the emphasis here is different: Japan above all wants raw materials, including chrome, and fuel including natural gas. In car manufacture in Uzbekistan Japan was pre-empted by Korea (Daewoo – also by the latter in Poland). Here too (as in Uzbek rice cultivation) Japanese advice can play a role.

Russia bestrides both spheres: that is, the Japanese both want their raw materials and offer them wanted manufactures, but the emphasis on consumer goods is less than in Eastern Europe and more on bulk supplies (tyres, rails). Japanese interest in long-distance communications is much greater in Russia. Japanese interest in one raw material (timber) is far greater and more immediate than in either of the other two groupings.

Although Japanese economic involvement touches a minority of the post-Soviet-bloc countries, it is also valid to emphasize that it does touch quite a number. This contrasts with China's economic involvement during the later decades before the disintegration of the Soviet Union. China (up to 1978) concentrated on Albania, obviously with political and ideological objectives, despite the not negligible economic burden. Japan, having (except in Russia's Far East) no political axe to grind and, as regards ideology, interested only in promoting acceptance of the market economy, spreads itself more widely. Unlike China, Japan does not place all its eggs in one basket.

In general, the economic objectives seem well-adapted to the preferences of the recipient country. Thus, Hungary is enabled to assemble cars which they want to do, Romania to enlarge its production of ball-bearings – useful for exports or for that country's multi-branch manufacturing – while funds are advanced to Albania's hydro-electric system, which generates almost all that country's electricity (the insanity of promoting steel production in Albania is not perpetuated) and to metal ores prospecting; heed is taken of Uzbekistan's need for bigger rice consumption; and intensive attention paid to Russia's timber resources and timber marketing. The Czechs are showered with advice to which, however, they are not in all cases receptive.

While this feature is probably exaggerated by our sources, major corporations figure very largely in Japanese economic involvement in all three major country groupings. It is not apparent that medium or small Japanese firms have taken much action, which is natural enough given that such involvement in any of the states under examination is considered to entail definite risks. However, part of the explanation here is likely to be that the activities of small firms receive little publicity. According to Glaubitz, 'hundreds of small firms' worked with the fourteen Japanese companies which in the mid-1970s conducted 90 per cent of all Japanese–Soviet trade (Glaubitz, p. 112, note 45). There are occasional other allusions to many small firms taking part. The prominence of major corporations is visible in all the country groupings, though international consortia are especially prominent in dealings with Russia, which probably reflects the special risks and difficulties that are apprehended there as well as the larger scale of operations.

Have new corporations come onto the scene in the post-Soviet time? To a large extent it would appear not. The corporations which appear in reports since 1991 are in the main the same as figured earlier. These have struck out in new directions, into new countries and new spheres of enterprise, but have scarcely been joined by others. This is perhaps the most telling illustration of native Japanese caution in business dealings.

5.5 MOTIVES FOR OR OBSTACLES TO JAPANESE INVOLVEMENT

It must be supposed that the classical motive of maximizing profitability, or more exactly responding to expected profitability, has generally been dominant. However, this can only rarely be substantiated in concrete examples. On the other hand secondary motives, contributing probably to profitability or to associated but less generically definable objectives, can be found based either on evidence (direct or indirect) or on inherent probability.

It has been noted already that size of population and involvement were positively correlated in the territories of the former Soviet Union. To correlate population and involvement is a much harder exercise to perform in Eastern Europe due to the complication of German reunification and the disintegrations of former Czechoslovakia and former Yugoslavia. It would seem, however, that in this region the correlation, while positive, is much less clearly so. Thus, Hungary emerges as first, regarding involvement, but (counting only Germany before reunification, and Czechoslovakia and former Yugoslavia before disintegration) seventh in population. It would appear that the Japanese have the countries of Eastern Europe more clearly in focus than they have the non-Russian successor states of the former USSR. This is not surprising – these successor states not having so far projected to foreigners distinctive images of themselves – yet is interesting, as it places Japanese perceptions in this respect on a level with Western European perceptions, despite Japan's being an Asian state. The individualities of the Eastern European countries are more clearly understood by the Japanese, as they are by other foreigners not directly from those regions (unless there is some special historical link, as between Korea and Uzbekistan).

To explain this situation, one may suppose that the immensity of Russia dazzles perception by the Japanese, so that other successor states of the USSR are scarcely seen, whereas in Eastern Europe no single country is perceived as equally dominant, either in population or otherwise. Alternatively, the explanation may be that in language, religion or culture the East European countries are more clearly differentiated from one another than are most of the non-Russian successor states of the USSR. (These latter in general have Islamic cultures and except for Tajikistan speak Turkic languages.) At any rate, the smallest or newest states – whether formed by disintegration of the USSR or of an East European country – have up to the time of writing attracted little Japanese economic involvement, and in most cases none.

Density of population is not likely to be scrutinized directly by investment executives, but is possibly significant since the Japanese economy has gained special experience in coping with high population density. That experience may help the Japanese to advise the Uzbeks on growing rice more intensively. On the other hand, *low* density of population in the co-operating country may be accompanied by ability to produce and export goods which Japan needs, such as Russian timber; it is also typical of territories which are crossed by long-distance overland transport, in which respect Russia is again indicated.

Income per head is doubtless considered in conjunction with population, but is a two-edged sword, as higher income per head is likely to enlarge demand in the local market, but on the other hand probably enlarges the local wage bill. Thus, wide distribution of a product within the country of manufacture, outside the localities from which the workforce is recruited, is desirable. Where the national as well as the local wage level is low, demand for the product within the country of manufacture will be restricted, whereas exports of it from that country will be stimulated, which is what has happened in the case of the Suzuki Swift.

How long the country has maintained itself as an independent entity, and how long it has been conscious of the existence of Japan, or Japan has been conscious of it, appears to be one other consideration. Russia scores highest not only because of its huge size but because of its lengthy history of contacts with Japan. No other country either of the former USSR or of Eastern Europe can compete in this regard. The fact that, historically, relations between Japan and Russia were often antagonistic dilutes this factor but without destroying it. The comparatively lengthy history of independent Albania (since 1912) perhaps helps that country by comparison with FYROM or Croatia, and the more continuous history of Hungary brings advantage to that country as compared with the Czech Republic, Slovakia or Slovenia. Certain of the East European countries have simply not existed as genuinely independent entities long enough for the Japanese to appreciate what they may be able to offer, their weaknesses, economic viability or reliability. Duration under some fairly stable political or economic regime is important too: the given country may – or may not – have had time to reform its economy satisfactorily, to adopt satisfactory legislation relating to privatization, land tenure, and so on.

Language is still another factor. The Japanese do not expect to be able to make use of their own language in international negotiations, but do appreciate being able to use some fairly commonly known language. This would not necessarily be the other country's native tongue. If it were, that would rule out the Hungarians, but in that country a lot of business can be conducted in English or German. Japanese problems in that regard in Albania are probably no greater than were surmounted by the Chinese during the period when they supported the Albanian economy, when presumably English or Russian were the common languages (see Hutchings, 1996, pp. 91–2). The successor states of the USSR can to a large extent conduct business in Russian – virtually a lingua franca of the former USSR – which, however, is still for Japanese (and others) a difficult foreign language. Where – as in Estonia, for example – there is antagonism to conducting business in Russian while the native language is virtually unknown by non-natives, this is an additional hurdle.

Most probably religion does not have any important influence, the two religions of Japan – Buddhism and Shintoism – being scarcely or not at all professed in any of the countries mentioned in this book, so their practices cannot give offence, or at most are regarded as quaint. In England, where an official Sumo contest was held, its Shintoist trappings were seen in that light.

It is highly important from the Japanese angle that a country should be in a state of peace. This does not guarantee Japanese economic involvement, but the contrary situation rules it out almost certainly. Thus, attention is focused on Russia, Kazakstan, Uzbekistan (the Uzbek leadership complacently drawing attention to its peaceful condition in contrast to certain other republics), Hungary, Germany, Poland, Romania or Czechoslovakia (and its successor states), not on Azerbaydzhan, Armenia (these two republics having been in conflict over Nagornyy-Karabakh), Georgia (civil war), Croatia, Serbia/Montenegro, or Bosnia-Hercegovina (independence wars). The conflict between Russia and Chechnya is apparently ignored because of the disparity in size of the combatants (Russia can hardly lose); Slovenia's brief independence war is also overlooked, as are disturbances accompanying Romania's 'revolution' which overthrew Ceausescu. It must be feared that the serious disturbances in Albania during the first half of 1997 will have a deterrent effect. FYROM is avoided probably for a combination of several reasons: its small size, short duration of independence, poverty and ostracism by Greece.

The stage of economic reform and privatization is very influential. Ukraine is largely ignored despite its imposing area and population, surely in part because of its slow and hesitant privatization (besides having little or nothing to spare that Japan really wants), whereas Hungary, though several times smaller, gained for this reason (among others) a head start. As noted already, time elapsed under a comparatively stable regime is important too or, more concretely, the Japanese take note of when economic transformation started and how far it has gone.

The Japanese are sticklers for straightforward and honest business behaviour. Thus, Poland's application for loan conditions to be renegotiated was rejected with disgust. This is normal Japanese business behaviour: negotiations are tough and perhaps prolonged, but once an agreement has been reached it must be strictly observed. Even in his own negotiations the author noticed this characteristic.

Does the country offer some commodity that Japan really needs? If it offers only manufactures, these must be very specialized for Japan not to be producing them. And Japan's culinary tastes are in some degree peculiar to itself. So sour cherries in brandy were Hungary's only success at Foodex. The list of items of this sort which can be supplied by Eastern Europe, Russia or other successor states of the former USSR but not by other countries of the world, is even more limited.

Geography, that is to say primarily distance, is important, though, due to the diverse size and irregular shape of countries and the influence of lines of communication, one that is especially hard to disentangle from other factors. It is also necessary to distinguish geography between countries from geography within a given country. The first evidently influences the Japanese preference for doing business with Russia relative rather than, say, Tajikistan or Estonia. The second encourages the Japanese to become involved in business in Russia's Far East much more than in European Russia. The location of a country is influential, for example the convenient locations of Poland and Hungary for distribution of goods within Central Europe. Bulgaria, say, would be much less suitable as a distribution point. Within a given country the most suitable site is chosen partly on geographical grounds, for instance Esztergom's nearness to Budapest and accessibility for both overland and river transport for Suzuki's Hungarian motor assembly plant. The ability to send freight by air is in this case a further advantage, whereas in some other instances that might attenuate the geographical factor. Economic geography may be affected also by the introduction of other means of transport, such as a pipeline, as the future may show for Turkmenistan.

How much capital a country can supply itself and whether international bodies such as the IMF will make a contribution necessarily exert great influence. Japan's Export-Import Bank (Eximbank) has played a significant role.

The relationship of an economy to other economies, in particular to adjacent ones and especially as regards trading and customs relationships, is seen as important. This, by the way, is illustrated in the argument in Britain by those who wish Britain to join the European Monetary Union (EMU) that to do so that will promote Japanese investment in Britain, though the list of desiderata mentioned so far in connection with the former USSR and Eastern Europe suggests that this is likely to be only one among a number of influential features. Similarly, the Japanese may find encouraging the adherence or intended adherence of a successor state of the former USSR to the CIS (Commonwealth of Independent States) or to some other international grouping, such as the intention to create a single economic area comprising Uzbekistan, Kazakstan and Kyrgyzstan (*Pravda vostoka*, 3 April 1994 – RN=22307). Conversely, withdrawal from or limited participation in such a grouping, or its dissolution, would discourage Japanese engagement. By itself, the dissolution even of CMEA (Council for Economic Mutual Aid) should have had a deterrent effect which, however, would have been counteracted by other simultaneous changes acting in the contrary sense.

Previous favourable experience by some other Japanese firm or firms is an encouraging feature, as was cited in certain reports about Japanese economic involvement in Russia. Japanese firms like to follow in well-trodden footsteps. Probably this is partly responsible for the scale of

Japanese engagement in Hungary. Likewise encouraging is any reconnaissance by Japanese bodies, such as JETRO, which customarily engage in that sort of activity. Conversely, of course, unfortunate experiences by others or by oneself will be a deterrent. Also expressive of Japanese caution is the fact that mainly large (often multinational) corporations are involved, and not infrequently consortia (see earlier section).

Political objectives are of two sorts: territorial and non-territorial. Japan seeks to recover Russian far eastern territories she sees as rightfully hers, which has probably swayed policy in the direction of providing sweeteners to Sakhalin. The brightly coloured trains donated to that island are an illustration. A parallel might be drawn with German Ostpolitik during the later years of the Federal German Republic. Elsewhere Japan has no territorial goals but wishes to support non-communist regimes, market economies and sound economic principles. Japan's interest in Russia is also in part to counteract the emergence of China (Kondrashov, 1997).

The extent of collaborative contacts between the two countries' economists, and whether Japanese advice in the running of the economy of the country has been accepted and/or Japanese appointed as advisers, should have some marginal influence. For instance, contacts between Japanese and German economists facilitate mutual understanding while the appointment of a former Japanese foreign minister as economic adviser to the Hungarian government must have boosted (or reflected) confidence.

Finally, there could be humanitarian aims and these may explain Japanese aid to Albania, but the lack of Japanese economic involvement in other deprived countries such as Armenia, Georgia or FYROM suggests that on the whole such motives are weak. Japan has, of course, no responsibility for those countries' economic plight.

The above considerations, or some of them, have influenced or are likely to have influenced the scale and type of Japanese economic involvement in individual countries or regions of countries. It is most difficult to estimate their relative importance. As regards the regions covered in this survey, such considerations also need to be weighed in relation to other major geographical regions, such as Western Europe or South-East Asia. These other major areas, in particular the last, have traditionally been the main arenas of Japanese economic engagement. However, to examine the entire field of Japanese overseas economic involvement would be a gigantic task and one which falls outside the scope of the present book.

Bibliography

A.St. (1997) *Romania libera*, 16 January.
ADN (1984) *Neues Deutschland*, 18 January.
ADN (1991) *Neues Deutschland*, 27 November.
ADN (1992) *Neues Deutschland*, 7 December.
ADN / ND (1990) *Neues Deutschland*, 19 March.
ADN / ND (1992) *Neues Deutschland*, 4 December.
ADN / ND (1993) *Neues Deutschland*, 23 February.
Agafonov, S. (1993) *Izvestiya*, 2 June.
Agzam, E. (1994) *Pravda vostoka*, 21 May.
Altmann, F.-L. (ed.) (1990) *Albanien im Umbruch* (Munchen: Sudost-Institut).
Anichkin, A. (1992) *Izvestiya*, 8 September.
Anon. (1977) *Rabotnichesko delo*, 13 October.
Anon. (1978a) *Nepszabadsag*, 12 November.
Anon. (1978b) *Magyar Hirlap*, 26 March.
Anon. (1979a) *Nepszabadsag*, 24 October.
Anon. (1979b) *Rabotnichesko delo*, 14 March.
Anon. (1980a) *Musaki Elet*, vol. 64, 17 October.
Anon. (1980b) *Nepszabadsag*, 6 May.
Anon. (1984) GDR-*Export-llka Journal*, March.
Anon. (1985a) *Heti vilaggazdasag*, 16 November.
Anon. (1985b) *Nepszabadsag*, 30 December.
Anon. (1985c) *Neues Deutschland*, 2 September.
Anon. (1986) *Scinteia*, 16 May.
Anon. (1987a) *Ekonomska politika*, 15 June.
Anon. (1987b) *Neues Deutschland*, no. 12, December.
Anon. (1988) *Nepszabadsag*, 6 August.
Anon. (1989a) *Nepszabadsag*, 15 June.
Anon. (1989b) *Nepszabadsag*, 2 January.
Anon. (1989c) *Nepszabadsag*, 1 April.
Anon. (1990a) *Nepszabadsag*, 2 February.
Anon. (1990b) *Sofiiski vesti*, 3 January.
Anon. (1991a) *Ekonomska politika*, 14 January.
Anon. (1991b) *Lidove noviny*, 21 January.
Anon. (1992a) *Nepszabadsag*, 1 October.
Anon. (1992b) *Nepszabadsag*, 6 March.
Anon. (1992c) *Pravda vostoka*, 20 October.
Anon. (1992d) *Eastern Europe and the Commonwealth of Independent States* 1st
    edn (London: Europa).
Anon. (1993a) *Bulgarian Telegraph Agency*, 1 April.
Anon. (1993b) *Ekonomika i zhizn'*, 12 August.
Anon. (1993c) *Gudok*, 6 July.
Anon. (1993d) *Hospodarske noviny* [daily] 28 December.
Anon. (1993e) *Nepszabadsag*, 22 April.
Anon. (1993f) *Nepszabadsag*, 4 February, 19 April.

Anon. (1993g) *Pravda vostoka*, 30 November.
Anon. (1994a) *Gudok*, 5 April.
Anon. (1994b) *Hospodarske noviny* [daily] 18 October.
Anon. (1994c) *Pravda vostoka*, 2 August.
Anon. (1994d) *Fletorja zyrtare e republikes te Shqiperise*, no. 8.
Anon. (1995a) *Hospodarske noviny* [daily], 23 November.
Anon. (1995b) *Hospodarske noviny* [daily], 27 April.
Anon. (1995c) *Hospodarske noviny*, 23 November.
Anon. (1995d) *Hospodarske noviny*, 3 March.
Anon. (1995e) *Narodna obroda*, 14 February.
Anon. (1995f) *Romania libera*, 28 April.
Anon. (1995g) *Fletorja zyrtare e republikes te Shqiperise*, December.
Anon. (1996a) *Le Monde*, 27 October.
Anon. (1996b) *Romania libera*, 17 May.
Anon. (1996c) *Romania libera*, 19 February.
Anon. (1996d) *Romania libera*, 29 May.
Anon. (1996e) *Romania libera*, 9 May.
Anon. (1996f) *Fletorja zyrtare e republikes te Shqiperise*, 1 September.
Anon. (1997a) *Finansovye izvestiya*, 18 February.
Anon. (1997b) *Gudok*, 16 July.
Anon. (1997c) *Romania libera*, 8 August.
Anon. (1997) *Sunday Telegraph*, 12 October.
Arkeyev, V. and V. Martynov (1992) *Gudok*, 19 March.
Arutyunyan, M. (1994) *Sovetskaya Rossiya*, 15 November.
Bashkimi (Tirana) [newspaper] (1995) 22 July.
Baskayev, K. (1996) *Finansovye izvestiya*, 15 March.
Bautzova, I. (1997) *EKONOM*, 17 April.
be (1994) *Frankfurter Allgemeine*, 13 October.
Bereczki, M. (1992) *Nepszabadsag*, 17 February.
Bezverkov, A. (1996) *Trud*, 25 January.
Bikmukhametov, R. (1987) *Izvestiya*, 5 June.
Bird, I. (1911) *Unbeaten Tracks in Japan* (London: John Murray).
Bisignani, J.D. (1983) *Japan Handbook* (Chico, Cal.: Moon).
Borisov, O. (1997) *Gudok*, 16 August.
Bossanyi, K. (1985) *Nepszabadsag*, 20 September.
Bratchikova, V. (1987) *Vodnyy transport*, 7 February.
Bratiloveanu, G.H. and M. Spanu (1985) *Monumente de Arhitectura in Lemn din Tinutul Sucevei* (Bucharest: Editura Meridiane).
Brezhnev, B. (1994) *Gudok*, 22 September.
Brown, A. *et al.* (eds) (1994) *The Cambridge Encyclopaedia of Russia and the former Soviet Union* (Cambridge: Cambridge University Press).
Bury, J.B. (n.d.) *A History of Greece* (New York: Modern Library).
Butler, T. (ed.) (1976) *Bulgaria Past and Present* (Columbus, Ohio: American Association for the Advancement of Slavic Studies), articles by John R. Lampe and Cyril E. Black.
B.V.J. (1993) *Nepszabadsag*, 24 April.
B.Zs. (1992) *Nepszabadsag*, 6 March.
Ceausescu, D. (1996) *Romania libera*, 12 October.
Chaplygin, Yu. (1997) *Business World*, 17 June.

Charodeyev, G. (1997) *Izvestiya*, 8 August.
Chibisov, V. (1997) *Gudok*, 3 July.
Chonkidze, I. (1995) *Gudok*, 21 February.
Christo, V. (1997–8) *Anglo-Albanian Association Newsletter*, Winter.
Cortazzi, Sir Hugh (1993) *Modern Japan: A Concise Survey* (London: Macmillan).
CTK (1996a) *Hospodarske noviny*, 11 April.
CTK (1996b) *Hospodarske noviny* [daily], 30 April.
Daily news (Sofia) [newspaper] (1995), 25 April.
Daniels, G. and R. Drifte (eds) (1986) *Europe and Japan: Changing Relationships since 1945* (Woodchurch: Paul Norbury).
Dannenberg, I. (1997) *Gudok*, 23 August.
Debski, W.S. (1995) *Trybuna*, 9 June.
Demchuk, N. (1997) *Sovetskaya Belorussiya*, 24 June.
Doleckova, M. (1992) *Hospodarske noviny*, 21 April.
Dostalova, I. (1997) *EKONOM*, 11 September.
dpa/ ADN (1992) *Neues Deutschland*, 31 March.
Drabova, A. (1992) *Hospodarske noviny* [daily], 7 July.
Durham, M.E. (1985, first printed 1909) *High Albania* (London: Virago).
Dzokayeva, T. (1994) *Delovoy mir*, 9 August.
EIU (Economist Intelligence Unit) (1997) *Country Report: Hungary*, 1st quarter.
Ellingstad, M. (1997) 'The Maquiladora Syndrome: Central European Prospects', *Europe-Asia Studies*, vol. 49, no. 1.
Eftov, V. (1994) *Vreme*, 28 February.
Ershov, Yu. (1997) *Business World*, 16 July.
European, The [newspaper] (1995) 16–22 November.
Fairbank, J.K., E.O. Reischauer and A.M. Craig (1973) *East Asia, Tradition and Transformation* (London: George Allen & Unwin).
Fedorov, L. (1997) *Finansovye izvestiya*, 6 March.
Fellegi, P. (1985) *Vecernik*, 5 February.
Florescu, R.R. and R.T. McNally, (1989) *Dracula, Prince of Many Faces* (Boston: Little, Brown).
Fodella, G. (ed.) (1983) *Japan's Economy in a Comparative Perspective* (Tenterden: Paul Norbury).
Frost, U. (1991) *Neues Deutschland*, 22 November.
Gal, Zs. (1987) *Nepszabadsag*, 7 February.
Galimov, Yu. (1994) *Delovoy mir*, 1 December.
Gati, J. (1979) *Heti vilaggazdasag*, 27 October.
Gerdina, T. and M.K. Baskar (eds) (1993) *Slovenija for Everyone*, 2nd rev. edn (Ljubljana: Vitrun).
Gergova, R.S. (1987) *Ikonomicheski zhivot*, February.
Gibbon, E. (1980 [1776–8]) *The Decline and Fall of the Roman Empire*, abridged by Dero A. Saunders (London: Penguin).
Glaubitz, J. (1995) *Between Tokyo and Moscow* (London: C. Hurst).
Gogidze, V. (1994) *Obshchaya gazeta*, 27 May.
Hall, R.B. (*c*.1962) *Japan: Industrial Power of Asia* (Princeton, NJ: D. Van Nostrand).
Hax, H., W. Klenner, W. Kraus, T. Matsuda and T. Nakamura (eds) (1995) *Economic Transformation in Eastern Europe and East Asia, A Challenge for Japan and Germany* (Berlin: Springer).

Hearn, L. (1894) *Glimpses of Unfamiliar Japan*, vol. 1 (Cambridge, Mass.: Riverside).
Herman, Z. (1993) *Ekonomska politika*, 14 June.
him (1995) *Frankfurter Allgemeine*, 3 May.
him (1996) *Frankfurter Allgemeine*, 19 September.
Hoeg, P. (1994) *Miss Smilla's Feeling for Snow*, trans. F. David (London: Harper Collins).
Holland, C. (1911) *Things Seen in Japan* (London: Seeley).
Hutchings, R. (1971) *Seasonal Influences in Soviet Industry* (London: OUP).
Hutchings, R. (1987) *Soviet Secrecy and Non-Secrecy* (London: Macmillan).
Hutchings, R. (1996) *Historical Dictionary of Albania* (Lanham, Md: Scarecrow)
Hutchings, R. (forthcoming) *Osteuropa-Wirtschaft*.
HV (1993a) *Heti vilaggazdasag*, 29 May.
HV (1993b) *Heti vilaggazdasag*, 20 July.
Hyoe, M. and D. Richie (eds) (1980) *A Hundred More Things Japanese* (Tokyo: Japan Culture Institute). Articles alluded to in this book are by Trevor P. Leggett, S. Trumbull and W. Murphy.
Infocentrum / German Agency BFA (1995) *Hospodarske noviny* [daily], 24 February.
Inoguchi, T. (1993) *Japan's Foreign Policy in an Era of Global Change* (London: Pinter).
ITAR (1997) *Gudok*, 19 February.
ITAR-Tass (1996) *Lesnaya gazeta*, 3 December.
JAC (1994) *Trybuna*, 4–5 June.
JAC (1995) *Trybuna*, 20 December.
Johnson, S. (1964) *Gay Bulgaria* (London: Robert Hale).
K.P. (1987) *Zycie Gospodarcze*, 1 February.
Kadare, I. (1986) *The General of the Dead Army* (London: Quartet).
Kalashnikova, E. (1997) *Gudok* (Commercial Supplement), 19 November.
Kalinkin, V. (1987) *Lesnaya promyshlennost'*, 24 December.
Kalinkin, V. (1997) *Lesnaya gazeta*, 22 April.
Karimov, I. (1995) *Pravda vostoka*, 13 April.
Keep, J. (1995) *Last of the Empires: A History of the Soviet Union 1945–1991* (Oxford: OUP).
Khasan, R. (1994) *Pravda vostoka*, 21 June.
Khoroshilov, A. (1995) *Lesnaya gazeta*, 3 October.
Khoroshilov, A. (1996a) *Lesnaya gazeta*, 14 May.
Khoroshilov, A. (1996b) *Lesnaya gazeta*, 2 April.
Khoroshilov, A. (1996c) *Lesnaya gazeta*, 31 August.
Khoroshilov, A. (1996d) *Lesnaya gazeta*, 23 March.
Khoroshilov, A. (1997a) *Lesnaya gazeta*, 8 April.
Khoroshilov, A. (1997b) *Lesnaya gazeta*, 29 April.
Kirby, E. Stuart (1981) *Russian Studies of Japan* (London: Macmillan).
Klvacova, E. (1997) *EKONOM*, 5 June.
Kohler, A. (1988) *Neues Deutschland*, 3 March.
Komiya, R. and R. Wakasugi (1991) *The Annals of the American Academy of Political and Social Science*, January.
Kondrashov, S. (1997) *Izvestiya*, 16 August.
Kovacs, B. (1991) *Nepszabadsag*, 16 December.

Kozlonskiy, V. (1993) *Rossiya*, 22 July.
Krauss, K. (1995) *Trybuna*, 3 November.
Kravchenko, Ye. (1994) *Kommersant*, 5 August.
Kryst (1995) *Trybuna*, 30 October.
k(sa) (1994) *Hospodarske noviny* [daily], 19 October.
Kucherenko, A. (1994a) *Gudok*, 23 October.
Kucherenko, A. (1994b) *Gudok*, 9 December.
Kucherenko, A. (1997a) *Gudok*, 11 January.
Kucherenko, A. (1997b) *Gudok*, 22 May.
Kucherenko, A. (1997c) *Gudok*, 25 March.
Kunilovskiy, G. (1997) *Gudok*, 22 July.
Kuz'menko, B. (1997) *Business World*, 8 April.
Lane, R.W. (1922) *The Peaks of Shala* (London: Chapman & Dodd).
Lashkevich, N. (1995) *Finansovye izvestiya*, 7 March.
Lashkevich, N. (1996) *Finansovye izvestiya*, 21 November.
Lashkevich, N. (1997) *Izvestiya*, 17 July.
Lavrinenko, Yu. (1997) *Gudok*, 11 June.
Lazar, G. (1996) *Romania libera*, 20 September.
Lazarov, B. (1984) *Sofiiski vesti*, 25 July.
Lensen, G.A. (1959) *The Russian Push toward Japan: Russo-Japanese Relations 1697–1875* (Princeton: Princeton UP).
Leskov, S. (1996) *Izvestiya*, 19 June.
Levina, L. (1987) *Lesnaya gazeta*, 24 May.
Levina, L. (1995) *Lesnaya gazeta*, 15 August.
Lubczyk, G. (1996) *Rzeczpospolita*, 3 October.
Magos, K. (1989) *Nepszabadsag*, 8 April.
Mamedov, S. (1993) *Finansovye izvestiya*, 27 March–2 April.
Manning, O. (1974) *Fortunes of War, vol. 1, The Balkan Trilogy* (London: Penguin).
Marbach, G. (1987) *Neues Deutschland*, 28 July.
Marcovici, I. (1995) *Romania libera*, 18 September.
Martynov, V. (1992) *Gudok*, 7 May.
Matkin, M. (1993) *Kommersant*, 28 July.
Mikinski, C. (1995) *Trybuna*, 21 March.
Mikulskiy, K. (1996) *Ekonomika i zhizn'*, 5 March.
Ministry of Foreign Affairs (1989) *Japan's ODA 1988* (Tokyo: Ministry of Foreign Affairs).
M.M. (1993) *Nepszabadsag*, 2 April.
Morinos, R. (1997) *Romania libera*, 18 June.
Morison, J. (ed.) (1992) *Eastern Europe and the West. Selected Papers from the Fourth World Congress for Soviet and East European Studies, Harrogate 1990* (New York: Macmillan), article by Frank W. Thackeray.
Moskvin, M. (1993) *Gudok*, 16 September.
Moskvin, M. (1995) *Gudok*, 26 May.
MTI (1983) *Nepszabadsag*, 28 October.
MTI (1984) *Nepszabadsag*, 21 July.
MTI (1985) *Nepszabadsag*, 12 December.
MTI (1986) *Nepszabadsag*, 5 July.
MTI (1988a) *Heti vilaggazdasag*, 16 December.

MTI (1988b) *Nepszabadsag*, 2 June.
MTI (1989) *Nepszabadsag*, 27 May.
MTI (1990a) *Nepszabadsag*, 16 January.
MTI (1990b) *Nepszabadsag*, 21 April.
MTI (1992a) *Nepszabadsag*, 7 November.
MTI (1992b) *Nepszabadsag*, 8 December.
MTI (1993a) *Nepszabadsag*, 18 May.
MTI (1993b) *Nepszabadsag*, 19 March.
MTI (1993c) *Nepszabadsag*, 8 November.
Murakami, Y. and Y. Kosai (eds) (1986) *Japan in the Global Community, its Role and Contribution on the Eve of the 21st Century* (Tokyo: University of Tokyo Press).
Namtalashvili, G. (1995) *Finansovye izvestiya*, 24 January.
Natek, K. *et al*. (1992) *Slovenija* (Ljubljana: Ministrstvo RS za informiranje).
New Albania Editorial Board (1984) *Albania* (Tirana: 8 Nentori).
Nicolescu, V. (1996) *Romania libera*, 24 September.
Nikolov, M. (1987) *Trud*, 22 April.
Nikolova, N. (1989) *Rabotnichesko delo*, 7 January.
Noland, M. (1990) *Japan and the World Economy*, vol. 2, no. 3.
O.Sz.A. (1993a) *Nepszabadsag*, 12 July.
O.Sz.A. (1993b) *Nepszabadsag*, 26 January.
Ochil, K. (1995) *Pravda vostoka*, 21 February.
Palin, M. (1997) BBC, 31 August.
Pan, A. (1996) *Gudok*, 9 August.
PAP (1991) *Trybuna*, 25 June.
Papadiuc, A. (1991) *Adevarul*, 28 May.
Peche, N. and K. Steinitz (1987) *Wirtschaftswissenschaft*, no. 9.
Pehlivanian, C. (1989) *Neues Deutschland*, 8 September.
Pernicky, R. and A. Hybner (1997) *EKONOM*, 23 January.
Petcu, M. (1995) *Romania libera*, 29 April.
Petrov, Yu. (1993) *Ekonomicheskaya gazeta*, 28 July.
pi (1995a) *Hospodarske noviny* [daily], 15 February.
pi (1995b) *Hospodarske noviny* [daily], 28 February.
pi (1995c) *Hospodarske noviny*, 6 January.
Pipa, A. (1990) *Albanian Stalinism: Ideo-Political Aspects* (Boulder, Colo.: East European Monographs).
Pis'mennaya, E. (1997) *Finansovye izvestiya*, 22 April.
Pitman, J. (1997) *The Times*, 29 September.
Polivka, M. (1996) *EKONOM*, 17 October.
Portanskiy, A. (1997) *Finansovye izvestiya*, 26 June.
Prelovskaya, I. (1992) *Izvestiya*, 6 January.
Radulescu, D. (1995a) *Romania libera*, 29 April.
Radulescu, D. (1995b) *Romania libera*, 14 October.
Radulescu, D. (1996) *Romania libera*, 23 March.
Radulescu, D. (1997) *Romania libera*, 7 November.
Reischauer, Edwin O. (1954) *Japan Past and Present* (Tokyo: Charles E. Tuttle).
Reuter (1996) *Hospodarske noviny* [daily], 23 April.
Richardson, D. and J. Denton (1988) *The Rough Guide to Eastern Europe: Hungary, Romania and Bulgaria* (London: Harrap-Columbus).

Rosich, P. (1997) *Finansovye izvestiya*, 20 February.
Russu, V. (1993) *Izvestiya*, 9 November.
R.Zs. (1991a) *Nepszabadsag*, 10 July.
R.Zs. (1991b) *Nepszabadsag*, 4 June.
R.Zs. (1993a) *Nepszabadsag*, 1 March.
R.Zs. (1993b) *Nepszabadsag*, 15 January.
R.Zs. (1993c) *Nepszabadsag*, 24 February.
R.Zs. (1993d) *Nepszabadsag*, 8 May.
Samarina, B. and B. Kuz'menko, (1997) *Business World*, 20–23 June.
Semenov, A. (1993) *Moskovskiy komsomolets*, 28 April.
Shchukin, R. (1996) *Gudok*, 10 December.
Shchurov, V. (1991) *Trud*, 18 March.
Shehu, A. (*c*.1997) *Studime Gjeografike*, no. 7.
Shimov, Ya. (1993) *Izvestiya*, 2 December.
Shirmanov, V. (1986) *Vodnyy transport*, 6 November.
Shitov, V. (1995) *Grazhdanskaya aviatsiya*, 1 March.
Shmyganovskiy, V. (1987) *Izvestiya*, 13 June.
Sieradzinski, J. (1996) *Trybuna*, 2 April.
Skripov, V. (1997) *Business World*, 12 February.
Stamov, S. (ed.) (1972) *The Architectural Heritage of Bulgaria* (Sofia: State Publishing House 'Tehnika').
Stanley, D. (1989) *Eastern Europe on a Shoestring* (Hawthorn, Victoria, Australia: Lonely Planet).
Stevenson, T. (1997) *Sotheby's World Wine Encyclopedia* (London: Dorling Kindersley).
Strange, R. (1993) *Japanese Manufacturing Investment in Europe: Its Impact on the UK Economy* (London: Routledge).
Strauss, R. *et al.* (1991) *Japan* (Hawthorn, Australia: Lonely Planet).
Sukhonos, A. (1996) *Delovoy mir*, 30 May.
Susumu, O. (1970) *The Origin of the Japanese Language* (Tokyo: Kokusai Bunka Shinkokai).
Sveshnikov, A. (1993) *Finansovye izvestiya*, 15–21 October.
Svistunov, S. (1996) *Finansovye izvestiya*, 3 December.
Syzdek, R. (1995) *Trybuna*, 6 October.
Szalay, A. (1993) *Nepszabadsag*, 15 February.
Szego, G. (1993) *Nepszabadsag*, 25 October.
Szot, E. (1997) *Rzeczpospolita*, 16 January.
Tarasov, A. (1997) *Sovietskiy Sakhalin*, 9 August.
Tell, R. (1995) *Rabochaya tribuna*, 18 February.
Terenche, C. (1997) *Romania libera*, 5 June.
Thackeray, Frank W. (1992) 'Pilsudski, Dmowski and the Russo-Japanese War: An Episode in the Diplomacy of a Stateless People' in John Morison (ed.) *Eastern Europe and the West, Selected Papers from the Fourth World Congress for Soviet and East European Studies, Harrogate, 1990* (New York: Macmillan).
Thornton, J. and N.N. Mikheyeva (1996) 'The Strategies of Foreign and Foreign-Assisted Firms in the Russian Far East: Alternatives to Missing Infrastructure' *Comparative Economic Studies*, Winter.
Todorov, D. (1996) *Duma*, 16 May.
TOMS (1990) *Trybuna*, 22 June.

Totev, K. (1984) *BTA Bulletin*, 10 May.
Treptow, K. (1992) *From Zamolxis to Jan Palach* (New York: Columbia UP).
Trofimov, V. (1993) *Izvestiya*, 20 May.
Trom, A. (1987) *Nepszabadsag*, 30 December.
Trom, A. (1989a) *Nepszabadsag*, 16 October.
Trom, A. (1989b) *Nepszabadsag*, 4 March.
Trom, A. (1990) *Nepszabadsag*, 13 January.
Trom, A. (1991) *Nepszabadsag*, 28 October.
Trom, A. (1993) *Nepszabadsag*, 2 April.
Tsvetkov *et al.* (1982) *Otechestven front*, 16 April.
Tuchkov, A. (1996) *Gudok*, 5 October.
Uegaki, A. (1993) *The Economic Review of the Seinan Gakuin University*, March.
Useynov, A. (1993) *Rossiyskaya gazeta*, 24 July.
Uz, A. (1993) *Pravda vostoka*, 14 December.
Uz, A. (1994a) *Pravda vostoka*, 7 June.
Uz, A. (1994b) *Pravda vostoka*, 6 October.
Vasilescu, A. (1996) *Romania libera*, 17 May.
Vels, V. (1993) *Gudok*, 17 August.
Vinogradov, B. (1996) *Izvestiya*, 18 December.
Vit, J. (1996) *Lidove noviny*, 9 January.
Vysotskiy, V. (1997) *Lesnaya gazeta*, 23 August.
Walewska, D. (1996) *Rzeczpospolita*, 13 November.
Wasilewski, J. (1995) *Trybuna*, 4–5 November.
Watson, J. (1996) 'Foreign Investment in Russia: the Case of the Oil Industry', *Europe-Asia Studies*, May.
Wessel, H. (1985) *Neues Deutschland*, 10 July.
Wilczynski, J. (1976) *The Multinationals and East-West Relations: Towards Trans-ideological Collaboration* (London: Macmillan).
Winnifrith, T. (ed.) (1992) *Perspectives on Albania* (London: Macmillan).
Wodz (1996) *Trybuna*, 29 April.
Woronoff, J. (1990) *Japan as – Anything but – Number One* (Basingstoke: Macmillan).
Yakovleva, Ye. (1996) *Izvestiya*, 14 February.
Yamamoto, K. (1995) *Illyria*, 19–21 January.
Yaroslavets, V. (1997) *Gudok*, 26 July.
Yermolayev, V. (1988) *Pravda*, 30 March.
Yevplanov, A. (1996) *Finansovye izvestiya*, 17 September.
Young, A. (1995) *Anglo-Albanian Association Newsletter*, no. 7 (Summer–Autumn).
Zhagel', I. (1997) *Finansovye izvestiya*, 8 April.
Zloch-Christy, I. (ed.) (1995) *Privatization and Foreign Investments in Eastern Europe* (Westport, Conn.: Praeger), articles by Ken Morita and Gabor Bakos.

Index

161

Index